FOOL'S PARADISE

ALSO BY STEVEN GAINES

The Sky's the Limit: Passion and Property in Manhattan

Philistines at the Hedgerow: Passion and Property in the Hamptons

Obsession: The Lives and Times of Calvin Klein

Simply Halston: The Untold Story

Heroes and Villains: The True Story of the Beach Boys

The Love You Make: An Insider's Story of the Beatles

Me, Alice: The Autobiography of Alice Cooper

Marjoe: The Biography of Evangelist Marjoe Gortner

The Club (NOVEL)

Another Runner in the Night (NOVEL)

FOOL'S PARADISE

Players, Poseurs, and the Culture of Excess
in South Beach

STEVEN GAINES

Crown Publishers
New York

Copyright © 2009 by Steven Gaines

Published in the United States by Crown Publishers, an imprint of the
Crown Publishing Group, a division of Random House, Inc., New York.
www.crownpublishing.com

CROWN and the Crown colophon are registered trademarks of
Random House, Inc.

Library of Congress Cataloging-in-Publication Data
Gaines, Steven S.
Fool's paradise / Steven Gaines.—1st ed.
1. South Beach (Miami Beach, Fla.)—Social life and customs.   2. Upper
class—Florida—Miami Beach.   3. Celebrities—Florida—Miami Beach.
4. Miami Beach (Fla.)—Social life and customs.   I. Title.
F319.M62G35 2009
975.9'381—dc22   2008036067

ISBN 978-0-307-34627-8

Printed in the United States of America

Design by Lauren Dong

10   9   8   7   6   5   4   3   2   1

First Edition

FOR ANTONY DIGIACOMO

Contents

One: SOCIALITES   1

Two: THE ISLAND OF BROKEN TOYS   13

Three: LINCOLN ROAD   23

Four: SANS SOUCI   34

Five: THE FONTAINEBLEAU   52

Six: EDEN ROC   72

Seven: TWILIGHT ON THE BEACH   81

Eight: THE MOST POWERFUL MAN IN MIAMI BEACH   99

Nine: SAVING SOUTH BEACH   111

Ten: LEONARD AND BARBARA   131

Eleven: THE MAYOR OF SOUTH BEACH   139

Twelve: INTO THE NIGHT   166

Thirteen: SOUTH BEACH STORY   189

Fourteen: WEDNESDAY NIGHT AT THE FORGE   199

Fifteen: MODELS   205

Sixteen: THE KING OF THE CITY   222

Seventeen: LIQUID   238

Eighteen: FOOL'S PARADISE   254

Bibliography   261

Acknowledgments   265

Index   267

We've got sand in our shoes. The truth of the matter is, Bill, it's pretty difficult to explain that to anyone who doesn't know what it means. It means a land covered with sunlight . . . warm and soft. It means pink and white houses . . . and purple bougainvillea and scarlet hibiscus. . . . It means palm trees . . . big fat porpoises playing in Biscayne Bay . . . and folks fishing from the bridges all day. Slim pale yachts and bustling motorboats, and hundreds of little sails fluttering like white butterflies over the water. Big smug liners and the battered freighters. Friendly faces— and never too big a hurry. And the skyline of the city with twinkling lights embroidered against a velvety moon glow . . . turquoise blue waters of the ocean lapping against white beaches and always the sun shining down in kindly warmth. . . . Bill, Sand in Your Shoes means . . . well it means Sand in Your Shoes . . . that's what it means.

—DAMON RUNYON,
in a letter to a friend in Hollywood

FOOL'S PARADISE

One

SOCIALITES

Moderation is a fatal thing. Nothing succeeds like excess.

—OSCAR WILDE

Even in a city where restraint is not considered a virtue, Amber Ridinger's bat mitzvah promised to be something special.

It was a balmy Saturday night in November, with air so soft and sweet you could almost taste it, and a big, chalk white moon hung over Miami. Outside of The Forge restaurant and Glass nightclub on Arthur Godfrey Road four klieg lights on the back of a flatbed truck were making loopy pink circles in the sky, part of a pastel halo that seemed to float over the city like the aurora borealis. Miles out to sea, the light show was visible to the thousands of passengers aboard the city-size cruise ships that had disembarked from the port of Miami an hour or so before, all in a line, bow to stern, heading off to the Caribbean like a string of diamonds on a navy sea.

The pink spotlights were part of the hoopla heralding the thirteenth birthday party of Amber Ridinger. At a cost of over $500,000, it was said to be the most expensive coming-of-age celebration ever held in Miami Beach, and the biggest party of its kind since Henry Ford's coming-out gala for his daughter at the Bath Club. More than two hundred guests were expected to attend, including New York Mets catcher Mike Piazza and his wife, former Playboy Playmate Alicia Rickter, who'd given Amber a $10,000 Cartier Pasha white-gold watch for her birthday. Even that largesse was surpassed by the singer and actress Jennifer Lopez, a family friend of relatively recent acquaintance, who presented Amber with the most lavish birthday gift of all—a $100,000, 30-carat diamond bracelet. Rap stars Ja Rule, Omarion, and Marques Houston were expected to entertain, and Amber herself was going to provide divertissement by introducing her own line of clothing called Gossip in an elaborate runway show. The music would be supplied by the superstar disc jockey DJ AM, best known to readers of *Us Magazine* as Adam Horowitz, the studly serial dater of Paris Hilton's posse. The bat mitzvah girl was also going to introduce her own signature fragrance, Amber No. 13, packaged in custom-designed crystal bottles with Amber's personal logo, each gift-wrapped in pink bows and placed on every table for the guests to take home. The *New York Post*'s gossip column, "Page Six," which doesn't do much bat mitzvah reporting, ran an item saying that Amber, an eighth-grade student at Miami Country Day School, was expected to wear a $26,000 purple-and-silver Dolce & Gabbana gown to her birthday party.

Amber was in "Page Six" because the bat mitzvah also had a publicist, Tara Solomon, of Tara Ink. Ms. Solomon, who hailed from Fort Myers, Florida, was herself a local celebrity and nightlife fixture, a bosomy version of Gidget gone awry, who also wrote an advice column for the *Miami Herald* called "Advice Diva." Ms. Solomon alerted the gossip columns and sent out press releases about the bat mitzvah, one of which was headlined BUTTERFLIES AND BLING—IT'S A BAT MITZVAH THING! The press release noted that "a limited number of escorted cameras will be allowed inside the venue," which is why the night of the bat mitzvah there was a wolf pack of jostling television news cameramen, reporters, and paparazzi in front of the faux eighteenth-century French facade of

The Forge, attacking en masse every time a stretch limousine or lollipop-colored muscle car pulled up to the VIP carpet to disgorge guests, mostly local Miami Beach celebrities such as Dr. Jeff Kamlet, the town's busiest addiction doctor; Thomas Kramer, Miami Beach's scandal-plagued Bad Boy real estate developer; Michael Capponi, the nightlife überpromoter and his model girlfriend Erin Henry; Elaine Lancaster, a staple of the social scene and beloved drag queen who is over seven feet tall in her wig; pop singer Vanessa ("A Thousand Miles") Carlton; Irv Gotti, the formerly indicted CEO of Murder Inc. Records; and stylish hip-hop impresario Damon Dash and his wife, fashion designer Rachel Roy.

Inside The Forge restaurant the bordello-like decor had been feebly disguised in keeping with the bat mitzvah's theme as an Amberland of "Butterflies and Bling." From the restaurant's ceiling in the Dome room hung what looked like a swarm of glittering bugs but were in fact synthetic butterflies, dangling on filament thread above the heads of the guests, along with a purported 42,000 sparkling Swarovski crystals, which supplied the bling. The walls had been draped in white satin, pink flower petals littered the floors, and the restaurant's $20 million wine cellar had been turned into a "Candy Land" where two Little People dressed in munchkinlike white overalls and wigs stood on a table spread with candies and sweets as well as a fountain spouting warm chocolate in which to dip strawberries. The Little People grinned gamely at the guests, who grinned back.

Around 9:30 p.m., Amber Ridinger herself arrived, emerging from the back of a stretch limousine in a flurry of strobe lights along with rap superstar Ja Rule and the platinum-selling singer Ashanti. Amber had dark eyes, pale pink lips, and dark hair piled on top of her head, a few strands of which escaped from under a diamond coronet and fell in her face. There was an endearing awkwardness to the thirteen-year-old as she made her way up the VIP carpet in her ill-fitting $26,000 Dolce & Gabbana gown while photographers shouted "Amber! Amber! Look this way!" like she was a movie star.

Inside The Forge, Amber's beaming parents were watching her arrival on a live video feed being shown throughout the restaurant on flat-screen televisions. "The party was really just meant to fulfill Amber's every vision and every dream," Loren Ridinger, thirty-eight, told a reporter. Mrs. Ridinger was dressed in a low-cut red print dress with spaghetti straps, and her husband, James "JR" Ridinger, fifty-five, was wearing a white tuxedo jacket with a white satin collar and a white shirt open at the neck. The Ridingers both had very white teeth, in contrast to their deep suntans, and they looked years younger than their ages.

The Ridingers had been identified that week with a thrift of description by the *Miami SunPost* as "money-heavy socialites." They'd materialized about ten years earlier from Greensboro, North Carolina, where they created a company out of their garage that sold household products over the Internet called Market America Worldwide, Inc. In 2006, Market America was grossing nearly $300 million a year in revenues, with annual sales projected to reach $1 billion by 2010. The firm was so rich that the Ridingers reportedly had $100 million in cash just sitting in the company's accounts. Back in Greensboro, Ridinger had run into some trouble with the SEC when he created a shell company to take Market America public and then sold shares without disclosing he had an interest in the company. Soon after paying the SEC a fine, the Ridingers moved to Miami. Like so many others, they were looking for fresh horizons and beautiful sunsets over the Everglades.

Miami Beach is a city of neophiliacs where people are mesmerized by shiny new things, and the newcomers du jour quickly rose to the top of the social strata—at least someone's social strata. They built a remarkable $25 million waterfront château-style house on North Bay Road, one of the city's toniest streets. The house had a formal living room with a trompe l'oeil ceiling painted with chariots and angels, and there were crystal chandeliers, gold-leaf-gilded crown moldings, and a marble bust of Beethoven. The Ridingers also had their own ballroom, in which they threw galas for the other money-heavy socialites. Mrs. Ridinger owned so many expensive Judith Leiber pocketbooks that they were locked in a display case in her bedroom. There was a stable of eighteen cars, including a Rolls-Royce Phantom, an Aston Martin, and a Mercedes McClaren—one of only five in the United States—and a staff of thirty-one, including chauffeurs and yacht crew. The couple also owned two boats, a $6 million 20-footer and an $18 million, 156-foot yacht, the latter of which they took to Manhattan in the summers to escape Miami's tropical heat. They kept it berthed at Chelsea Piers while they lived in a penthouse suite at the Ritz-Carlton Hotel. The couple was also known for their generosity to charities and their friends. They'd befriended an impressive variety of A-list celebrities, including singers Jennifer Lopez and her husband Marc Anthony, and Madonna, who was wary of most people and hard to get to know, yet who felt comfortable enough with the Ridingers to use their six-room guest cottage instead of staying in a hotel when she was in Miami.

Tara Solomon hit a home run for the Ridingers in the press. Amber's birthday party made the front page of the *Miami Herald* and the cover of the *Style* section of the *New York Times* and was featured in the *South Florida Sun-Sentinel*. Amber's pink-carpet arrival was seen on the 11:00 p.m. news on several local TV outlets in Miami, and it was featured in segments on *Inside Edition, Access Hollywood,* and *Geraldo at Large.* MTV ran a news story about the party called "Torah Down the House," and on CNN, in a segment about expensive parties for teens, Loren Ridinger was seen saying to Amber, "You're a great kid and don't be mad at Mommy if everything's not perfect."

There was just one thing that wasn't perfect.

Amber Ridinger wasn't raised Jewish.

Her father had been brought up Methodist, and the family celebrated Christmas—but Amber's maternal grandmother, who died when she was only seven months old, *was* Jewish, which made Amber's mother Jewish, and in Miami Beach, that's enough to throw a bat mitzvah. Rabbi Zev Katz, thirty-four, who officiated at Amber's extravaganza, admitted he did not perform a bat mitzvah ceremony. The bearded and jovial Rabbi Katz was the quintessential Miami Beach Lubavitcher rabbi, who could be found weekdays with his "Chabad House on Wheels," a panel bus, which he parked at a crosswalk on Lincoln Road and used to solicit fellow Jews to lay *tefillin*. He didn't want to convert Gentiles, he wanted to bring Jews further into the fold, and so he'd embrace Jews or the nearest thing to it, like Amber. The eminently likable Rabbi Katz explained that Amber hadn't recited a haftorah, one of the most traditional parts of the ceremony, and that the event took place not in a synagogue but in the parents' North Bay Road château, and that Amber simply made a speech and Rabbi Katz blessed her.

But hey, this is Miami Beach.

It also turned out that Loren and JR Ridinger weren't exactly "dot com millionaires" as described in the press, although a portion of their company's business—mainly consumer polls about their products—was conducted online. Market America has been compared in the press to the Amway company model, which the Ridingers adamantly deny is a fair comparison. Purportedly, Market America has 100,000 "distributors" who pay $600 in start-up fees and about $150 a month to stay "active" in the company. Each salesperson is expected to recruit two more. Market America is so wildly popular that the company has been able to fill convention halls and stadiums as large as the Carnival Center in Miami for sales conferences, one of the highlights of which is testimony by the company's top earners to the riches and spoils Market America has brought them. In fact, Amber's extravagant bat mitzvah was an example of one of the tenets of Market America's marketing strategy—that the senior officers and top earners of the company conspicuously show off the rewards of their hard work—cars, homes, luxury goods—thus inspiring new conscriptees and making Amber Ridinger's bat mitzvah a possible tax deduction.

·THAT SAME balmy weekend, across the still-warm waters of Biscayne Bay in Coral Gables, a wealthy suburb of the city of Miami, the condescending but codependent older sister of louche Miami Beach, there was another party of socialites taking place.

There were no paparazzi or sound bites or spotlights in the sky.

There was a photographer, hired by the hosts, who politely took posed pictures of guests during cocktails.

This party was a $1,000-a-seat black-tie gala at the elegant Biltmore Hotel to kick off a three-day celebration called "A Very Wolfsonian Weekend," marking the tenth anniversary of the Wolfsonian–Florida International University Museum in Miami Beach. The honorary chairs of the event were Carnival Cruise Lines' vice chairman and COO Howard Frank and his wife Mary; Miami Design Center developer Craig Robins; and hotelier André Balazs. Guests included architects David Schwarz, Luis Pons, and Chad Oppenheim; publishing heiress Jan Cowles; high-end real estate developer Walid Wahab; photographer Iran Issa-Khan; artist and writer Michele Oka Doner; banker Enrique Carrillo; art dealer Marvin Ross Friedman; interior designer Pepe Calderin; and Modesto A. Maidique, president of Florida International University, who was being honored, along with Michael Holden, a vice president of JP Morgan, and the Wolfsonian Museum's founder, the remarkable Mitchell Wolfson Jr., affectionately known as "Micky."

Micky Wolfson is the scion of one of the most prominent families in Miami Beach's history. Mitchell Sr. built the Wometco chain of movie theaters in greater Miami—including the world-famous Capri on Lincoln Road. He also started the city's first television station, WTKK, which he built into a small network in southern Florida. Mitchell Sr. was also an inspiring civic leader during wartime—and the first Jewish man elected mayor of Miami Beach, in 1943, who patriotically resigned as mayor to fight in World War II. When Mitchell Sr. died in 1984, Micky inherited $84.4 million and began to use it to satisfy a lifelong craving: collecting.

Micky was a collector of *things*. All sorts of things, it turned out. It started with a collection of hotel keys when he was a child and turned into the Wolfsonian Museum, a trove of curiosities comprising 70,000 objects and 36,000 books, all from the period of 1885 to the end of World War II, each one of them with its own backstory, provenance, or significance in history. Much of the collection is identified as "decorative propaganda," which are curios relating to the Fascist and Nazi movements in Europe. It includes a "banned books" section that contains a 1941 copy of *Mein Kampf* in Braille; Hitler's silverware; a silver cocktail shaker from World War I shaped like a bomb; and Nazi wall hangings. The remainder of the collection contains eccentric pieces that can't be categorized: Queen Victoria's soup tureen; King Farouk's matchbook collection; and the massive finial that once capped the Woolworth Building in New York City. Another curious thing about this collection is that it's housed in a 56,000-square-foot, 1926 Mediterranean-style converted warehouse on Washington Avenue and 10th Street in Miami Beach, incongruously situated amid Cuban and Thai restaurants, slice-of-pizza joints, and sleazy storefront nightclubs with blacked-out windows. Wolfson used to pay to store his collection in this warehouse, but when he began to run out of space he bought the whole building in 1985 and renovated it into a seven-story museum and research facility.

In 1997 Wolfson gave the Wolfsonian Museum and all its contents to the Florida International University to bring it fiscal stability and longevity. The museum is still heavily indebted to the generosity of corporate donors as well as many of the 600 guests who assembled for the dinner dance under the barrel-ceiling ballroom at the Biltmore Hotel that mid-November night. The elegant hotel is a National Historic Landmark built in 1926 by architects Leonard Schultze and S. Fullerton Weaver, who also built the Waldorf-Astoria in New York and The Breakers in Palm Beach. The majestic main building is 76,000 square feet and had the largest hotel pool in America when it was built, a shimmering lagoon 250 feet long that wrapped around covered piazzas and cabanas. Its best-known architectural detail is a fifteen-story copper-covered bell tower modeled after the Moorish Giralda Tower in Seville, Spain.

The evening of the party, guests were served cocktails and hors d'oeuvres on a tiled patio overlooking the manicured gardens of the hotel. They were summoned to dinner by "Wolfsonian Fanfare," commissioned especially for that evening by composer and conductor Michael Ruszczynski and played by members of the New World Symphony orchestra. The menu that night included baked stuffed apple with country sausage, supreme of halibut, and duck consommé. Key lime bars, inspired by the hotel's first menu eighty years before, were served for dessert. The Peter Duchin society band played, and although Duchin was eighty years old—and many of the guests were not that much younger—he managed to get the crowd up on the dance floor.

When dinner and speeches were over, a writer new to the area approached Arva Moore Parks, Miami's grande dame historian, author, and publisher, who played a central role in the $55 million renovation of the Biltmore Hotel that culminated in 1987. Ms. Parks warned the writer that the great pitfall of writing about Miami Beach would be to make a factual error and that the watchdogs of the city's legacy would be lying in wait. She gave the visitor a pop quiz: Who was the architect of the hotel in which he was sitting? The visitor guessed Addison Mizner. Ms. Parks adopted an "I told you so" look, and then informed the visitor that the architect/builder was Schultze & Weaver. Ms. Parks's abashed petitioner used his last moments holding her attention to pose a question. "If the guests tonight in this ballroom constitute Miami society," he asked, "who is Miami Beach society?"

Ms. Parks thought for a moment, scrunched up her nose, and said, "There isn't any."

Then she got up and did a mean Charleston with her husband.

"MIAMI BEACH *evolved* into a nonsociety," Micky Wolfson said, a bit dolefully. "Miami Beach is one of the few society-less cities in the world. There is nothing sacred. No tradition."

Wolfson, sixty-seven, was dressed in a European-cut, belted sports jacket and dark slacks, looking very spiffy. He was not in Miami Beach but in Manhattan, in one of the two apartments he keeps in a building on Park Avenue South, one for himself and one for guests. The peripatetic collector passes through Manhattan often on his travels to Europe, where he lives half of the year, busy acquiring objects for a second museum he is creating outside of Genoa, Italy, this one called Wolfsoniana, which will specialize in Italian, Austrian, and German decorative and propaganda arts. When he is in residence in Florida he no longer stays in his hometown of Miami Beach. Years ago he felt compelled to move away from Miami Beach to a duplex in a high-rise apartment building in Miami, where he can look at the hurly-burly of the city across the bay without actually being there. He feels a sense of loss by what has happened across the bay. After all, he named the reminiscence he wrote (with the artist Michele Oka Doner) about growing up in the city *Miami Beach: Blueprint of an Eden.*

A Princeton graduate with a degree in art history, Wolfson considers tradition, civility, conviviality, and good conversation essential elements in any society. "But there is no conversation now in Miami Beach," he said. "There are monologues. There are diatribes. But there is no conversation." He shrugged. "Nowadays people identify themselves with a sports team.

"There used to be society in Miami Beach," he continued. "The kind that would be recognized as society in other parts of the country. But all the society that was there, that celebrated itself, and was grudgingly admired by others, their circle and their clubhouses do not house them anymore. Those people are gone. I think I'm the last of a generation, the last of the old-timers. There is no continuity," Wolfson said. "The people who had been coming to Miami Beach since the forties began to die out and the town was left forlorn and open to all kinds of takers and comers. It completely lost its identity. Its identity died. It died with a generation, and its identity was renewed by Yankees who saw the marketing possibilities."

The society who Mickey Wolfson was referring to were the local men and women of "Old Miami Beach," citizens who had lived there since it was incorporated in 1915 and had been active in the community and church in the 1920s and 1930s but had no wealth. There was also a seasonal meritocracy of "tradesmen millionaires," men who were wealthy but without position, or, as *Time* magazine described them, of "unspectacular fortune." A 1936 *Fortune* magazine portrayed the winter residents of Miami Beach as "the sediment of middle-class society" and "minor capitalists" and called the resort "What God had left over when he created Palm Beach." Miami Beach was, as author Polly Redford called it, "a second-rate WASP resort." Jane Fisher, the first wife of the creator of Miami Beach, the real estate developer Carl Fisher, wrote in her autobiography, *Fabulous Hoosier*, that "Palm Beach society . . . thought we were scum."

Even so, *Fortune* estimated that 600 millionaires had winter homes in Miami Beach, among them Elmer Maytag, the washing-machine manufacturer; Mark Honeywell, the inventor of the thermostat; Leonard Florsheim, who started a chain of shoe stores; William Hoover, who manufactured vacuum cleaners; Sebastian Kresge, who owned a chain of five-and-dime stores; and Harry M. Stevens, concessionaire. The wealthy included some Jews, such as John D. Hertz, the founder of the Yellow Cab Company and a car-leasing firm; and Julius Fleischmann, of the margarine company. There were also the men of what Polly Redford called "oil-can society": W. M. Griffin from Fort Wayne, Indiana, made "pumps." W. O. Briggs made auto bodies in Detroit. C. A. McCulloch was in the utilities business in Chicago. Moe Annenberg owned the *Daily Racing Form.*

In his 1952 book *The Last Resorts,* Cleveland Amory described the difference between the "hotel society" of Miami Beach and the "cottage society" of Palm Beach. In Palm Beach the only place one wants to be seen is at "the club" or on the society pages of the Palm Beach "shiny sheet," as it's called. On the other hand, in Miami Beach, according to Amory, when a sightseeing boat pulled close to one of the small residential islands in Biscayne Bay so a group of tourists could eyeball some of the big mansions and expensive yachts, the owner of one of the houses came out on his dock, clasped his hands over his head as if he had won a prizefight, and posed for pictures.

"It's a city of characters," commented Wolfson, "which is what drew writers like Damon Runyon and Walter Winchell." Wolfson admonishes critics for expecting too much. "Miami Beach was founded on the idea that people wanted to use their money to pay for toys. So Miami Beach is a city of playpens and playfulness. It never had a pretense for anything more than being a celebration of playfulness. It wasn't meant to be anything except one of the world's greatest resorts."

Two

THE ISLAND OF BROKEN TOYS

Miami Beach is like a Dickens novel with a tan.

—AFTER DARK: SOUTH BEACH ARTS &
ENTERTAINMENT CHANNEL

What is Miami Beach?

The city is a chimera. In eternal flux. If you walk a few blocks in any direction and look at the buildings and at the faces of people on the streets or listen to the chatter, you could be in any of four or five different places—Tel Aviv; Saint-Tropez; Rio de Janiero; Berlin; Coney Island.

People are in a good mood in Miami Beach. Visitors say they feel better just being there. It stays lighter longer in the winter in Miami Beach than in most other places because the city lies closer to the equator than any other resort in the continental United States, and daylight lingers. Some residents posit that all the rounded corners and curved buildings enhance a feeling of smooth well-being. Others say it's simply the spectacular beauty, the palm trees and sunshine, the translucent sea, so many different hues of aqua and green that it looks like a canvas from a paint-by-number kit.

Miami Beach's original intent as a naughty playground for

wealthy adults has been well served. It has a full-throttle, seven-days-a-week party in progress, as if the city is caught in some eternal spring break. There are thousands of bars, clubs, restaurants, and überhip hotels with jaw-dropping architecture and room rates that run anywhere from $100 to $10,000 a night. Perhaps most important, there is an ever-replenishing stock of good-looking young men and women who go there to party and have sex. Sex is the city's favorite pastime. In South Beach two is never enough; the prevailing style of sport fucking is a ménage à trois—usually two men and one woman (although that's not written in stone). This only slightly complicates the matter of pickups in a city where it seems there are a lot of bisexual women. It also helps that the preferred South Beach drug is Ecstasy, which floods the brain with serotonin, the feel-good neurotransmitter that helps lubricate inhibition and stir the libido. You can buy a tab of Ecstasy in Miami Beach as easy as a pack of gum— or score a gram of cocaine with little more difficulty than ordering a mojito on Ocean Drive. "Everybody in this town is on drugs and drinks almost every night," notes Dr. Jeff Kamlet, the city's primo drug counselor to the local glitterati. "This is a total party environment. It's a mixture of easy availability of drugs and the nightlife. People who like to party come here to live and vacation, and they party like there are no consequences."

As much as the power faction that runs Miami Beach is enthralled by its international reputation as a seaside Sodom, behind the world-class facade it suffers are the insecurities, intrigues, rivalries, and bitchiness of an insular southern boondock. Its power structure is cliquish, gossipy, and xenophobic, terrified that under the shellac of sophistication Miami Beach is going to be revealed as second-rate. Although 13 million tourists spend their way through town every year, Michael Aller, the director of tourism and conventions, voices the generally held perception that "maybe only one hundred and fifty people run all of Miami Beach. Maybe even less. Everybody knows each other here. This is a very small town." For a small town there's a big fat money pie to carve up: the gross city product is $6.5 billion—per capita one of the highest in the nation.

The place is not just small psychologically but physically, too. The author David Rieff described it as a "toy city." It takes less than half an hour to cross Miami Beach on foot from bay to ocean. It's little more than a barrier reef, 7.1 square miles, half of it dredged out of the ocean floor to give it more landmass. The full-time 95,000 residents—among them Cubans, South Americans, Spaniards, Russians, Israelis, and Germans—make Miami Beach the second most densely packed city in America next to Manhattan. Oddly, the city government isn't quite certain what the 95,000 population figure represents. Many part-time residents live somewhere else but declare Miami Beach as their primary residence because of tax advantages: there are no city or state income taxes for full-time Florida residents. In the 1960s and 1970s the city had a better idea of the size of its population when seasonal renters had their electric meters turned on and off. Before then the city used to weigh the garbage to estimate how many tourists visited in the winter.

Contrary to the indelible impression that Miami Beach is still a ghetto for old Jews on pensions, fewer than 20 percent of the 95,000 residents are Jewish, according to surveys conducted by the University of Miami. Some 60 percent of the population of Miami Beach are Hispanic, and the average age hovers around thirty-seven years old, not ninety. The Jewish decline began three decades ago, not because old people moved away but because old people died off and were not replaced with the next generation. The last kosher hotel closed in 2005, and the one large reform synagogue, Temple Emanu-El, has been struggling financially for over a decade. Although there are still pockets of Orthodox Jews, and the Talmudic University remains in evidence on Alton Road, the fruit stores, kosher butchers, shoe-repair stores, and bakeries that used to line Washington Avenue have been replaced with slice-of-pizza joints, motorcycle-wear shops, Thai restaurants, and discount shoe stores. Wolfie's, the legendary delicatessen where the waiters put silver bowls of pickles and cole slaw and a basket of freshly baked onion rolls on every table, is now just a childhood dream to a bunch of aging baby boomers. But Miami Beach is not about staying the same.

What remains unfailingly constant is the extraordinary weather. Between the trade winds softening the air and the Gulf Stream warming the waters, it's paradise in the winter months. It's one of the few places on the mainland in which subtropical plants and fruits will grow all year round. The weather cooperates with tourism in that it rains mostly out of season*—75 percent of the average annual rainfall occurs between May and October. In winter the average daytime temperature is 76 degrees, but in summer, when the temperature hovers in the mid-90s, the broiling intensity of the sun is intolerable. The air is so wet and thick that you can perspire just sitting still. People move very slowly. Even drivers in cars stopped at traffic lights take their time moving when the light changes to green. (Perhaps this is not due to the languid pace but to the fact that so many drivers are on their cell phones. Miami Beach has the largest concentration of cell phones in America, and there's no local law that prohibits driving and dialing. Everybody in Miami Beach seems to be talking on a cell phone, and there is a joke that you can tell an Israeli from a Latino in Miami Beach because the Israelis are talking on two cell phones at once.)

Although most tourists never differentiate between the two, Miami Beach and South Beach are not synonymous. South Beach is the lower third of Miami Beach where most of the hotels and clubs

---

*There is no official answer to how long a "season" is in Miami Beach. The chamber of commerce would like tourists to believe that the season starts in November and ends around Easter, but tourism doesn't really pick up until January and it falls off at the end of March.

are located. Also, Miami Beach is not a part of the city of Miami but a distinct and separate municipality, with its own government and tax base, as well as its own culture. The city of Miami has long lived in the shadow of the little sandbar across the bay. Sixty years ago *Time* magazine noted that "one of Miami's claims to fame is that it is the city near Miami Beach." While Miami city has gained prestige as the financial center of Latin America, it still has the third worst poverty rate in the nation, and for cities with a population of more than 250,000, Miami has the lowest median household income in the country—only $24,000. Meanwhile the city of Miami Beach, whose median gross income is $89,000, longs for its own respectability, like a hooker who wants to be asked to stay for breakfast. In a town where the firefighters wear uniforms courtesy of Izod, body image is a preoccupation, and Shaquille O'Neal is a reserve police officer, residents are sensitive about being thought superficial.

Local boosters point out with pride that since 2002, Miami Beach has been the host city to Art Basel, the American venue of the spectacular international arts fair that the *New York Times* called "a carnival of excess for anyone seeking a vaguely highbrow justification to head somewhere warm in the winter," adding that art at Art Basel was sold with "garage-sale efficiency." It was efficient enough that $500 million worth of art changed hands at the 2007 exposition, much of it privately before the exhibition even began, piggybacked with two dozen other simultaneous satellite art fairs. Although the sexy, overwrought city, with its hundreds of dramatic hotels and party settings, is a worthy backdrop to Art Basel, the art fair is in reality just another of the conventions that pass through the 1.2 million-square-foot convention center and fill the city's hotel rooms. When Art Basel leaves, it takes its culture with it. In 2007 an official of Art Basel denied persistent rumors that the organization was planning to move the fair to Los Angeles in 2010.

Truth be told, in Miami Beach there are more tattoo parlors than libraries, more spray-tan parlors than schools. (There are seven public grade schools and one high school.) There are more bars per capita than in any other city in America, and there is one building referred to as "the clubhouse" that is dedicated solely to Alcoholics Anonymous meetings, twenty-four hours a day, alternating in English and Spanish.

Miami Beach may be self-involved but it is not particularly self-examining. It has no indigenous newspaper, although the *Miami New Times* frequently casts its acerbic eye on it, the *SunPost* newspaper keeps an office and reports from there, and the Beach is somewhat grudgingly covered by the *Miami Herald*, the way the *Wall Street Journal* would cover Asbury Park, New Jersey.

It's not much of a town for books, either; there's only one bookstore/café, Books & Books on Lincoln Road. One would imagine that in a beach town there would be a big market for books, but sunbathers on the beach don't seem to be reading. Rather, they're all staring at the nearly naked bodies surrounding them. When Mitchell Kaplan, the owner of Books & Books and the founder of the Miami Book Fair, was asked by the *Miami Herald* if he thought Miami was lowbrow, he replied, "We have an image that everybody here has fake boobs. Well, some people with fake boobs are very intellectual."

While a $446.3 million Miami Performing Arts Center has been built across the MacArthur Causeway in the city of Miami, the city of Miami Beach spent years debating whether to give a long-term contract to Cirque de Soleil in the Arthur Godfrey Theater, where touring companies of Broadway shows appear. Miami Beach's major cultural calling card is justifiably the New World Symphony, an orchestra of brilliant young music students directed by the famous conductor Michael Tilson Thomas. The city is building a new concert hall designed by Frank Gehry for the New World Symphony, which will be the resort's pride and joy. (Another prestigious architectural addition to Miami Beach in the works is a building by Jacques Herzog and Pierre de Meuron—but this one is a parking garage.) Aside from the unique Wolfsonian Museum and a small Jewish museum in a preserved old *shul* dedicated to the story of the Jewish saga in Miami Beach, there is only one fine-arts museum, the Bass, founded in 1963 by Johanna and John Bass and refurbished from a former public library, with a collection of 3,000 works of art, including the living room furniture of the town's most famous hotel designer, Morris Lapidus. Unfortunately, in 1968 a team of art experts declared seventeen paintings to be forgeries.* There is a larger museum, the World Erotic Art Museum, which is 12,000 square feet and houses 4,000 pieces, run by Naomi Wilzig, the widow of a New Jersey banker with a penchant for historic dildos. "Let's face it," former Miami Beach mayor Neisen Kasdin said, "people in Miami Beach talk a lot about the Art Deco district, but to the rest of the world, Miami Beach is sex."

It is also a city with an "end of the world" mentality, or as W. Somerset Maugham said about Monte Carlo, "a sunny place for shady people." In 1940 *Time* magazine characterized Miami Beach as "a prime destination for Americans on the make, on the lam, or on a pension." The city has always enjoyed its outlaw reputation; it didn't allow the Gideons to put Bibles in hotel rooms until 1948. Modern-day Miami Beach is a petri dish of regenerated lives, a nourishing environment for the dispossessed who need a second chance. The city itself has redefined its identity half a dozen times since it was incorporated in 1915. Observes Esther Percal, one of the top real estate brokers, "People come here with a lot of baggage." It is of no small consideration to those with baggage that because of Florida's Homestead Act, no one can take your home

---

*In the Miami area, the most valuable art is not in museums but in the private museums of a handful of wealthy local collectors. The Rubell Family Collection, started in 1964 by Don and Mera Rubell, has twenty-seven galleries and a 30,000-volume research library, and is considered one of the finest contemporary art collections in the world. But it's in Miami, not Miami Beach.

even if you declare bankruptcy or are convicted of paying for your Bentley with your company's junk bonds.

Elaine Lancaster, the female impersonator nonpareil and Miami Beach socialite who is so popular that she was given the key to the city of Miami Beach as well as the key to the city of Miami, explains, "This is the island of broken toys. This is a place where people get away with things they would never get away with any-place else in the world. That's what draws them here."

Almost everything in Miami Beach has come from somewhere else, including the palm trees (the original nuts were brought from Trinidad), the flamingos (brought from the Bahamas by entrepre-neur Carl Fisher and replenished when they died), and the beach (which had to be widened with sand from up the coast). Other parts of Miami Beach have been tailored, nipped, tucked, or engorged as well, including nineteen man-made islands that were dredged from the ocean floor and added off its western shore to increase the landmass. Even its blunt southern tip at Government Cut was circumcised to accommodate larger ships entering the port.*

MIAMI BEACH is deliberately missing three features usually found in American cities: It does not have homeless shelters, black neighborhoods, or cemeteries. The many homeless people who live in South Beach would sleep on the beach all year round if they were allowed, and each night they are rounded up by a posse of

---

*Curiously, although Miami Beach is associated with plastic surgery, in part because of the success of the pansexual plastic-surgery saga on TV, *Nip/Tuck,* the best plastic surgeons are still in New York and Los Angeles. Plastic surgery in Miami Beach is apt to look extreme—breasts too large, lips too puffy—and many middle-aged men and women sport a tight, caught-in-a-wind-tunnel look. Plastic surgery, on average, is half the price of surgery in New York and LA, but you get what you pay for.

"homeless police" and brought to shelters across Biscayne Bay in the city of Miami.

There is no African American neighborhood in Miami Beach because blacks were never welcomed. At its roots, Miami Beach is a city in the Deep South that remained segregated long after the rest of the South, its bigotry hidden under the guise of a resort city of white transients. Until the 1960s, African Americans were only allowed in Miami Beach during the day if they had a job there, and at night they were checked for "night passes," signed by white employers, at the causeway entrances.* During World War II when the U.S. Army used Miami Beach as a basic training camp, black soldiers were segregated from the USO, and in 1953 the Betsy Ross Hotel on Ocean Drive allowed black delegates from the Churches of God in Christ convention to stay there, but would not allow them into the dining room. Celebrities were not exempt. When the African American singer Lena Horne headlined the Fontainebleau Hotel, she wasn't allowed to sleep there; after the show she was driven to a hotel in Liberty City, a black section across Biscayne Bay, to spend the night. The reason why the singer Nat King Cole premiered what would become his classic song "Mona Lisa" at the Eden Roc was because he was told that black entertainers had to use the side door at the Fontainebleau. The first African American entertainer allowed to stay in Miami Beach was Harry Belafonte, who was given a room at the Eden Roc Hotel in 1963. Racial tensions in Miami between whites and blacks were exacerbated in the 1970s when the newly arriving Cuban population (regarded as the "Jews of the Caribbean" for their industriousness) found immediate

---

*Fisher Island, which is often touted as the most expensive zip code in America, was once owned by a prominent black businessman named Dana A. Dorsey, who bought the island to start a resort for African Americans who were prohibited from vacationing in Miami Beach. Carl Fisher bought the island from Dorsey in 1919.

acceptance, jobs, and assimilation, while black citizens were still regarded as inferiors.

In 1990, under pressure from Cuban and Jewish leaders who were angered by Nelson Mandela's support of Fidel Castro and Yasser Arafat, the city of Miami Beach decided to officially snub the great South African leader. Recently freed from prison, Mandela was scheduled to visit Miami Beach as part of a seven-city tour of the United States. He checked in and out of his Miami Beach hotel suite without so much as a basket of fruit from the city. Angered and affronted, American civil rights activists called for a national 1,000-day boycott of Miami Beach hotels and businesses by all people of color. It was a powerful protest. Large corporations with African American employees stopped booking their conventions in Miami Beach, simply to avoid becoming part of the controversy, and in the first 365 days of the boycott, the city of Miami Beach lost $50 million in revenues. Anxious to reconcile with black leaders, the city fathers in 1993 promised to guarantee a loan for the construction of the first black-owned-and-operated hotel and convention center in Miami Beach, which everybody in Miami Beach immediately began to refer to as the "Black Hotel." Nowadays Miami Beach depends deeply on African Americans for income in the off-season. The Winter Music Conference every March is almost all R&B and hip-hop and attracts an estimated 40,000 people of color to its eighty-five parties; and Memorial Day weekend in South Beach has become unofficially known as the "black weekend," when an estimated 100,000 African Americans come to Miami Beach to celebrate.

As for cemeteries, burials are against the law in Miami Beach. Youth, not death, is the selling point, and in any event, because the soil is so porous, a coffin would bob to the surface within ten years of being inhumed. Like everything else in Miami Beach, its very foundation is liable to shift.

Three
LINCOLN ROAD

Miami Beach is where neon goes to die.
—LENNY BRUCE

"No, madam, this is not a switchboard," Michael Aller said pleasantly into his cell phone. "You have reached the tourist hotline *directly*. This is Michael Aller, *Mr. Miami Beach*."

Mr. Miami Beach listened patiently.

"I'm sorry," he said, "but that particular footrace is already over. It started four hours ago. There's another race tomorrow, which includes the handicapped, and there's one next week—if you're still here in Miami Beach. Well, thank you for coming. *God bless.*"

Aller, sixty-seven, snapped his cell phone shut and placed it on the marble table in front of him next to his Louis Vuitton tote-all. He was perched on a stool at a table inside the Van Dyke Café on Lincoln Road, taking shelter from one of those baby squalls in Miami Beach that materialize with no warning and then evaporate into blue sky. It was a Saturday in January, and Miami Beach locals know that January is the coolest and most unpredictable month weatherwise, although the resort-industry professionals don't want the tourists to know that, especially Michael Aller, for whom there is no such thing as a bad month in Miami

Beach. "Mr. Miami Beach" is the self-proclaimed sobriquet of a man whose official job title is Chief of Protocol of Miami Beach and Tourism and Convention Director, a powerful position in a city whose lifeblood is tourism and its tributaries.

Aller is a small, pear-shaped man with a sweet grandfatherly face. He was wearing khaki slacks and a polo shirt with a plastic I LOVE MIAMI BEACH pin on it. He had a good manicure and the faint aroma of Kouros surrounded him, the same Yves Saint Laurent cologne he's worn for more than 30 years. Aller is one of the last of a generation of Miami Beach old-timers, with a twist—he is openly gay. ("How will you recognize me?" he asked a writer incredulously over the phone. "I'm old, I'm fat, I'm Jewish, and I'm gay.")

Aller's cell phone rang again, but this time instead of answering "Miami Beach Tourist Bureau" he turned off the ringer and let his voice mail answer. He remarked that his phone rings so frequently because it's printed on every official tourist guide and pamphlet published by the tourist board of the city of Miami Beach, and he produced a stack of flyers from his tote-all to prove it. He said he never gets tired answering questions about footraces and hotel availability. "Never," he said flatly. "I love what I do."

He grew up in Detroit, Michigan, an only child. His father's company supplied much of the marble and stone used in the construction of the Fontainebleau Hotel, and as part of his payment the Fontainebleau's owner, Ben Novack, gave Aller's family an apartment at the Fontainebleau in winter months, from Thanksgiving to Easter. "You've heard of Eloise at the Plaza?" he asked. "Well, I was Michael at the Fontainebleau. I was nine years old when I first was taken there." Every morning Aller, dressed in short pants and blazer, would go down to the lobby and say hello to Novack, who would pat him on the head. Aller's parents, he once explained, had two cabanas at the Fontainebleau, one where his father played gin rummy and another where his mother played canasta. He told a reporter that his father made so much money playing gin rummy that he "became a limited partner in two hotels and a shopping center just on the winnings from card games."

In 1980, after spending nineteen years in the nursing-home business in California, Michael Aller moved to Fort Lauderdale and took a job selling shirts. In 1987 he was back in Miami Beach, where he became manager of the Burdines Polo Shop for $5.50 an hour. A ham at heart, with the singing voice and delivery of an old vaudevillian, he used to entertain at parties and charity events, singing "Mammy" like Al Jolson or doing Georgie Jessel impersonations and insulting people like Don Rickles. Aller was so popular that he and some friends rented a seventy-eight-foot catamaran on weekends and turned it into a "floating cabaret," with Aller acting as host and stand-up comedian. He later had a local public-access cable-TV show, *Michael Aller's Miami Beach Is My Beat,* and eventually he went to work for the chamber of commerce. He became head of tourism just as the city began to burgeon in the mid-1990s.

The rain ended as quickly as if a faucet had been turned off, and the warm sun rolled across the wide street. The sidewalks were crowded with café tables and umbrellas, and a low concrete median of reflecting pools and thick landscaping of palms and hibiscus and oleander ran down the center of the road. Within a moment there was a return of the pleasant cacophony of squawking parrots (blown over from Parrot Jungle Island by Hurricane Andrew), and the people returned, too, materializing from nowhere into the sunshine to resume the seemingly irresistible ritual of strolling along Lincoln Road. This is the center of a city that has no center. Like the citizens of an old eastern European town, many people in Miami Beach take a weekly *spaziergang* on Lincoln Road. On a typical day in season, some 15,000 of the hoi polloi will wander up and down the patterned sidewalks of this broad pedestrian mall, eight blocks long and a hundred feet wide.* It is a mesmerizing parade of tourists and locals, the high and the low, politicians, hookers, humans and dogs, pocketbook thieves and movie stars, strolling back and forth or sitting under the colored umbrellas at the café tables, watching the people watching them.

However, this is not the Croisette in Cannes; while there are many beautiful and fashionable women and men, it is more like the cast of the barroom scene in *Star Wars* is passing by. The scene fascinates with the expectation of which great beauty or monster might saunter by next. There are women in skimpy clothing with Miami Beach Goddess breasts as well as anorexic stick figures with collagen-filled lips. There are street performers—a man with no arms who paints with his feet, and a woman covered in white makeup who stands immobile and pretends she's a statue. There are bicyclists weaving in and out and people walking dogs— sometimes with multiple dogs on tangled leashes—and barking dogs are everywhere, and every hundred feet or so there are bowls of water for thirsty canines put outside by the shop owners. There are more than 200 shops, flashy clothing stores with satiny embroidered shirts and high prices, expensive shoe stores with cheap European merchandise at high prices, a Pottery Barn, housewares stores, art galleries, sunglass shops, a Banana Republic in what was once an old bank, an Apple Computer shop, and a Victoria's Secret, which allegedly pays $60,000 a month for its visibility on the highly trafficked street.

Sitting at the Van Dyke Café, it's difficult not to notice all the gay men ambling down the street, intimidatingly beautiful, tanned from the beach and muscular from hours at the gym and the use of steroids and human growth hormone, all part of the Miami Beach

---

*Lincoln Road is technically twelve blocks long, but only eight are part of the pedestrian mall.

gay subculture.* Under Michael Aller's command the Chamber of Commerce mounted a major campaign to make gay men and lesbians feel welcome at the resort. It's because of Aller that in all of the Miami Beach tourism paraphernalia, photographs of male partners and female partners are featured along with heterosexual couples and families. Like the official Miami Beach advertising brochures say, "The Magic's in the Mix." This was done not just to champion equality but because where gays go, gay money follows. Gays have more disposable income than straight families, and they spend big bucks on travel and vacations. They also buy real estate and help gentrify neighborhoods. Gay men became one of the cornerstones of Miami Beach's most recent revival, attracted to the cheap rents and the laissez-faire attitude of the indifferent locals.

In the 1980s the Beach became a mecca for HIV-positive men when there were few treatments and life expectancy was short. South Beach, where people lived in the present and sensation was paramount, seemed the perfect place to spend their last years, and according to Florida International University, in the late 1980s and early 1990s Miami Beach became the single greatest destination for gay men newly diagnosed with AIDS. *Out* magazine described Miami Beach as "a palm-lined cliff that mighty buffaloes throw themselves over." By 1995 one South Beach AIDS support foundation estimated that one in three gay men in Miami Beach had HIV, and between 1999 and 2001 South Beach had one of the highest "conversion" rates to HIV positive in the country. These gay men

---

*In 1960, Miami Beach historian Harold Mehling wrote in his book *The Most of Everything* that ". . . the Beach is plagued by a rampaging problem of overt homosexuality and lesbianism. Whatever the lure for sexual deviates is, they respond in large numbers and can be found any evening clogging the vicinity of Lincoln and Alton Road. . . . There they promenade in public as a mild form of enjoyment. The Miami Beach police allow the deviates to 'cluster' on the theory that they will at least be isolated. . . ."

sold their life insurance policies for cash and spent their retirement funds. Then something unexpected happened—after the initial onslaught of AIDS, Miami's gay citizens didn't all die. New medicines were developed and many who thought they'd never leave South Beach alive went on to thrive and prosper. Suddenly South Beach was no longer the charming, inexpensive town the gays had helped gentrify; rents were high and going higher and condominiums were priced in the millions of dollars. Thousands of gay residents went on a pilgrimage north, to the Wilton Manors area of Fort Lauderdale, which now has the third-largest gay population per capita of any city in America. The former Warsaw Ballroom on Collins Avenue, one of the most famous gay nightclubs in the United States, is now Jerry's Famous Deli, and the legendary gay club Salvation is now an Office Depot. Although the gay population in Miami Beach is still very visible, their numbers have shrunk to such a degree that as of this writing there are only two gay bars left on Miami Beach.

ONE COULD only imagine what Carl Fisher, the real Mr. Miami Beach, the brilliant showman and salesman who invented the resort, would have thought of Lincoln Road today, a street he built to be the "Fifth Avenue of the South." The café in which Aller was sitting, the Van Dyke, was the tallest building in Miami Beach when Carl Fisher built it in 1924, and it was the first to have an elevator, in which prospective land buyers could ascend to Fisher's real estate offices and purchase plots of land. "If you look up there," Aller said, pointing to the sixth floor, "you'll see a balcony from which he sold property. He took customers out on the balcony because it was too much of a jungle to be sold from land level, so he stood up there and pointed out pieces of property to sell them."

Fisher was a hard-drinking man who cussed and smoked cigars and spat in a spittoon. Several biographies have been written about the extraordinary Mr. Fisher and his myriad endeavors, not the least of which was raising Miami Beach from a snake-infested swamp, but the most amusing—and probably most apocryphal— account of his life is called *Fabulous Hoosier,* written in 1947 by Jane Watts Fisher, Carl's first wife, who after her divorce continued to live in Miami Beach, where she was a celebrity. Although Carl Fisher remarried, after his death Jane played the role of the widow and gave all the interviews when the press came calling. She was such a fabulist that no one knows what parts of her book or stories are true, yet what better historian for Miami Beach? She married Carl Fisher in 1909 when she was fifteen years old and he was thirty-five. She claimed she first laid eyes on him in the Indianapolis sky sitting in an automobile hanging from a balloon in a publicity stunt. He owned the largest automobile dealership in America and used all manner of promotional ploys to sell his product, including tossing a car off the roof of a building and then starting it up to show it could take rough handling.

Fisher was born in 1874, and his vision was diminished by 50 percent from the time he was a child because of severe astigmatism. It stopped him from accomplishing very little: He opened a bicycle shop in the 1880s when he was only a teenager, and despite his vision problems he raced bicycles and automobiles, and in 1904 he set the automobile speed record of two miles in 2:02 minutes. That same year, he craftily bought the patent to a sealed, gas-filled acetylene car headlight from its disgruntled inventor and started the Prest-O-Lite manufacturing company, which gave drivers the ability to see at night and revolutionized the automobile industry. Fisher sold Prest-O-Light to the Union Carbide Company for $9 million a few years later. He also conceived and built the Indianapolis Speedway in 1909 to help promote auto racing, and in 1912 he raised $10 million from his pals in the auto industry to build a coast-to-coast paved highway, the Lincoln Highway, named for Abraham Lincoln, his idol, to encourage the use of automobiles for travel instead of trains. For the same reason, he also built the Dixie Highway to create a southeast corridor for vehicles, which eventually led him to Miami's door.

In 1912 Fisher bought a vacation home in the city of Miami, and he wasn't there long before he heard a story about a bridge—the longest wooden bridge in the world, 2½ miles in length, built with 2,100 wood pilings—that was left half finished sticking out into Biscayne Bay. It seemed that an old Quaker, John Collins, originally from Moorestown, New Jersey, and now an avocado farmer on the barrier island across the bay sometimes called "Ocean Beach," was trying to build a bridge between the island and the mainland to get his avocados to market and had run out of money halfway. Fisher loaned Collins $50,000 to finish the bridge, and in return he was given 200 acres of swamp on Miami Beach, and then bought 210 acres more.

When Fisher first visited the island, it was nearly primeval, covered with bugs, rats, snakes, mosquitoes, and biting horseflies so voracious that, according to Jane Fisher, they would hungrily cover a man from head to foot so it looked as if he was wearing a black suit. The horseflies' incessant biting was so intolerable that mules brought to the island to help clear it went berserk and jumped into the water and drowned. On the upper beach there was a House of Refuge shack for shipwreck victims, and on the southern end, a bathhouse and casino whose sunbathers were brought across Biscayne Bay by sixty-foot double-decker ferries and led to the beach through tropical undergrowth so otherworldly that the owners named it "Fairy Land." According to Jane, the first time they walked the beach together Fisher drew a diagram in the sand with a stick and said he was going to build the greatest resort in the world, the Riviera of America.

Fisher built his Riviera from the ground up, quite literally. He drained the swamps and had giant scythes pulled by donkeys cut the palmetto roots into two-foot-long stumps, over which he poured sixteen acres of sand from the bottom of Biscayne Bay, like pouring plaster over lath, and allowed it to settle and "sweeten" in the sun. He platted the land, promoted it, and sold it. During the great Florida land boom of the 1920s, which Fisher helped kick off, there were reports of real estate appreciating 1,000 percent in a single week.* Fisher built mansions, nightclubs, and polo and yacht clubs, and in 1925 he created Lincoln Road to be the resort's centerpiece.

At the eastern end of Lincoln Road, directly on the ocean, he built his own beautiful mansion, The Shadows, at a cost of $65,000, and on the western end he built a bold archway of coral rock. In between Fisher laid out a boulevard in brilliant white coral, one hundred feet wide. He built the road with sidewalks double the width of an ordinary street because he had the idea that the inner lane would be for window-shoppers who wanted to stroll leisurely down the street, while an outside pedestrian lane would accommodate those on a less casual promenade. Chauffeur-driven automobiles would be able to follow slowly in the road. All the chic New York stores opened on Lincoln Road—Sulka, Saks Fifth Avenue, Bonwit Teller, Peck & Peck, FAO Schwarz, and Lilly Daché, the Fifth Avenue milliner.

Miami Beach wasn't Fisher's only creation. In 1926 he tried, and failed dismally, to build a summer resort at Montauk, New York, on the eastern tip of Long Island, "a summer Miami Beach," he called it. But the Great Depression wiped out most of his cash, and his Montauk project went bankrupt in 1932 and sucked him

---

*Much of the land rush in Miami Beach in the 1920s was aided by the "Binder Boys," a group of fast-talking opportunists named for an unusual Florida real estate law that allowed a buyer to tie up a piece of property for ninety days with only a small deposit by signing a binder. That gave the speculator ninety days to sell the binder at a profit. A man could parlay $100 into $1 million. The Binder Boys, who were mostly Jewish and not too appreciated by the locals, met every morning at the Ponce De Leon Hotel for breakfast.

under with it. He'd divorced Jane Fisher in 1926 and married again, but he never had children. As Montauk failed and his role in Miami Beach and self-respect faltered, he began to like his booze even more. He developed cirrhosis of the liver in his fifties but could not abate his drinking, and toward the end of his life he had special suits made for him with two sets of buttons to expand when his body retained fluids. He died in 1939 at age sixty-five and was buried in Indianapolis.

"LET'S TAKE a ride in my car," Michael Aller said. "I want to show you something." The waiter at the Van Dyke refused to give Mr. Miami Beach a check for his soft drink, and Aller walked around the corner to where his big pearlized-white Cadillac with MR. MIAMI BEACH plates was illegally parked. (The local police won't give him a check either, he said.) He used some of his favorite hand lotion he had just purchased and popped the bottle in the trunk. In the backseat of the car was a Mickey Mouse doll, seat-belted in. Mickey Mouse is Aller's theme. For decades he's worn a Mickey Mouse figure on his lapel and on the face of his watch, and his office is filled with Mickey Mouse memorabilia, because, he told the *Miami Herald*, "Everything in life is Mickey Mouse. I don't let anyone or anything upset me. Whenever I start to lose it, I just remember Mickey."

As he drove up Collins Avenue, he reminisced about meeting the comedian Georgie Jessel when he was a child and going on the road with him as a teenager, and how Miami Beach was paradise for him now and he never left town, perhaps only for a week or two in summer because "Why would you want to leave paradise?" He went on about his eyesight getting worse and that he only listened to audiobooks, and Sunday afternoon was the only day he turned off his phone. Suddenly there it was, up ahead, Aller's destination. "Look! See!" he exclaimed. "What do you see?"

It turned out that what Aller wanted to show me was something that wasn't there anymore: A Miami Beach landmark was missing—a ten-story wall, 120 feet wide, at Collins and 44th Street, where the street turns to the west. On the wall had been a trompe l'oeil mural, painted in 1985 by New York artist Richard Haas, of two classical figures on either side of an archway that showed what the viewer would see if the wall had not been there—the world-famous curved edifice of the Fontainebleau Hotel. Then, when you turned the corner, there was the real Fontainebleau Hotel. The wall, which had stood for forty-eight years, had been torn down, and the view now was of a shockingly big, thirty-six-story white concrete condominium honeycomb of apartments with tiny terraces. Peeking out almost modestly from behind it was a sliver of the iconic curve of the Fontainebleau, which was going through a $400 million makeover. This new incarnation of the Fontainebleau, they say, will set the standard for the next generation of Miami Beach hotels—big Las Vegas–style resorts with condominium complexes, high-end retail shops, four-star celebrity restaurants, and nightclubs that will draw headlining stars back to Miami Beach.

For the half a minute that Michael Aller sat behind the steering wheel of his car waiting for the light to change, gawking at the new building, he looked very much like part of the city's past staring at its future.

Four

SANS SOUCI

This was the asshole of the world, Florida, as far as I'm concerned, when it comes to architecture and interior design.
—Morris Lapidus

"*That lying horror La-peee-dus!*" Bernice Novack unexpectedly cried out, rocking forward in her chair and folding her arms across her stomach as if she had a bellyache. "I've always called him La-*peee*-dus because that was his real name," she said.

For the past hour, Bernice Novack's voice had barely risen above a shy whisper until she heard the name Morris Lapidus, yet after all these years just the mention of her ex-husband's nemesis sent her into a paroxysm of anger. She was sitting in a folding chair amid the clutter of her son's crowded Fort Lauderdale office, looking very small and delicate. She was still beautiful, even at eighty years old, and it was not hard to understand what had made Ben Novack become so infatuated with her fifty-five years before.

Her son, Ben Jr., fifty, was observing his mother from behind a large desk covered with stacks of file folders, model boats, snow globes, and collectible plates from various U.S. cities. Behind him the office's white shutters were closed against the afternoon sun. From this office in one of two homes he owns next door to each other in a gated Fort Lauderdale community, Ben Jr. runs a convention-booking company, a business he learned by rote from growing up behind the scenes at the Fontainebleau, the hotel his father built and operated for twenty-three years. He doesn't look like his father, who was short and wiry and dark—Ben has blue eyes and bushy hair—but there is something taut and difficult about him, much like his father was said to have been. Although his office was a jumble of cartons, overflowing file cabinets, and antiquated printers and fax machines stored in the corners, Ben Jr. himself was precise and demanding; in the bathroom he shared with his office staff there were not one but two signs insisting occupants WASH YOUR HANDS BEFORE LEAVING.

Ben Jr. and his mother are deliberately not easy to find. They are not listed in the phone directory, and people they once knew in Miami Beach never see them anymore, or have a handy phone number. Miami Beach may only be forty-five minutes away on I-95, but for mother and son it's another place in time. They rarely go there and they stopped driving by the Fontainebleau years ago; it was too painful. They don't like to talk about it either, and Bernice only rarely gives interviews. "If she wanted to talk," said Lisa Cole, the former publicist for the Fontainebleau Hotel, "she could tell some stories. She probably witnessed some outrageous things. She was there for it all. But she'll take it to the grave."

When the Fontainebleau was the world's most famous hotel, Bernice was its First Lady. She was the perfect accoutrement. She lived in a duplex penthouse apartment, and she was always perfectly coiffed and poised and dressed in what seemed like an endless array of beautiful clothing and evening gowns. She met the prime minister of Israel and dined with Ed Sullivan, Jerry Lewis, Walter Winchell, and Joan Crawford, who arrived at the hotel with a makeup case full of vodka, and whose mere appearance in the lobby was enough to prompt a round of applause from the guests. There are photos of Bernice in a two-piece swimsuit with her arm around Esther Williams's waist at the hotel's pool, and there's a photo of her and Ben and Ben Jr. with John F. Kennedy, to whose inauguration she was invited (JFK stayed in Suite 1784 at the Fontainebleau while Marilyn Monroe stayed in Suite 1782). Monroe was no stranger to the Fontainebleau. Her husband Arthur Miller's father stayed in the hotel near the end of his life and Monroe visited him there. The desk clerk didn't recognize her and "thought she was a prostitute," the hotel's longtime doorman Mac McSwane told a journalist. "She was nice but very dumb."

Bernice remembered when Mia Farrow, in T-shirt and jeans, "a little waif, a tiny little thing," sat crying on the front steps of the hotel. On a break from shooting *Rosemary's Baby* in New York, she surprised her then-husband Frank Sinatra and he refused to let her up to his suite. He sent down an envelope full of money and told her to go home. Bernice adored Sinatra, despite all the gangster rumors and violence that surrounded him. He once gave her a pair of emerald earrings with a note that read, "If you don't cotton to these mothers you can always sell them to Swifty," meaning Swifty Morgan, the Fontainebleau's resident loan shark, who sat in a cabana all day and took markers or jewelry from guests, often to pay gambling debts incurred in the Fontainebleau card room.*

"I had quite a life," she said. But she doesn't want to dredge all that up again.

Then there's Ben Jr., who does not allow his mother to give unfettered interviews. This is because almost everything ever written about the Fontainebleau makes him furious. Sitting behind his desk he huffs and puffs indignantly over bits of hotel lore repeated to him, stories that helped make the Fontainebleau a legend. "It's a

---

*The Fontainebleau's publicist Lisa Cole related that one day a man had to hock his wife's jewelry to pay his gambling debt, and the next day his wife saw another woman wearing her diamonds.

shame," he said. "They all make such great mythical stories—the spite wall, the staircase to nowhere—but they're only imaginations that people have perpetrated over the years." Ben Jr. is so angry about the imaginations that he'll consent to an interview only if he is granted—in writing—the opportunity to refute every story about his father that others tell. For the record, he refutes almost every single one of them.

The story that irritates mother and son the most is the issue of who really designed the Fontainebleau's iconic curve: Was it the owner and creator, Ben Novack, or the architect and designer, Morris Lapidus? Ben Jr. dismissed Lapidus as "nothing but a draftsman." He claimed, "Nobody knew Jack Diddly about Morris Lapidus before my father." The theory is that because Morris Lapidus outlived Novack, he had the advantage of rewriting history without Novack around to refute it, and Lapidus took his fair share of credit while portraying Novack as an egotistical liar. In fact, Lapidus disliked Novack so much that he intentionally misspelled his name as *Novak* throughout his two autobiographies, the last one appropriately titled *Too Much Is Never Enough*. "I thought about taking him on," Ben Jr. said, "but then I thought, 'What am I taking on a ninety-year-old man for?'" The Novack family still took pleasure by intentionally pronouncing the name Lapidus with its Old World emphasis every time they said it.

BERNICE DRAZEN met Ben Novack during World War II at La Martinique nightclub on 57th Street in New York, where she had gone for a drink with her girlfriends. She was twenty-two years old and a successful photographer's model. Ben knew one of her girlfriends and joined the women at their table. "It was not love at first sight," she said. "First of all, he was seventeen years older. But there was something about him. He was charming and vulnerable, and there was the way he walked and swayed his shoulders." He was five foot six and something of a dandy. He had a tightly trimmed mustache that looked like two insect wings on his upper lip, and he regularly wore hand-tailored sport jackets, pocket squares, and cuff links of semiprecious stones. Due to a childhood swimming accident, he wore a large, flesh-colored hearing aid in his right ear with a wire that ran down to a microphone in his pocket, despite which he kept asking Bernice to repeat things for him.

He was married, it turned out, to a woman named Bella, who stayed behind in Miami Beach when he came to New York on business, or to play, like that night Bernice met him at La Martinique. Of course, Bernice was married too, to a solider who was off in Europe fighting the war.

"People who don't hear well want to talk," Bernice said. Ben was full of bombast and braggadocio. He owned a hotel in Miami Beach called the Cornell, and he had big plans for the future. He was putting together a partnership to build a hotel of a class never seen before in Miami Beach, an elegant and sophisticated inn on the ocean with a penthouse nightclub and its own restaurants and shops. He was going to give it a fancy French name, the Sans Souci—"without care."

Bernice smiled remembering it. "That Ben," she said. "He always wanted to build his grand hotel."

WHEN BEN Novack first arrived in Miami Beach in February of 1940, the city was at its glittering, giddiest best. It was what *New York Herald Tribune* society columnist Lucius Beebe described as "the last Gomorrah, the ultimate Babylon, the final Gnome-Rhône-Jupiter-Whirlwind, superdeluxe, extra-special, colossal, double-feature and Zombie-ridden madhouse of the world." Less hyperbolic but just as impressive was a 1940 story in *Time* magazine, which featured the city's mayor, John Levi, on the cover, declaring the resort a "unique U.S. phenomenon" and "like no other town in the U.S. or in the world."

While other cities were still struggling to recover from the Great Depression, Miami Beach just brushed itself off and continued on as if the crash had hardly happened. Its growing reputation as an escapist playground made the resort more popular than ever. The kind of visitors changed, from wealthy industrialists who owned second homes to tourists who needed hotels in which to stay. In the early 1940s, despite the government's wartime plea for patriotic citizens to curtail pleasure travel, a whopping 3 million tourists a year came to visit southern Florida.

Novack arrived in Miami Beach with a crazy scheme to buy a fleet of boats and import bananas from Cuba, although some people who knew him back then remember him selling expensive wrist-watches to get by. It quickly became obvious to him that he should stick with the family business, hostelry. Miami Beach was in the midst of a hotel-building frenzy that had begun in 1935. *Architectural Forum* magazine called it a "Boom Over Miami." The year Novack arrived, an astonishing forty-one new hotels opened their doors. Novack's father, Hyman Novack, had built and operated the famous Laurel's Country Club on Sackett Lake in the Catskill Mountains, and Novack grew up in the front office. After his father died Novack tried to run the Laurel's with his brother, but they didn't get along, so he quit. His next venture was a haberdashery called Kemp and Novack in New York on Sixth Avenue, but again he quarreled with his partner, and they closed up shop and liquidated the store. When he got to Miami Beach he rallied some partners for cash—one of his specialties would be finding partners—and he signed a $20,000, one-year lease on the 111-room Monroe Towers at 30th and Collins, where his first wife, Bella, helped change the sheets and towels and he fixed the plumbing.

It was World War II that made him rich.

At first the war scarcely seemed to faze Miami Beach. Business was good, the band played on, and the song was a rumba. The rich continued to take vacations and the city became a safe haven for international café society and wealthy Europeans. There were some modest attempts at patriotism—there were metal collection drives, and the bathing beauties painted their fingernails red, white, and blue—but for the most part the city continued on with its frivolity until the Germans posted U2 boats in the shipping lanes just off the coast.

It came as a rude awakening for the rollicking resort when in February of 1942 the U.S. Army designated Miami Beach as one of several cities in which to billet thousands of soldiers for basic training before they were shipped out to duty. Within a matter of weeks the Army Air Force requisitioned more than 180 hotels, 100 apartment buildings, and 18 private homes to be used as offices and barracks, as well as the Nautilus Hotel, which was converted into an army hospital, and the Miami Beach golf course, which was leased for a dollar a year to be used as a parade field. The army took over 70,000 hotel rooms, for which the government paid from $1 to $10 a night. "Basically my father walked into a deal where the army took a contract out with him and his hotel was filled with troops," explained Ben Jr. "He raked in the profits and he did so well that he got another hotel and did the same thing, and then another hotel with an army contract." Novack parlayed his good fortune into buying a stake in the Monroe, then the Cornell, and eventually he operated the formidable Atlantis Hotel on the ocean, built in 1936, which the army used as a reception center for servicemen. "Boy, did my dad clean up!" Ben Jr. said. "He got rich!"

In 1944, Dolly De Milhau, a correspondent for *Town & Country* magazine, reported "Next time you're wondering where anybody is, I suggest you come down to Miami Beach, park a camp chair . . . and just sit and wait. Sooner or later everyone you've ever known or heard of is sure to wander by." The Duke and Duchess of Windsor visited Miami Beach in 1940 (but stayed at the Biltmore in Coral Gables), and the football player John Sims "Shipwreck" Kelly and his fiancée, glamour girl Brenda Frazier, the "debutante of the century," rented a house on Pine Tree Drive and invited Howard Hawks for dinner. William Kissam Vanderbilt was in residence at his home on Fisher Island. Damon Runyon owned a home on Hibiscus Island, and Walter Winchell spent winters at the Roney Plaza, where Al Jolson lolled away hours on the beach every day toasting himself the color of a coffee bean. Eleanor Roosevelt rented a house on Golden Beach and gave talks at Miami Beach High School. Statesmen Harry Truman, Douglas MacArthur, and Winston Churchill vacationed in Miami Beach after the war, and Churchill, who rarely took vacations, spent several weeks painting on the beach. Churchill somehow found the time and inspiration to write the historic speech he gave that March of 1946 at Westminster College in Fulton, Missouri, in which he coined the phrase "iron curtain."

Miami Beach already had the reputation of "an open city, nakedly acknowledged to be a funhouse exempt from moral and legal restrictions," as Miami Beach historian Harold Mehling described it. It was true that the nightclubs and saloons were boisterous. One Beach favorite, the Five O'Clock Club, served free drinks at five in the afternoon and at five in the morning, and at both times the place was packed. Kitty Davis's Airliner on Alton Road was decorated to look like the inside of a plane. Jack Dempsey was a partner in the Vanderbilt Hotel and worked the bar and shook hands with customers. Roberto's Mexicana Bar featured transvestite bartenders and waiters, and the men at the Club Ha Ha wore makeup and sang dirty songs to the customers. At La Paloma in the city of Miami, male customers wore evening gowns, as was their pleasure, before the club was shut down and the owners sent to jail. There was also a nude floor show of beautiful women at La Boheme nightclub. Possessing more mainstream appeal was Lou Walter's Latin Quarter, with its buxom showgirls à la Ziegfeld. In 1941 alone, Hildegarde, Jane Froman, Milton Berle, Martha Raye, Shecky Greene, and Sophie Tucker entertained at Miami Beach nightclubs, and the music of the great Latin bands of Tito Puente, Tito Rodriguez, and Xavier Cugat filled the balmy night air.

Many of the patrons in these nightclubs and bars were what *Life* magazine described politely as "playboys and expensive demi-mondaines." The tourists in Miami Beach, said *Fortune* magazine, "bring their pleasures and their morals with them from the North." *Fortune* estimated that 20,000 "lone women" visited Miami every season and that "casual acquaintances are easily made. . . . An unat-tached girl, if she so desires, may pay her winter's expenses from the pocketbook of a man picked up in any bar." There were so many B-girls in bars that the Miami Beach city council passed an ordinance requiring that clubs notify patrons how much money was owed after each round of drinks. There was also a popular 1941 movie musical extolling the ease with which a young woman could meet a rich husband called *Moon Over Miami* starring Betty Grable and Don Ameche. Conveniently, Miami Beach was also a divorce mill that rivaled Reno—it only took ninety days to declare residency, and over 10,000 couples were divorced in Dade County a year. In 1942 one woman sued for divorce on the grounds that her husband was "interested chiefly in wine, women, song, and slow horses."

There were lots of slow horses. Since the legalization of pari-mutuel gambling in 1929, three horse tracks and four jai-alai fron-tons were built within easy reach of Miami Beach, and at the southernmost tip of South Beach a dog track called Miami Beach Kennel Club opened, operated by sports promoter Ted Rickard but allegedly bankrolled by Al Capone for $1 million. Going to the track to "watch the dogs" became one of the most popular

diversions on the Beach. Capone also had interests in the Villa
Venice, a casino on Ocean Drive and 14th Street; in the Hangar
Room casino; and in the Palm Island Club, which was on the same
exclusive residential island where Capone made his home.

In 1928 Capone bought a Spanish-style, two-story mansion
on Palm Island surrounded by high walls and dense shrubbery.
The house had been built by the beer brewer Clarence Busch, and
Capone added a $75,000 thirty-by-sixty-foot swimming pool that
could be filled with either salt or fresh water. Capone's house
became one of the city's biggest boat-viewed tourist attractions.
Those who dared to get close enough could see men patrolling the
premises carrying rifles. It was said that Capone slept in a four-
poster bed with a chest of money at the foot, and that every afternoon he held poker games for his pals—played only with $1,000
bills. He obviously got sand in his shoes because he liked Miami
Beach so much that he called it the "Sunny Italy of the New
World." Capone was a good neighbor, well behaved, polite, and
generous. He tried to grease his way into the community's good
graces by making generous donations to local charities, and he
once gave a party for Miami Beach's firemen, at which his staff
sported shoulder holsters and guns. But the *Miami Herald* ran
articles and editorials reminding everyone how murderous he
really was, and soon the charities began to return his money, his
house was raided, and he was brought up on charges as a public
nuisance. Carl Fisher himself testified at a court hearing that
Capone's presence in Miami Beach was bringing property values
down. Capone got to stay, but he wasn't around very much. For
most of the 1930s he was in and out of prison for tax evasion, and
he only moved back to Miami Beach to die of syphilis-induced
dementia.

Capone helped to establish Miami Beach's reputation as a gangster and gambling haven and an easy port for bootleggers. Writer

Helen Muir claimed that there were so many gangsters in Miami
Beach in the 1940s that they met around 11:00 a.m. on 32nd and
Collins "like show people of vaudeville days meeting by the Palace
to swap trade information." As a public service the *Miami Herald*
began to run a column called "Know Your Neighbor," which featured photographs and rap sheets of crooks and gamblers who had
come to town to live. Later, a group of anonymous citizens called
"The Secret Six" was formed to expose hoodlums who had moved
into the area, and a local radio station began to carry a show called
The Sinister Plot in which a different gangster was featured each
week, a forerunner of TV's *America's Most Wanted*.

As tourism began to grow in the 1930s and 1940s, casino
gambling became a crucial attraction. Author Ted Koefed described
Miami Beach as "an illegal Las Vegas, with an ocean, instead of
a desert. . . ." Just north of the resort there was plenty of action
at Ben Marden's elegant Brook Club in Surfside, or at the Sunny
Isles Club, where tourists happily rubbed elbows with nattily
dressed mobsters and their girlfriends. There were also dozens
of less elegant places to gamble called "rug joints," run by gangsters
in private homes to which any hotel doorman could direct a
tourist.

Every big hotel in Miami Beach had to have an on-premise
bookie for the convenience of the guests, and an estimated two
hundred bookies worked on the Beach. In 1948 *Time* magazine
described bookmaking in Miami Beach as "an industry" and
reported that the police chief, P. R. Short, explained, "We don't
intend to bother the bookies. They don't bother us." Perhaps that
was because although Short's salary was only $7,500 a year, he was
earning ten times that amount in bribes. The bookies usually
worked out of beach cabanas that the hotels rented to them for the
season, and they were in competition with each other for spots at
the best hotels. The owners began charging them for the franchise,

and in some cases the bookies paid as much as $50,000 for the use of a cabana for a season. In the mid-1940s a group of five men—Jules Levitt, Charles Friedman, Harold Salvey, Ed Rosenbaum, and Sam Cohen—put an end to the rent gouging by hotel owners by forming a group called the S&G Syndicate (the initials possibly standing for Stop and Go) to control and protect gambling in Miami Beach. The S&G Syndicate was so successful that by 1949 it was collecting $40 million a year in bets placed with bookies. Hotels that were not controlled by the S&G Syndicate were raided by the police, and their bookies were harassed.

It was Tennessee senator Estes Kefauver who finally put an end to the organized bookmaking and illegal gambling casinos. Kefauver was the head of the Senate Special Committee to Investigate Organized Crime in Interstate Commerce, which very effectively ferreted out organized crime throughout the country. The Kefauver Committee, as it became known, investigated crime in fifteen U.S. cities, often grilling gangsters in televised hearings watched by 30 million Americans. In 1949 the committee launched a massive investigation into Miami Beach gambling. "Criminals from all over the nation were able to act freely in the Miami area," found the Kefauver Report, "because the concentration of economic power they brought in from the outside enabled them to . . . corrupt substantial portions of the community."

THE GREATEST realization of pharaonic desire may not be to build a mausoleum for the world to remember one's glory, or a palace in which to live that is the envy of one's peers, but to build a hotel, to create a unique physical and psychological environment in which people will pay money to sleep and eat and play. The owner of the hotel is omnipotent, a god-like ringmaster of his living creation. The desire to build and run a hotel never attracted small personalities, and Miami Beach hotelmen were kindred spirits, mavericks, gamblers and scrappy guys with oversize personalities.

In the 1940s the hotel owners started to compete with each other with gimmicks and amenities to attract guests. The Royal Palm at 15th and Collins Avenue boasted a shower, bath, telephone, and radio in every room. The Versailles at Collins and 34th Street offered running ice water and steamed heat for chilly nights. The White House on Ocean Drive advertised running saltwater, for in-room bathing, and the Normandy Plaza at 69th and Collins had a roof solarium for nude bathing. In 1947 the first $1 million hotel was built, the Sherry Frontenac, which had two towers connected by a bridge and twelve shops in the hotel, and it was the first hotel to provide entertainment in its own nightclub.

Yet no hotel helped usher in the modern era of Miami Beach glitz and ersatz glamour, or held the public's sway, more than the 246-room Saxony Hotel, which was built in 1948 at a then astonishing cost of $5 million. It was named for its millionaire owner, George Saxon, the famous "punch board" king of Chicago who manufactured the important component in slot machines. The hotel's architect was Roy F. France, one of the holy trinity of local Miami Beach architects (the other two being Henry Hohauser and Lawrence Murray Dixon), who had designed hundreds of beautiful apartment buildings, public spaces, and elegant hotels in Miami Beach, including the grand Whitman Hotel in 1936, right across the street from the Saxony. The sleek, modernistic, slightly fan-shaped Saxony was a block wide and sixteen stories tall. It was nicknamed the "Ivory Tower" for its luxurious penthouse nightclub. The Saxony was the first completely air-conditioned hotel on the Beach, and guests ascended to their room floors in a glass-enclosed elevator that ran up a track on the outside of the building.

The year it opened it was awarded the Miami Beach Hotel Owners Association "Hotel of the Year"* award.

Shortly after the Saxony opened, Novack assembled a group of investors to talk about building a hotel that would top the Saxony, to be built on a plot of land just one block south of it. His partners included Ben Marden, a nightclub operator; Danny Arnstein, the owner of the Yellow Cab Company of Chicago and New York; Harry Toffel, a wealthy dress manufacturer they called "Little Harry"; and "Big Harry," Harry Mufson, the "tire king." Mufson was an elegant man, pleasant and easygoing, but with a quick temper, particularly when he'd had a few. He liked to spend his day playing cards and drinking gin and tonics in a cabana at the Cornell Hotel—which Novack once operated. Mufson had made his money in an automotive tire business that he and his younger brothers started in the Bronx, New York, in 1930. They called it the Vanderbilt Tire and Rubber Companies, a name they chose because "Vanderbilt" sounded classier than "Mufson." The brothers built the company into a national chain of 37 tire franchises with outlets in Macy's, Bamberger's, and Sears, Roebuck stores, and in 1945 they sold the company to the B.F. Goodrich tire company for $6 million. Harry Mufson and his brothers all moved to Florida, where they opened the first of a chain of ten auto-supply and tire stores on the Tamiami Trail they called Jefferson's.

Jefferson's was so successful that it again made the brothers millionaires, but Mufson's heart wasn't in tires or the auto-supply business. Mufson was taken with the fast-paced, high-stakes, booze-and-broads world of Miami Beach hotel life, and he bought the small Cornell Hotel to get his feet wet before becoming partners with Ben Novack in building a grand new hotel, the Sans Souci.

---

*Miami Beach historian Howard Kleinberg writes in his book *Woggles and Cheese Holes* that there is "no evidence of such a formal declaration or award by any organization." Be that as it may, it was a real thing in the public's mind.

In 1948 Novack and Mufson hired Roy F. France, and encouraged France to eclipse his own work on the Saxony. France took the commission, but when he presented his architectural sketches Novack was unhappy. Instead of the innovative design he expected, the drawings looked like all the rest of the L-shaped hotels on the Beach: six stories of pancaked floors painted a tropical white with horizontal bands of windows. Novack wanted something more unusual, but France refused to make changes according to his client's whimsies. Novack had already paid France a portion of his fee, so instead of firing him, Novack made inquiries to find another architect who would embellish France's work and give it some pizzazz. At the suggestion of his friend Charles Spector, a vice president of the A.S. Beck shoe store chain in New York, Novack met with a top retail-store designer named Morris Lapidus, an unlikely choice to gussy up a hotel.

MORRIS LAPIDUS, who was forty-six at the time, was a tall man with broad shoulders, a receding hairline, and bushy sideburns. He was always fastidiously groomed and dressed, and almost every day of his life he wore a sport jacket and slacks or a suit to work, always with a perfectly tied, butterfly bow tie—his signature piece of attire. Although he sometimes looked as though he might have just stepped off the floor of the House of Commons, he was not a visiting lord but rather a Russian Jewish immigrant who lived in a relatively modest but strikingly decorated house on East 8th Street in Flatbush, Brooklyn, New York. From the way he carried himself, and his high opinion of his work, one would assume he designed skyscrapers, not retail shops.

But he had designed some of the most famous retail shops in the world. By the late 1940s, when Lapidus was introduced to Ben Novack, he had already created some 450 storefronts and interiors, including the showstopping A.S. Beck shoe store on Fifth

Avenue and the steel-and-glass Bond clothing store on State Street in Chicago, one of the most photographed storefronts of the decade. In the process he'd become something of a marketing strategist. "I am an architect by training but a mob psychologist by insight," Lapidus said of his work. He began to look at retail space as "a machine for selling" and developed three basic categories for store design: ornamentation, color, and light. He had a "moth theory" that posited that customers were attracted to brightly lit areas where premium merchandise should be displayed. He observed that "people don't walk in straight lines like ants," so his interiors were open spaces with meandering, curved parameters and dramatic recessed lighting. He devised ornamentation that he referred to as "intentional nonsense to amuse customers." His ceilings had jigsaw-shaped recesses backlit by neon; his walls had random Swiss cheese cutouts; and he sometimes separated open spaces with rows of tension poles that the critics named "bean poles." He also favored an amoeba-like shape that was called a "woggle" by another critic, and these shapes and lighting effects and curving walls became what Lapidus referred to as his "bag of tricks."

Lapidus had been a drama student at New York University and an aspiring stage designer. He graduated from Columbia University's architectural school in 1925, and his first job was for the architectural firm of Warren and Wetmore—the architects of Grand Central Terminal in New York. Lapidus's first major assignment was to design the details of the bathrooms for the Atlantic City Convention Center, but he soon graduated to designing the interior details of the Palais Royale, a New York speakeasy owned by Bugsy Siegel. Never before had he worked on a hotel. Only once had he submitted a plan for a hotel, but he forgot to put bathrooms in the rooms, and so, after time, retail shops became his métier.

Novack's grand idea was that the behavioral design techniques Lapidus was successfully using to create retail space would work as well for hotels. Lapidus agreed to tinker with Roy France's design in exchange for a modest fee of $18,000. Novack and Mufson arranged a meeting between France and Lapidus in France's Miami Beach offices, where Lapidus produced plans for additions and changes. France, an accomplished and well-respected architect, was undoubtedly furious, and he dismissed Lapidus's plans as not physically feasible; there were stresses and strains and stairways that could not be built on a foundation of sand. The meeting ended abruptly, and outside on the sidewalk Novack and the partners agreed that Lapidus should take over and that Novack and Lapidus would doctor France's design to suit them, Roy France be damned.

To celebrate they invited Lapidus to dinner at Harry Mufson's house that night. Lapidus got a taste of what was in store for him. The partners got into a brawl over whether the nightclub in the new hotel should be big and brassy or small and intimate. Ben Novack wanted small and intimate. Within minutes Novack was snarling insults at his partners to "stick to the tire business" and "stick to your dresses," and "the air became blue with more four-letter words than I knew existed," Lapidus wrote. Ben took Bernice by the arm and said, "We're getting out of here, the deal is off." The deal wasn't off, but angry threats and life-and-death crises became daily events.

The Sans Souci was in fact the showstopper hotel of 1949. It ushered in a new standard in luxury and design in Miami Beach. Architecturally the building sported many easily identifiable Lapidus touches—such as the architectural fin of blue glass tiles that ran up the front of the building, at the top of which the sans-serif name **Sans Souci** was bathed in blue-white light, visible for miles up and down Collins Avenue. "There were native coral stone walls," Lapidus wrote, "with splashing fountains and lush tropical foliage growing in the most unlikely places." The swimming pool was in the shape of a Lapidus squiggle, and at night the colored lighting on the pool and decks and gardens "turned the areas into an exotic fairyland." The lobby had undulating walls, cheese holes, and bean poles on which hung globelike birdcages with branches and leaves instead of birds, because the birds would have left droppings on the furniture and guests. The promotional material boasted, "In Paris it's the Eiffel Tower . . . in London, Buckingham Palace . . . and in Miami Beach, the Sans Souci." When Mohammad Reza Pahlavi, the shah of Iran, visited Miami Beach, he and his entourage leased Sans Souci's entire top floor, and Novack redecorated all the rooms to their pleasing.

The Sans Souci was unquestionably deserving of the accolade "Hotel of the Year," yet the Saxony won the award again that year, and again the year after that, for three years in a row. It irritated Novack, but in the long run it hardly mattered. He had ambitions that would dwarf any award the Hotel Owners Association could bestow. He was going to build not just the "Hotel of the Year" but the hotel of the *century*. He knew what the public wanted and how to give it to them. Glamorous. Expensive. Dramatic. Big. Very big. "I want to build," he said, "the world's most pretentious hotel."

Five

THE FONTAINEBLEAU

All the rivers of the very worst taste twisted down to the delta
of each lobby in each grand Miami Beach hotel . . .
—NORMAN MAILER, 1968

Ben Novack never stopped pursuing Bernice from the night he met her at La Martinique nightclub. He phoned whenever he was in town, he begged her to come out to dinner at 21, and he sent her extravagant gifts from Miami Beach, including a Joe's Stone Crab dinner on dry ice. At one point she was told by her modeling agency that she was booked on a photographic shoot in Havana. A few days later she was flown to Cuba with another model, a photographer, and a makeup artist. "But when I got there," she said, "it was Ben! He had set up the whole thing to look like a job, just so he could spend time with me." She was taken with his romantic, soft side, although she was one of few people to see it. "He used to write poetry," Bernice said, "and he played the piano for me and he loved romantic musicals, like *Brigadoon*."

Eventually Novack divorced his wife, and the divorce so depressed him that he had what Bernice described as a "nervous breakdown" and he went away to Arizona for a time to recuperate.* The Novack family contends that Harry Mufson helped perpetrate Novack's psychological break with a mean practical joke. Evidently Mufson was getting a little sick of Novack's shrill grandiosity, and Mufson emptied all the furniture out of Novack's office at the Sans Souci and changed the locks to goad him. When Novack arrived to find the door to his offices locked and his furniture gone, he panicked and thought he was going crazy. When the practical joke was revealed, Novack was humiliated. This prank inflamed the growing one-upmanship and enmity between Novack and Mufson. Yet it was Harry Mufson who called Bernice in New York to tell her how sad and forlorn Novack was without her and that she should call to cheer him up.

In 1952, seven years after they met, and after Bernice's marriage to her soldier husband had been annulled and an engagement to another man had been broken, Bernice and Ben were married by a justice of the peace in a small ceremony at the Essex House in New York. Then she packed her belongings and moved to the Sans Souci hotel.

It was a tough transition. The Sans Souci was booked solid, the lobby overflowing day and night with guests and gawkers. There were days Bernice didn't feel like leaving her room. While some hotel owners kept a separate residence, "Ben always lived in his establishments," Bernice said. Novack was happy living in a big impersonal transient place, where the lobby was like his living room only it had strangers wandering through it. He had learned from his father's hotel in the Catskills that being a hotelier was not a nine-to-five job. "A hotel owner is always on the premises and he must be a good host," Novack told a reporter. "He must have a warm, pleasant manner. Otherwise he has no business being in the business."

---

*One thing that probably upset him was that Bella's family owned the land on which the Sans Souci was built, and because of the divorce he had to come to some sort of settlement that was probably not cheap.

For Bernice, life in a hotel was aimless. She had given up her modeling career and all she had was time on her hands. She didn't know a soul in Miami Beach except for the spouses of Ben's partners. "The wives and I didn't get along," she recalled. "They were very cold to me and so much older. Here I was, a model. They wanted to sit in a cabana and play cards all day and I wasn't interested." So she sat by herself most of the time and wondered what she'd gotten herself into.

In any event, she didn't live at the Sans Souci for very long. In July of 1952, Ben Novack announced to the *Miami Herald* that he and a syndicate had made a deal with the heirs of Harvey S. Firestone, the late chairman of Firestone Tire and Rubber Company, who died in 1938, to buy his oceanfront estate on Collins Avenue and 44th Street for $2.3 million, a considerable sum in the 1950s. The estate had 950 feet of oceanfront, the largest privately owned piece of oceanfront in Miami Beach. Harry Mufson told the *Miami Herald* that they would demolish the thirty-year-old mansion and replace it with a behemoth hotel—550 rooms—at a breathtaking cost of $10 million (which would escalate to $16 million by the time the job was done). The new hotel "would be gigantic," Mufson bragged to the *Herald*. "Twice as big as anything on the Beach."

Nobody was cheering. Novack had at first said he was going to buy the Firestone estate to conserve the land as a public park and prevent another hotel from being built on it. The Firestone estate was figuratively and literally a line in the sand in Miami Beach. It was the curtain raiser on Millionaire's Row, a cavalcade of oceanfront mansions that lined Collins Avenue from 44th Street to 59th Street. Harbel, as it was called, was a stately Mediterranean villa bounded by palm trees, built in 1919 by James Snowden, a partner in Standard Oil. It was the setting of elegant parties at which Thomas Edison and Henry Ford and other notable men of their day joined Firestone's table. Harbel had become a showcase for Carl Fisher's vision of Miami Beach's luxurious lifestyle.

More important to many, it marked the zoning demarcation between residential and commercial buildings. Conventional wisdom was that the nearly four hundred existing hotels below 44th Street were enough for Miami Beach, and there was still hope that the northern part of the Beach would retain its residential aspect, like Palm Beach, instead of becoming a commercial quagmire, the ocean view lost to a wall of hotels. Harvey Firestone's heirs disagreed; they wanted the right to sell the property at the highest price for the best possible use, and beginning in 1943 they challenged the zoning ordinance in court, initiating a series of lawsuits that took seven years to wend their way to the State Supreme Court, where in 1950 the Firestones were awarded a commercial rezoning. Novack and his partners bought the estate two years later.

Or so his partners thought.

Shortly before the closing—just two or three days before the terms of the deal would expire, according to some versions of the story—Mufson discovered that the seed money Novack had used to bankroll the Firestone property—$15,000—came out of the coffers of the Sans Souci hotel and that the Sun N' Sea Corporation's name wasn't on the deed to the Firestone estate, only Novack's name. It was a double cross. Bernice and Ben Jr. don't remember the details except that "Ben didn't get along with Mufson," according to Bernice. Novack and Mufson nearly came to blows at the Sans Souci, and the next day Mufson and the other partners consulted a lawyer.

With Mufson and his partners' money gone, and just twenty-four hours before the day of closing, Novack worked the telephones late into the night, calling old friends and acquaintances, trying to raise the funds before the deal fell through. According to Ben Jr., his father called just about everybody he ever knew in his entire life, begging, "Trust me, just send me the money, I'll send you the contracts later."

Said Ben Jr., "He put together the most unusual partnership of people you ever heard of. Some of the people he got weren't his choice, but they were willing to cough up the dough." Among the eleven original partners in the new hotel were Herbert Glassman, who made millions in the taxi and limousine business; auto dealer Joseph Cherner, who opened the first shopping center in the United States in Shirlington, Virginia; Abe Rosenberg, the owner of a large spirits distributor called Star Liquor; Jules Gorlitz, the president of the Sea Nymph bathing suit company in New York; and possibly a few unnamed investors, such as Sam Giancana from Chicago. In Miami Beach there was a joke that Novack had about as many partners as his hotels had rooms.

Novack also secured a $5 million building loan, the largest such loan in the history of South Florida.

Before the end of the year Harry Mufson and five other stockholders in the Sun N' Sea Corporation filed suit against Ben Novack to halt the construction of the new hotel. The court refused to stop construction, but in settlement Novack divested himself of his Sans Souci stock and the partners paid him $1.5 million for the land he owned upon which the Sans Souci stood. Harry Mufson hated Novack from then on. It wasn't just about the money; in the Wild West world of Miami Beach hotel owners, there was blood of honor spilled on Collins Avenue.

IN DECEMBER of 1953, when Novack was asked who would be the architect of his new hotel, he claimed he blurted out the first name that came to him—Morris Lapidus. But that wasn't true. By the time Novack uttered the name Lapidus, the hotelier had already consulted with several prominent architects whose design fees for a $12 million building were in the range of $500,000. Some architects refused to work with Novack, putting him in the life-is-too-short category. So when pressed, Novack said Lapidus's name. It certainly was news to Lapidus when he read in the *New York Times* that he was going to design Novack's new hotel. Hardly a flattering way to be offered a job, but in truth Lapidus was so grateful to be able to design an entire building from the ground up that he was willing to suffer almost any of Novack's indignities. Since his work on the Sans Souci, Lapidus had been in demand as a "hotel doctor" who put the frills and finishing touches on half a dozen hotels on Collins Avenue, among them the Nautilus, Delano, Biltmore Terrace, and Algiers, which featured a semicircular glass-walled lobby that hung out over Collins Avenue and bellhops dressed in tunics and fezzes. But none of these buildings carried Lapidus's name as the architect, and he got little public credit for his work.* "I had never been the architect for a complete new building," he lamented.

Lapidus made what he called a "ruinous" deal with Ben Novack. He agreed to design not just the building but the entire hotel, inside and out, including landscaping and lobbies, wall sconces and wallpaper, chandeliers, sofas, and staff uniforms—all for only $80,000.

At the start of their collaboration on the Fontainebleau, Lapidus presented Novack with twenty-six drawings for the hotel. "These are for me?" Novack asked sweetly. "May I do anything with them I want?" When Lapidus said of course he could, Novack ripped up the drawings and tossed the pieces in the wastepaper basket.

Lapidus decided that since any idea that wasn't Novack's own would be rejected out of hand, he would nonchalantly mention

---

*Lapidus's son Alan, also an architect, claimed that his father took more credit for the total design of these hotels than he deserved and that the architects of record complained to the American Institute of Architects, from which Lapidus was expelled.

concepts to Novack in passing, like a posthypnotic suggestion, and then wait for Novack to regurgitate the idea back to him a week or two later, at which time Lapidus would act as if Novack was a creative genius.

As for the big question of whose idea it was for the now world-famous shape of the hotel, Lapidus claimed it came to him while riding the BMT subway in New York. To prepare Novack, he kept telling him that every hotel on Miami Beach was boxy and square and that Novack should think of "curves and circles, curves and circles." Lapidus said that weeks later when Novack showed him a sketch for a curved building, he commented, "That's terrific," and kept his mouth shut.

Bernice tells a different story that she claims is the gospel about the design of the Fontainebleau. One day when she and Novack were living at the Sans Souci, Ben borrowed her sketchpad and charcoal and took it to the bathroom with him, where he sat on the toilet sketching. A long time went by—over an hour—and Bernice finally knocked on the door and said, "Ben, are you all right?"

And Ben said, "I'm all right. I'm designing the Fontainebleau."

When Lapidus heard this story he countered, "Ben Novack couldn't design a toilet."

WHEN THE war with Harry Mufson erupted, Ben and Bernice fled the Sans Souci and moved into the abandoned Firestone mansion, which became the construction headquarters for the new hotel. Novack used the large formal dining room for the general contractor's office and the adjoining breakfast room as his inner sanctum, guarded by a secretary named Miss Gabby. Bernice sequestered herself in one of the large bedrooms and watched in awe while around her a hotel was created from the foundation up. The concrete trucks lined up all down Collins Avenue, while a crew of

1,200 men* worked dawn until dark, swarming over a seventeen-story skeleton composed of enough steel to build a skyscraper one hundred stories tall. Finally the Firestone mansion itself had to be bulldozed to make way for seven acres of formal gardens designed after the *petit jardins* of the Palace of Versailles, at their center a fifty-four- by fifty-four-foot fishpond. Novack was on the job site every morning, dressed in work clothes, supervising each bolt and nail. Years later when Conrad Hilton asked Novack how he managed to build such a massive hotel in less than a year, Novack answered, "Put on a pair of overalls."

Novack wanted a big hotel, and big it was. Truckloads of materials were delivered in quantities so large they were measured in miles: 25 miles of carpeting at a cost of $600,000; 1 mile of fluorescent tubing; 140 miles of electrical wiring; 50 miles of telephone wires. There were also 8,000 lightbulbs; 2,000 mirrors; and enough plumbing fixtures for 800 homes. More than 100 miles of plumbing pipe connected the swimming pools, fountains, kitchens, 1,000 toilets, and 40 bidets. Truckloads of white and pink and black marble for the lobbies and public spaces were unloaded on forklifts. It seemed as though the hotel was being glazed in marble. In the main lobby alone there was half an acre of white marble on the floor, inlaid with repeating black marble bow-tie shapes.† "We're full of marble," Novack proudly told a reporter.

The hotel's interim name was "Estate," but before long Novack settled on "Fontainebleau," although the correct French

---

*Novack was opposed to trade unions and the men who built the Fontainebleau Hotel were nonunion. Midway through construction one of the bearing pillars in the hotel was dynamited in a sabotage attempt, thought to be the work of the unions, but the building held firm.

†Morris Lapidus always wore bow ties, and most observers believe that the floor motif was the architect's way of leaving his imprint. Ben Jr. denies that the bow-tie pattern had anything to do with Lapidus and claims that it was just a coincidence.

pronunciation eternally escaped him. He, and everyone in Miami Beach, pronounced the name FOUN-tin-blew. Novack first became aware of the Royal Château de Fontainebleau in 1951. He was on a driving vacation in France with Bernice and they accidentally came upon it. As it happened, the Château de Fontainebleau was an apt inspiration for Novack's new hotel. Originally built in the twelfth century, with architectural makeovers through the centuries by Henry II, Catherine de Medici, and Napoléon Bonaparte, it was always considered the height of gilded glamour, and its mannerist interior design inspired the expression "Fontainebleau style" in France. Ironically, Ben and Bernice never actually laid eyes on the château. "We didn't stop to look at it," Novack said, "but we liked the name, kind of catchy."

When Novack told Lapidus he wanted the interior of the modern hotel to look like a French château, Lapidus showed him pictures of a château in a book. "Not that French château," Lapidus recalled Novack saying; "I want a modern French château." Novack wanted to invent his own "Fontainebleau style" called "Modern French Provincial," otherwise known as "Miami Beach French." How faux French Provincial furniture was going to mesh with— and fill up—a modern building that size was anybody's guess. Lapidus actually went on a $100,000 shopping spree along Manhattan's Third Avenue, then lined with expensive antique stores, and had the furniture shipped back to Florida. When he returned he found the marble statuary being used by workmen as sawhorses. It hardly seemed to matter how the statues were treated, because eventually many of the antiques were stripped to their wood and painted with gold paint because they hadn't been shiny enough.

Nearly a year passed of having to deal with bellicose Ben Novack, and Morris Lapidus was exhausted and broke. He estimated he'd already worked double the amount of time he had allotted for his fee of $80,000. He was supporting two residences—an apartment in Miami Beach and his house in Brooklyn—and his creditors up north were hounding him. Without telling his wife, Bea, Lapidus emptied out their savings account to pay the bills and borrowed money from friends. According to his version of events, faced with personal bankruptcy he met with Novack and asked to renegotiate his fee. After some haggling, Novack agreed it would be fair to pay him an additional $40,000—but only if the other investors consented.

In November of 1954, a few weeks before the opening of the hotel, Novack gave a grand tour of the new hotel for all the partners, which ended on the deck of the impressively large 6,500-square-foot swimming pool. This was the moment that Lapidus chose to take Novack aside and ask if it would be a good time to tell the partners about the additional $40,000 that Novack had promised.

"I don't understand what you're talking about," Novack said. "What forty thousand dollars?"

"You remember, Ben," Lapidus recounted saying. "The forty thousand dollars' extra fee that we agreed would be paid to me. You said to wait until the partners saw the hotel."

"I can't understand you, Morris," Novack responded. "What are you talking about?" Novack looked incredulous. "I never said I'd pay you another forty thousand dollars."

Lapidus lost his mind, literally. He wanted to kill Novack. As Novack turned to walk away, Lapidus picked up a three-by-six piece of construction lumber lying on the pool deck and began to chase after Novack with it, swinging the lumber at Novack's head. Lapidus recounted, "I had no control over myself—running—screaming—flailing the length of timber . . . I only knew that I wanted to crush that timber on my client's skull." Novack ran from Lapidus as the startled guests stared in disbelief while Lapidus chased him around the pool, waving the lumber and loudly chanting, *"He must die! He must die! He must die!"*

The next thing Lapidus remembered was that he was on his

back on the deck pinned down by several of the investors while a man splashed pool water in his face. He was so distraught that, he recalled, "It took about three of the partners to restrain me."

The architect was eventually paid the additional $40,000, but only after he was made to apologize to Novack for trying to kill him. Novack maintained that he had never promised the money to Lapidus in the first place and that because of his hearing problem, or faulty hearing aid, he must have misunderstood the conversation.

"I can't say anything good about the man," Lapidus said. "Bad, bad, bad."

SHEATHED IN a veneer of 85,000 square feet of aquamarine glass that took on the color of the sky during the day and shimmered in the sultry air at night, the arcuate Fontainebleau Hotel dominated everything around it, the sky and ocean merely a backdrop to its beauty. It was so instantly recognizable around the world that for the first twenty-four years of the hotel's existence it never had a name sign. It opened on December 20, 1954, with a party for 1,600 people, including New York mayor Robert Wagner, who flew to Miami with a contingent of international press. There was such a crush of people on opening night that much of the carpeting was ruined and had to be replaced. Patti Page sang the "Fontainebleau Waltz" in the La Ronde Room, and above the hotel whenever an Eastern Airlines jet arrived or departed Miami International it tipped its wings in salute. "Everything was in French," reported the *Miami Herald*, "including the confusion." (The restroom doors were marked MESSIEURS and MESDAMES.) The guest of honor was the mayor of Fontainebleau, France, who was stupefied by the hodgepodge of style and furniture and the twenty-four different colors Lapidus had mixed together. The nicest thing he could say about the hotel was that while the outside was very strong, the inside was a "bouillabaisse."

Fish stew or not, it was as promised "a monumental show-place . . . that . . . dazzled visitors," said the *New York Times*, but only in retrospect. When the hotel first opened, it was the subject of great ridicule. To comment that the hotel was overdone or garish was beside the point. The Fontainebleau wasn't built for traditional aesthetic reasons. It was shameless, built to amuse the senses, to shock and surprise. "I wanted people to walk in and drop dead," Lapidus said. He created a world that "would represent for [guests] the dream of tropical opulence and glittering luxury, influenced by the greatest mass media of entertainment of that time, the movies. . . . So I designed a movie set! I never for a moment let Ben Novak [sic] know what I was doing. For him I was expressing his ideas of what a luxury hotel should be."

The sheer volume of open space in the main lobby, with its eighteen-foot ceilings, was as marvelous as was the ridiculous incongruity of marble statues and busts on pedestals placed throughout it with no particular design scheme, so it seemed—Greek statuary mixed with terra-cotta cherubs and marble Roman busts, potted palms, a faux nineteenth-century grand piano, ornate wall clocks, then stretches of open marble with black inlaid bow ties almost as if there was not enough furniture to fill it, until another furniture setting appeared next to a paneled wood wall. The central lobby was supported by majestic columns that had no base or capitals, and recessed into the lobby ceiling were four crystal half-ton chandeliers that Lapidus had had fabricated in Belgium, each made of 1,800 pieces of crystal that needed to be disassembled by hand twice a year and individually washed in soap and water.

The Fontainebleau was the only hotel on the Beach that had a formal nighttime dress code; women wore cocktail dresses with mink stoles and men wore suits with ties. The doorman, Floyd "Mac" McSwane, who worked there for twenty years, kept extra jackets and ties in his locker. Getting dressed up for a night at the

Fontainebleau was part of the fun, and Lapidus cleverly gave the guests a dramatic way for them to display their finery with the "staircase to nowhere." The white marble staircase hugged a curved wall painted with a scene of the ruins of the Roman Forum. It allowed hotel guests the opportunity to take an elevator to the mezzanine and walk down the staircase, stopping at the "return," where the staircase changed direction and women could pivot while everyone in the lobby watched, as if they were at a fashion show. Watching people walk down the "staircase to nowhere," the women in gowns and diamonds and furs, was one of the hotel's most popular attractions.

As Ben Jr. pointed out, the staircase to nowhere "didn't go nowhere." It connected the lobby with the mezzanine, where there were hotel offices; a writing room with comfortable chairs and desks, an important part of every hotel in the 1950s, where guests could send home postcards and letters on Fontainebleau stationery; a "TV Theater," which featured one of the earliest large-screen television sets and rows of chairs for people who didn't want to watch TV in their rooms; and a large card room, full of smoke and gamblers, with high-stakes pinochle and poker games. On an average day in season, hundreds of thousands of dollars would change hands, on the weekend sometimes a million, and when the mobsters and movie stars were playing, a folding wall would be drawn to separate the VIPs from the more public tables.

Novack showed himself to be the consummate hotelier. Behind the scenes the Fontainebleau was a huge, complicated piece of machinery with dozens of components that all operated under his command. There were 847 full-time employees—1 employee per 1.4 guests—and hundreds more in parttime help. Behind the walls of the lobby were banks of switchboard operators manning phone boards with plug patches for the hotel's hundreds of telephones, and since there was no voice mail at the time, messages were written by hand and one of the hotel's small army of bellhops, dressed in impeccable Fontainebleau uniforms, slipped a copy under the guest's door, with a second copy left in the room box. For more urgent calls, one of the page boys would wander through the lobbies and out by the pool and beach summoning guests by name.

Because there was constant wear and tear on the furniture in the 550 rooms, Novack outfitted the basement with its own furniture repair shop and hired two full-time craftsmen to run it. There was also a full-time television repairman; four staff gardeners; and a team of laundresses who worked round-the-clock in an industrial-size laundry plant bigger than that of most metropolitan hospitals, washing thousands of sheets and towels a day. The amount of mail in and out of the hotel was so voluminous that Novack had to create an in-house post office to deal with it.

The food service and cuisine of the hotel's seven restaurants was overseen by a septuagenarian *maître de bouche* with the suspiciously grand name of René de la Jousselinière de Villermet de la Godsrary. To store food for its hungry boarders, the hotel maintained six walk-in freezers the size of trucks. The Fontainebleau also had its own bakery and its own butcher department with a staff of full-time butchers; Novack would no doubt have raised the cattle and chickens to supply his kitchens if he had had the chance. It took a total of 80 cooks working in eight kitchens over 30 gas ranges to prepare an average of 2,000 meals a day, including food for 24-hour-a-day room service.

The main dining room, the Fleur de Lis, was pure Lapidus magic. It looked like the set of a Jean Cocteau movie, with high gray walls and giant bisque and papier-mâché figurines of Louis XV and his courtiers on pedestals, interspersed with bizarre electrified candelabra fashioned from tree branches and antlers. Patrons entered the Fleur de Lis room by stepping up on a raised carpeted platform bathed in pink light so they could be seen by everyone in the dining room before descending a few steps onto the restaurant level to be seated. The pixilated ambience of this restaurant so amused John Jacob Astor that he gave several dinner parties there instead of at his nearby mansion, and the chairman of Revlon cosmetics, Charles Revson, once held a party at the Fleur de Lis that depleted the hotel's entire caviar supply.

Novack created the Fontainebleau to be self-contained, so that a guest would never have to leave and spend money elsewhere. The hotel's lower level was named the Rue de la Paix, and it had more than thirty retail shops, including a shop for women's formal wear where live mannequins modeled Dior evening gowns; a linen shop with $2,500 lace tablecloths and $50 napkins; a stock brokerage so guests could keep an eye on their investments; a furrier, who did such a good business in selling mink stoles late at night that he stayed open until dawn every day; and a barber shop where a down-on-his-luck former lightweight boxing champ named Beau Jack shined shoes. The lower level also featured a spacious "elegante" coffee shop/Jewish delicatessen called the Chez Bon Bon, which was intended to look like an Old World Viennese pastry shop, with plastic hedges along the walls and alcoves in which bisque figures balanced cornucopias of food on their turbans.

One of the hotel's most popular amenities was simple compared with all the rest—a "gymnasium" with *schvitz* baths, both Turkish and Russian, where a heavyset old man hosed you down after a good sweat with water so icy cold it was a miracle more men didn't have heart attacks. Up on the roof there were separate men's and women's solariums, human broilers where guests could lie naked in the sun coated in suntan oil, or get a naked massage from a bulky eastern European type dressed in white pants and T-shirt. There was also, although not advertised in promotional materials, a *mikvah,* or ritual cleansing bath, for Orthodox Jewish women in the basement.

The Fontainebleau proved to be a spectacular background for dozens of films and television shows, including Jerry Lewis's 1960 film *The Bellboy,* with actor Alex Gerry playing the part of the obsequious "Mr. Novak" [sic]. The hotel's Boom Boom Room was the hangout of Sandy Winfield II, the dashing young detective played by actor Troy Donahue in the 1960–62 hit television series *Surfside 6,* and the opening scene in the 1962 James Bond movie *Goldfinger* took place in one of the hotel's 250 double-decker cabanas, in which Margaret Nolan gave Sean Connery a massage while outside a team of shapely female water-skiers skied on the six-lane, Olympic-size swimming pool.* The Fontainebleau also made appearances in the action movie *The Specialist,* with Sylvester Stallone and Sharon Stone; *The Bodyguard,* with Kevin Costner and Whitney Houston; and *Scarface,* with Al Pacino as Tony Montana, a Marielito Cuban drug dealer who looks out from the magnificent hotel's rear terrace and murmurs, "This is paradise. This is paradise." Yet the hotel—and Miami Beach— probably never had any better publicity than from 1966 to 1970 when each week a CBS TV announcer uttered the words, "*From Miami Beach, the sun and fun capital of the world, it's the Jackie Gleason Show!*"

The Fontainebleau boasted yet another distinction: It was the most robbed hotel on Miami Beach, a candy store for thieves. The hotel was rife with room burglaries. Even Novack reported to the police the theft of his "piggy bank," which, he said, was filled not with loose change but with $15,000 worth of $100 bills. Since guests brought their best jewels to wear at the Fontainebleau, each room had its own safe-deposit box in a wall behind the cashier's desk in the lobby, but not every guest took advantage of the locked box, and in two years over $250,000 worth of jewelry was stolen from guests' rooms, including a $70,000 jewelry heist that took

---

*This entire sequence at the Fontainebleau was fabricated. Ben Novack Jr. points out that the scenes inside the cabana were shot on a Hollywood set and that the Fontainebleau's pool was not long enough for the water-skiers to gain enough speed to stay aloft, so they were superimposed into the shot. In the film James Bond calls the Fontainebleau "the best hotel in Miami Beach."

place while a clothing manufacturer and his wife were playing canasta by the pool. Novack hired twenty plainclothes men to patrol the hallways twenty-four hours a day, commanded by former New York City Police Department lieutenant James Gillace, whose remedy for the thievery was to suggest that if the women didn't wear so many diamonds at night, there'd be less stolen.

THE FONTAINEBLEAU turned Lapidus into an object of ridicule from both critics and peers, winning him the sobriquet "The Liberace of architecture." The reviews were unmerciful. The *New York Times*'s Ada Louise Huxtable called the Fontainebleau "aesthetic illiteracy." Architect Robert Anshen described it as "a monument to vulgarity." *Art in America* decried that the building was "hedonism's vacuum in a materialist culture." A friend of Lapidus who was an editor at *Architectural Forum* called him and said, "Morris, what the hell did you do? You created a monstrosity," and the magazine went on to label the hotel a "building of sucker-traps." *Look* called it "a mammoth dental plate." (*Look* also noted that there were "116 jokes in circulation about the Fontainebleau," for example, "The Fontainebleau is the only hotel to have wall-to-wall carpeting on the beach.") Even the architect Frank Lloyd Wright, usually reticent about critiquing his colleagues, described the Fontainebleau as an "ant hill."*

Belittle it as they may, the hotel took its place in American culture, but it would take thirty years for scholars to admit that the Fontainebleau inaugurated the postmodern movement in architecture. What began as "a condescension to the client," as Lapidus called it, became an internationally known style.

---

*When Lapidus finally met Frank Lloyd Wright years later, he was introduced to Wright as an architect who had "done some work" in Miami Beach. Wright said, "You've done some work down there? Well, if I was you, I wouldn't talk about it."

"You asked who designed it?" Novack snapped to a reporter. "*I* did. It was my idea to have the curved building, it was my idea to decorate it, it was my idea to build it, it was my idea to pay for it. Lapidus helped. He was part and parcel of me. He's a very clever man," Novack said, lapsing into the third person, "but Ben Novack designed that building."

BEN AND Bernice Novack's apartment on the fifteenth floor of the Château building at the Fontainebleau was known as the Governor's Suite. It was a four-bedroom oceanfront duplex with marble floors, formal dining room, billiard room, and piano bar—all with floor-to-ceiling windows. The view was a spectacular panorama of sea and changing sky. It was the kind of apartment you see only in movies (and sure enough, a scene in the 1960 movie *Ocean's 11* was shot in its billiard room), yet after a short time it lost its luster for Bernice. The disquieting reality was that save for her clothing and a few pieces of jewelry, nothing belonged to her. "Everything was owned by the hotel," she said—the Limoges dishes upon which she ate, the bed in which she slept. She didn't choose the sofa in the living room or the curtains for her bedroom. There was no grocery store at which to buy milk or shop for dinner, no laundry, no dishes in the sink, no beds to make. Instead there was room service and chefs cooking her meals to order, a bar that was automatically restocked, and fresh linens on the bed every day—life in a completely impersonal world.

"I was never happy living in the hotel," she asserted, and she asked Ben to buy a house nearby so she could make a life away from the hotel, but he didn't want to be away from the Fontainebleau—ever. "The Fontainebleau was his *life*," Bernice said. "It was his baby, his wife, his mistress, all his dreams and ideas together."

Bernice's part in this dream was as the beautiful trophy wife.

She was always on stage, an object of curiosity for the guests and the staff. She was expected to be the most fashionable woman in the hotel, as she was, impeccably turned out at all times, in an amazing array of outfits, even just walking to her cabana by the pool. "You are always in a glass cage when you're the wife of the owner," she explained. "People stared at me. They'd say, 'There's the owner's wife' or 'There's Mrs. Novack.' I didn't care for it. I didn't like the 'front' of the house." In her many years as the Fontainebleau's First Lady, she is remembered as the very pretty woman at Ben Novack's side who smiled and kept quiet. "It was not an easy life," she acknowledged. "It was very difficult, believe it or not."

Ben Jr. was born a year after the hotel opened, and like his mother he had his part to play in the drama that was the hotel— the dauphin. But being the little prince of the Fontainebleau was an especially tough role for a kid, particularly for a rambunctious boy like Ben Jr. "He was in everybody's hair," remembered Lenore Toby, the Fontainebleau's longtime publicist. "We used to call him 'Benjy' because he was a little tyrant, and he hated it. '*My name is Benjamin*,' he used to say. He had no discipline whatsoever, and his supervisors were the security guards in the hotel. They brought him up, and as a result that's what he wanted to be, a security guard."

"Let me tell you, I never had a childhood," Ben Jr. said. "I was always among adults. I had several nannies but I didn't know what it was like to be a normal kid playing in the neighborhood. I lived on the seventeenth floor of a hotel, and if I met some kids they were only around for four days with their parents on vacation." Even a simple birthday party was a "major ordeal," with a self-conscious artificiality that took away any real joy. The other children came to his birthday parties dressed in their best clothing and bearing expensive birthday gifts. They were brought to the hotel by their parents, passed through security, and ushered up into the private apartment. They ate a meal served by room service and a birthday cake made in the hotel's kitchens in an atmosphere of complete unease.

There was also a kidnap threat on Ben Jr., perhaps as a result of his father's tough stand against building and trade unions, or perhaps something else, it was never made publicly clear. When it happened Novack Sr. decided against telling Bernice and Ben Jr. and the Miami Beach police secretly trailed the youngster for weeks. "It was the worst environment for a child," Ben Jr. admitted. "But I grew up very quickly. And now I wouldn't change anything."

Six

EDEN ROC

The hotels are all beautiful—even the hideous ones!
—JULIE HARRIS AS RUTH ARNOLD IN THE PLAY
THE WARM PENINSULA, 1959

Harry Mufson was banned from the Fontainebleau, but he was curious to see for himself what all the fuss was about, so one day he put on a disguise and snuck inside. He looked around and thought, "I can do better."

In June of 1955 Mufson bought the 8½-acre parcel one site north of the Fontainebleau, which had been the estate of Albert Warner, one of the founding brothers of Warner Bros. Studios. Mufson announced to the press that he was going to build a hotel even more elegant and luxurious than the Fontainebleau. It was going to be called the Eden Roc, named for the gardens of the grand Hôtel du Cap Eden-Roc in the south of France, and the architect would be none other than Morris Lapidus.

The Eden Roc and the Fontainebleau would be separated only by a parking lot.

Novack was gutted with rage. He called Lapidus and demanded that he not design the Eden Roc, but Lapidus didn't see why he had to give up the commission. For Lapidus there was no downside; he would have two of the largest, most lavish hotels in Miami Beach right next to each other, and as a bonus it would aggravate Ben Novack.

In retaliation, Novack forbade Lapidus to ever set foot in the Fontainebleau again. He was banished from his own creation. The two men hated each other so much that they even insulted the hotel they had created together. Novack told a reporter from the *Saturday Evening Post* that Lapidus's contribution to the Fontainebleau "stinks," and in response Lapidus told the reporter, "Frankly it's not the kind of place I'd care to stay in myself."

Harry Mufson turned out to be almost as ignorant a client as Novack. Lapidus recounted that when he suggested there be a Baroque influence in the interior of the Eden Roc as opposed to the French Provincial used in the Fontainebleau, Mufson shouted in exasperation, "I don't care if it's Baroque or Brooklyn, just get me plenty of glamour and make sure it screams luxury!" Lapidus once showed Mufson a $10,000 copy of the statue *Winged Victory* that he wanted to place at the entrance of the hotel and Mufson demanded, "Where's the head? For ten grand I want a head!" Yet the men got along well enough to make a buying trip to Europe together, spending a total of $2 million on furnishings for the lobby and public spaces of the hotel.

The Eden Roc opened in December of 1955, just one year after the Fontainebleau, at a cost of $13 million. Although it was smaller and not as striking as the Fontainebleau, it was nevertheless a handsome, gracefully designed building with a grand driveway, a long striped portico, and an edifice with two full-length vertical panels of sparkling glass tiles tinted in gradations of green to emulate the depth of the sea. On its roof was what looked like an ocean liner's smokestack with the name Eden Roc spelled out in neon. The public space was just as overdone but felt less staged than the Fontainebleau's lobby did, although somehow familiar. All of Lapidus's bag of tricks were evident: There were white marble floors inlaid with large black fleurs-de-lis (instead of bow ties), and there was a sunken circular seating area with columns similar to the ones at the Fontainebleau, and—no surprise—a floating staircase that seemed to go nowhere that looked about the same as the one in the Fontainebleau and was in the same general place in the lobby. As with the Fontainebleau, grandiose names abounded. The lobby was called the Grand Lobby, the formal dining room was the Mona Lisa Room, and the bars were the Café Pompeii and Harry's Bar, the latter named not after Harry Mufson but after the famed Harry's Bar in Venice.

The Fontainebleau by itself was a showstopper, but the two hotels side by side on Collins Avenue was a sensation. All anybody talked about that season was the Fontainebleau and the Eden Roc right next to each other, and Lapidus and Mufson feuding with Novack, and after a while all the talk began to drive Novack insane. The Eden Roc siphoned away business and publicity, and, most important, it took away some of his pleasure in the Fontainebleau. The Eden Roc was in his face forever. He could not live that way, and he decided that he would hurt Harry Mufson in the worst possible way he could think of: He would take away the sun.

In 1956 Novack took a 99-year lease on the parking lot that separated the Fontainebleau and the Eden Roc and went "back to the bathroom," as Ben Novack Jr. put it, to design a new wing for the Fontainebleau.* Ostensibly what Novack wanted to do was add more guest rooms and build a much larger ballroom to attract convention business. The new wing, to be called the Chateau building, was a rectangular slab that was a good complement to the main building's arc. The problem was, as described by Ben Jr., that there was a fourteen-foot setback from the neighboring property to the north—the Eden Roc—and to build a 40,000-square-foot,

---

*Even though Novack had banned Lapidus from entering the Fontainebleau, he still had the temerity to ask him if he was interested in designing the new wing. Lapidus passed.

pillarless ballroom that could accommodate 3,000 people, the wall facing the Eden Roc would have to be solid to support all the weight. That would be a blank wall, seventeen stories tall, painted gray, only fourteen feet from the Eden Roc, and not only would everyone in the Eden Roc have to look up at an ugly blank gray wall, but every day, beginning around noon, the tall gray wall would block the sunlight from the Eden Roc pool. It cast what the *Miami Herald* described as "an immense blob of cool shadow over the pool most of the day." The finished wall had only three windows in it, the dining room windows of Ben Novack's new penthouse apartment, so, as the story goes, he could spit out the window at the Eden Roc.

Ben Novack Jr. refutes that his father ever spit at the Eden Roc or that he built the wall to block the sun for spite. "My father didn't give a shit what was going on next door," he said. "My father didn't even realize that the state of Florida is at a slight angle northeast and at twelve thirty in the afternoon the wall would cast a shadow over the Eden Roc," he added, with a smile. "Meanwhile, the result was the most godawful ugly wall."

Mufson and his partners in the Eden Roc sued Novack over the wall and the shadow it cast, but the court held that the Eden Roc had no air rights to the space and that the courts could not compel a building—or Novack's handiwork—not to cast a shadow.*

The shadow over the Eden Roc's pool became a national news story and threatened to ruin their business, and at tremendous cost Mufson and his partners were forced to build a second large pool, this one up on a deck on the north side of the hotel, away from the "Spite Wall." They also instituted what was called "anti-shadow" attractions, including waterskiing on Indian Creek and free yacht rides. For many

---

*In 2001 the Delano and Surfcomber hotels sued the builders of the new W hotel being built out of the Ritz Plaza, claiming that the W's seven-story structure would cast a shadow over their pool complexes.

years the perception prevailed that the Eden Roc's swimming pool got no sun. The reservation clerks went to great pains to point out that a sunny new pool had been built, yet the Eden Roc, in many ways a more elegant hotel than the Fontainebleau, would always be perceived to live in its shadow.

THE EDEN ROC, like the Fontainebleau, became a favorite haunt of underworld figures. "The boys," as the mobsters were called, rented cabanas by the year. Jules Levitt, one of the biggest bookies on the Beach and a partner in the infamous S&G Syndicate, was arrested in one of the cabanas of the Eden Roc for taking book, and in 1961 the Florida state attorney general's office asked that the switchboard be shut down because of all the bookmaking. There was also one hapless guest who found a gun in her night-table drawer and, thinking it was a cigarette lighter, pulled the trigger and put a bullet in the wall. At some point the disgusted Eden Roc shareholders filed suit against Mufson and his partners for being in league with the bookies.

Harry Mufson might have been hooked up with his share of gangsters and bookies, but he loved the hotel business and he was good at it. He was generous to the people who worked for him, and the staff of the hotel had no complaints. When there was an employee strike, Mufson put on an apron and washed dishes in the kitchen. One night when Pearl Bailey wasn't able to appear in the nightclub, Mufson picked up the check for the entire audience. Mufson booked Barbra Streisand to headline the hotel's nightclub just as she was starting out, and he loaned her his car because she was so broke. On the second night of Streisand's run he bought out her contract because the nightclub was half empty. Mufson liked rubbing elbows with celebrities, and sometimes he'd invite the big stars staying at the hotel to his house on Pine Tree Drive for dinner. It irked Novack when Mufson was invited to travel to Europe with Frank Sinatra to see the Ingemar Johansson–Floyd Patterson title fight in Sweden.

Mufson was a nice guy, but he was also a heavy drinker and smoked two packs of cigarettes a day. He spent too many late nights at Harry's Bar. In the late 1960s he bought the grand old Roney Plaza Hotel, and he was making plans for its major renovation when he had a heart attack and nearly died. At his doctor's insistence, Mufson sold the hotel in 1968, and the following year he reluctantly sold his shares in the Eden Roc and retired permanently from the hotel business. He remained active with the family chain of Jefferson stores, which he sold to Montgomery Ward for $37 million in stock. In 1973, four years after selling the Eden Roc, he died of a second massive heart attack in his Collins Avenue apartment at the age of sixty-four.

The new owner of the Eden Roc was one of Mufson's partners, fifty-year-old Morris Landsburgh, who was already a celebrity in Miami Beach. He was an elegant man who was twice named one of America's best-dressed men, and he had large real estate holdings in Miami Beach hotels, including the Deauville, Sherry Frontenac, Casablanca, Versailles, Crown, Saxony, and Sans Souci, the latter of which Landsburgh bought from Harry Mufson. He owned a Rolls-Royce automobile, which he kept parked right on the ramp of the hotel, and he was known for ceremoniously bowing to guests and saying "Good evening, you all." Landsburgh made his fortune despite having a silver plate covering half of his head and being deaf in one ear, the result of a run-in with an ice truck when he was a little boy. He was also the inventor and proponent of the "American plan" for hotels that included two meals a day included with the room charge.

Ten years before Landsburgh bought the Eden Roc, he and his business partner, Sam Cohen, took controlling interest in the Flamingo Hotel and Casino in Las Vegas for $10.6 million, a deal brokered by Meyer Lansky, who received a $200,000 finder's fee.

The fee was paid to Lansky in installments from the $10 million that Landsburgh and Cohen were skimming from the Flamingo's gambling proceeds, charged federal agents. In 1973 Landsburgh and Cohen pleaded guilty to federal charges of income tax evasion and of conspiring with Lansky to defraud the Internal Revenue Service. Landsburgh and Cohen were each given a one-year prison sentence but served only half their time, in a minimum-security prison in Florida. They passed the days playing tennis and cards, and they were served meals cooked by the chef at the Eden Roc.

After Landsburgh and Cohen's release in 1973, they were forced to give up their liquor license at the Eden Roc and they sold the hotel to Howard Garfinkel, a Miami Beach real estate investor whose portfolio included several large apartment buildings. Garfinkel was a tall, heavyset man who wore large diamond pinkie rings, owned two Rolls-Royces (one for him and one for his wife), and had a mansion on Pine Tree Drive. He didn't know much about running a hotel, but he was a fanatic about the hotel's appearance. He kept a chart of the positions of every sofa and table in the lobby and had the staff paint over the tire smudges on the white curbs of the hotel's grand front driveway. Once an hour a maintenance man polished away the fingerprints on the bronze doors to the elevators. People were mighty impressed with Howard Garfinkel until he made the mistake of pledging $3 million to the University of Miami to expand its art museum. When the money was not forthcoming it was discovered that Mr. Garfinkel was—surprise!—an ex-con who had defrauded two banks in New Jersey for $200,000. Soon the paychecks at the Eden Roc began to bounce and employees staged a lobby protest, chanting "We want money!" It wasn't great for business, and on June 5, 1975, the Garfinkels declared bankruptcy. Morris Landsburgh and company, acting with a court trustee, took back $6 million in mortgages on the building and reopened it under their auspices while they tried to find another buyer. Landsburgh never lived to see it sold. Like Harry Mufson, he too died of a massive heart attack, one February morning in 1977 at the age of fifty-eight, in his Collins Avenue apartment.

A dizzying procession of wannabes and owners followed. In 1978 Bob Guccione, anticipating that gambling would be legalized in Miami Beach, made a $15.5 million offer to buy the Eden Roc but withdrew it when it became clear the gambling bill would fail. In May 1980 the Saudi Arabian sheikh Wadji Tahlawi bought the hotel, calling it "a lovely lady in need of a face-lift," and professed he was "in love" with the Eden Roc and would never sell it. He spent a paltry $7 million on renovations, painted it beige, and added some fountains in the lobby and smoky mirrors in the elevators, but he refurbished only three floors of rooms. He gave a gala at the hotel at which a Bengal tiger named Caliph was paraded through the ballroom. Wadji Tahlawi saw no pitfalls in a devout Muslim owning a hotel in which the guests were predominantly Jewish. "Jew or Moslem," he said, "you are talking about a different idea of how to get to paradise." But the Jews only believed in a paradise here on earth—Miami Beach—and when it became clear no Jew would stay at a hotel owned by an Arab, he sold it to Budapest-born developer Tibor Hollo for $22.5 million in December of 1981.

Among many other holdings, Tibor Hollo was the developer of the 42-story, $750 million Venetia office complex, shopping center, and condominium skyscraper on Biscayne Bay that had more floor space than the Empire State Building—with a mortgage almost as big. By 1991, after the country skidded into a hiccup of a recession, Tibor Hollo's real estate investments began to go south, one by one, and he never had the money to make the necessary renovations on the Eden Roc. By then the hotel had $30 million in mortgages against it and it wound up in the hands of a court-appointed receiver. In 1992 hotelier Ian Schrager and entertainment impresario David Geffen toyed with the idea of buying the Eden Roc for $12 million, and Schrager had a construction and design team pore over the hotel before they decided to opt out. In October 1992 the New York real estate investor Irving Goldman's family bought the hotel from the Federal Deposit Insurance Corporation for $14.6 million, and they sunk $28 million into a long-overdue renovation. The Goldman family ran the hotel for six years before selling it for $45 million to the Blackacre Capital Group and Destination Hotels & Resorts, an international organization that ran twenty-three hotels in the United States.

The hotel is now known as the Eden Roc Renaissance Beach Resort & Spa, and in 2007 it went through a much needed $170 million upgrade that included the addition of two new ballrooms totaling 14,000 square feet, a 5,000-square-foot rooftop convention hall, a new spa, and a Starbucks. There was only one problem with the Eden Roc's spiffy new look—that ugly Spite Wall. The owners of the Fontainebleau at that time said they would consider demolishing it and build in its stead a twenty-story glass tower with five hundred hotel rooms connecting the Eden Roc with the Fontainebleau. But that turned out to be too ambitious a project and the idea was dropped. The Miami Beach Historic Preservation Board suggested that if the Spite Wall was going to remain, perhaps windows could be put into its bleak blank side. But it turned out that cutting windows into the facade would necessitate massive steel reinforcements because of the way Ben Novack had deliberately built it. "I don't know why the building was built this way," said project architect John Nichols, "but it was." It turned out that the Fontainebleau structural plans no longer exist.

Since the blank wall looked like it was there to stay, the corporation that owned the Eden Roc decided the best thing to do was build their own blank wall to face it. The Eden Roc added a condominium addition, and now there are now two windowless walls facing each other, only fourteen feet apart by measuring tape but as wide as the Grand Canyon in spirit.

Seven

TWILIGHT ON
THE BEACH

*Welcome to Miami Beach, ladies and gentlemen, where
everything's cheaper than it looks.*

—ATTRIBUTED TO NEIL YOUNG

Next to the Mob-run hotels of Las Vegas, the Fontainebleau was
Frank Sinatra's favorite haunt. He headlined the Fontainebleau's
La Ronde Room almost every winter during the 1950s and 1960s,
and when he wasn't working at the Fontainebleau he stayed
there on vacation. Sinatra sold out La Ronde weeks in advance,
and the maître d' made $5,000 a night in tips from guests trying
to get a good table—money he had to split with Ben Novack,
who also demanded half of the tips of the parking valets out front.
Sinatra liked the hotel so much that he used it as a location for several movies, including 1959's *A Hole in the Head*, a film he produced and starred in as a down-on-his-luck owner of the Cardozo
Hotel in South Beach, and *Tony Rome*, a cheesy 1967 private-eye
flick costarring Jill St. John as a broad who lives in a suite at
the Fontainebleau and slings lines like "This stink-pot town. Didya
know the women outnumber the men twenty to one? It's a
man's town."

In Sinatra's twenty-year association with the Fontainebleau, he
never paid for anything, not his room, meals, booze, or even

the lounge chair and TV set he threw off the balcony of his fifteenth-floor penthouse suite, called the Frank Sinatra Suite—at least it was on the nights he was staying there. The only thing Sinatra paid for was his hookers.

And the hotel never paid him anything—the most he received was a $6,000 ring that Ben Novack gave him to show his gratitude. Just how this could be, that one of the world's great entertainers worked the Fontainebleau for two decades for free, was possibly explained in a Justice Department memo that asserted Sinatra worked gratis because the Fontainebleau was Mob controlled and it was his obligation. Novack always heatedly denied that his hotel was connected to the Mob, and Ben Jr. also protests, "We couldn't keep anybody out of the hotel! It was a public place!"—but at the very least the hotel was a "hangout for hoodlums," as the Florida attorney general's office called it.

Sinatra was as taken with mobsters and the Mafia as a school-boy with a crush, and an FBI informant who had observed Sinatra with mobster Joe "Stingy" Fischetti at the Fontainebleau believed the singer had "a hoodlum complex." Fischetti had been one of Sinatra's tightest buddies since the men had met two decades before in Las Vegas. It was Fischetti who supplied Sinatra with hot and cold running hookers. He and his older brothers, Charles and Rocco, were said to be cousins of Al Capone. Fischetti was allegedly assigned to watch out for Sinatra in Miami Beach by Mafia kingpin Frank Costello, and the two became so thick that at one point Sinatra insisted Fischetti be put on the Fontainebleau payroll as his "talent agent." In 1962 Novack paid Fischetti almost $40,000; he was mysteriously dropped from the books the following year.

Fischetti was small time compared with Sam Giancana, the head of the Chicago Mob, who kept a suite at the Fontainebleau. Giancana ran the lucrative gambling rackets in pre-Castro

Cuba and made an estimated $40 million a year from illegal sources. Sinatra was so starstruck by the Mafia kingpin that he gave Giancana a star-sapphire pinkie ring as a friendship gift (which Giancana was reportedly loath to wear unless he was with Sinatra). Giancana was a little man who drove a pink Cadillac and wore sharkskin suits, alligator shoes, and a toupee. In July of 1959 when Giancana's daughter was married in a lavish wedding at the Fontainebleau, the *New York Post* reported that the bride's father "stole for a living." He did a lot more than steal; Giancana was reputed to have ordered the murders of more than two hundred men and was himself arrested three times for murder. In 1961 he was almost certainly involved in a discussion that took place in the lobby of the Fontainebleau in which he offered the CIA the help of the Mafia in assassinating Cuban leader Fidel Castro.

Giancana would often meet with Meyer Lansky in the rooftop solarium, where it was isolated and they could talk. Lansky was a legendary figure in the world of gangsters, a Jew who was revered as the financial brain for the Mob and the man who controlled organized crime in South Florida. Lansky had run the casinos in pre-Castro Cuba with Giancana, and it was Lansky who masterminded the Mob's infiltration of Las Vegas in the 1950s. He was probably most famous for arranging to split the money skimmed from Vegas casinos into nine shares, seven to be distributed among all the Mob families and two for himself. Lansky and Giancana spent a great deal of money at the Fontainebleau—"God did they spend money!" Ben Jr. said. Lansky kept to himself; he used the pay phones in the lower lobbies, or ate lunch at the coffee shop and left, but Sinatra, Fischetti, and Giancana would hang out together and amuse themselves by throwing cherry bombs off the balcony of Sinatra's suite.

Although Ben Novack fancied himself Sinatra's good friend—he frequently boasted that he stayed at Sinatra's home in Los Angeles—the singer treated him like another of his flunkies. Late one night in the Poodle Lounge* after a show, Sinatra and his sycophant buddies were sitting around a table when Sinatra discovered his glass was empty and there was no waiter nearby. He picked up an ice bucket filled with ice and water and turned it over on Novack's head. "You run a fucking lousy hotel," he snarled.

Violence followed Sinatra around the Fontainebleau, and although the staff was thrilled to see him, they were afraid of him as well. In 1967, when Sinatra was shooting *Tony Rome* at the hotel, what started as a kibitzing match between him and comedian Shecky Greene, who was acting in the movie, turned mean. Around four that morning a bunch of hoods attacked Greene in the Fontainebleau lobby with a blackjack. "Five guys were beating me up and I hear Frank say, 'That's enough,'" he told a reporter. Greene's head bandages can be seen in the movie. That same year an old man who worked at the hotel was so excited to see Sinatra in the coffee shop that he grabbed Sinatra's hand and the singer's bodyguards pounced on the duffer and beat him up.

It was Sinatra who arranged the infamous meeting between John F. Kennedy and Sam Giancana at the Fontainebleau on April 12, 1960, during which Kennedy asked for Giancana's support in helping him win crucial districts in Chicago that the Mob controlled. Giancana delivered the Chicago precincts and Kennedy was elected president, but instead of showing gratitude to the Mob benefactor, JFK allowed his brother, then Attorney

---

*Author Lewis Lapham described seeing Novack in the Poodle Lounge almost every night of the week, sitting at a table in the corner, "with his hat on, a cigar in his teeth, and an expensive sport coat thrown carelessly over his shoulder. He sits among good-looking blonde girls and heavy-set men who speak in hoarse whispers of their winnings and losses at the track. Petitioners continuously present themselves at his table, asking for a room, or a tip on a horse, or an introduction to a big-name talent booked into one of his nightclubs."

General Bobby Kennedy, to vehemently attack organized crime. Some of the mobsters held Sinatra responsible for what they felt was a double cross. Reportedly, in 1961 when two screenwriters working with Sinatra arrived at his Fontainebleau penthouse suite, they found the singer locked in his bedroom. Earlier, he'd lifted the silver dome covering the dinner that the room service staff had brought to his suite and he'd found the skinned head of a lamb.

IN 1967, after years of persistent rumors that organized crime was in control of the Fontainebleau, Clarence Jones and James Savage, two investigative reporters from the *Miami Herald*, attempted to untangle a nearly incomprehensible paper trail of mortgages, deeds, and obfuscating transactions in the Fontainebleau's thirteen-year real estate history. The lengthy front-page article called the Fontainebleau "a jungle of corporate and financial manipulation" and claimed that much of the twenty-two acres on which the hotel stood was owned by "gamblers and hoodlums."* The *Herald* contended that the ownership of the Fontainebleau had passed into the hands of a syndicate with the improbable name of the Minneapolis Combination, a front for Mob brains Meyer Lansky. The article claimed that Max ("Little Maxie Eder") Raymond wasn't really a gentleman who owned the linen shop downstairs but a gangster and the hotel's "resident muscle." An ex-con and accused murderer, Raymond was the man to see for getting into the private high-stakes card games held behind closed doors, which was his

---

*It would later be revealed in local police documents that as early as 1956 one of Novack's nervous partners, investor Ben Jaffe, who owned a 40 percent interest in the hotel, requested that law enforcement conduct an investigation into Mob infiltration.

"concession." The article also naively claimed that Raymond was the Mob's in-house connection who kept an eye on Novack.*

The immediate result of the *Herald*'s accusations, which made national news, was that Novack's banking relationships turned glacial. Whatever loans, investment money, or mortgaging he was involved in or would need in the future from banking institutions was finished. The *Herald* article would likely ruin him financially, and Novack felt compelled to fight it, not just to save face but to stay solvent: He filed a $10 million libel suit against the *Herald* and its writers. Yet he was stymied from the start when the *Herald*'s lawyers refused to turn over the reporters' notes and material upon which the article was based, claiming they were covered by the shield law protecting journalists from revealing sources.

Novack's getting into a protracted legal pissing contest with the *Herald* did not make the mobsters who hung out at the hotel very happy, and overnight they vanished from the premises.

The *Herald*, then owned by the powerful Knight-Ridder newspaper group, was determined to defend itself, and just to show that the owners meant business, the first person their lawyers subpoenaed for deposition in April 1967 was Frank Sinatra. In an absurd parody of real life, Sinatra gave his deposition not in a lawyer's office but in his penthouse suite at the Fontainebleau, where he was shooting the movie *Tony Rome*. He was in full movie makeup and his Los Angeles attorney, Milton Rudin, was at his side. Sinatra swore that in all the years he'd been appearing at the Fontainebleau he had no idea how

---

*The truth may have been darker and more complicated. It's now generally believed that Joe Fischetti ran the Fontainebleau for the Mob. Years later a memo from former assistant U.S. attorney Martin McNamara to Henry Peterson, head of the Organized Crime Strike Force in Washington, D.C., made the accusation "Joe Fischetti and Ben Novak [sic] of the Fontainebleau are regarded as being fronts for substantial investments of hood money . . ."

much he was paid. He admitted that he "met" Sam Giancana but insisted that he never stayed at the Fontainebleau when the mobster was in residence. He also admitted that it was possible he played pinochle in the card room "for a dollar or two" but was not aware of any gambling. Most important, he denied he knew of any connections between Novack and Giancana, or Meyer Lansky.

In April of 1968, as the trial date drew close, Sinatra was subpoenaed again, and this time he barricaded himself in his hotel suite to avoid process servers. That night, on stage in La Ronde Room, the process servers were waiting for him in the audience. "We're having a wonderful time in Miami Beach," Sinatra caustically told the audience. "Get a subpoena every day." When he was ordered by a judge to show up for his deposition or be held in contempt of court, he left town. In all, nineteen witnesses whom the *Herald* called for deposition, including Meyer Lansky, took the Fifth instead of answering questions.

The *Herald* lawyers might not have gotten any incriminating information, but they made their point. Novack's lawsuit could prove very uncomfortable to the Mob, and two days before the trial was to begin, Novack dropped his $10 million libel claim. In return the newspaper published a statement saying that an insurance company was titleholder of record of the land on which the hotel stood, and that Novack was sole owner of the operating company. Otherwise the newspaper never apologized or retracted any of its accusations.

IN JUNE 1968, two months after the libel lawsuit with the *Herald* was settled, Bernice and Ben Novack divorced after sixteen years of marriage. By then, Bernice said, "I had not been happy for a long time. I didn't want to live at the hotel and he would never buy me a house. He was fooling around. He was attractive and rich and women were after him. After all, he owned the world-renowned Fontainebleau." Ben evidently thought that Bernice was fooling around too, because in 1966 he had a private detective shadow her from May 16 to October 1 (and then stiffed the detective agency for the fee and was sued for $7,800). "Mind you, while he was having me followed he was going out with somebody else at the time," Bernice said. "She was a bitch. She used to come to the hotel while the divorce was going on. She really pursued him and I guess he fell in love with her."

"Bernice ended up throwing Ben out of the suite," said the hotel's publicist, Lenore Toby. Ben moved into another suite with Ben Jr. until the couple were divorced and Bernice moved out, taking with her a truckload of items and furniture, some of which a court of law did not believe she was entitled to, including twenty cases of sparkling soda mix and a $10,000 set of china. Ben withheld $15,000 in alimony and a judge held Bernice in contempt of court until she returned the goods along with a portrait of Ben Jr. Ben asserted that since Bernice had custody of their son, at least he deserved the portrait to look at.

In January 1969, seven months after his divorce became final, Ben married the woman he had been seeing, a union that lasted only three years before she filed for dissolution in December 1971. He never married again, although he was rarely without female companionship.

In 1978, ten years after their divorce, Ben Novack, claiming he was broke, sued Bernice to have his alimony reduced or terminated, and lost. "I didn't come out of it with too much," she said, laughing at the thought of having her alimony terminated. "Little more than my jewelry. Not even a car."

PERHAPS BERNICE got out just in time.

Ben Novack was broke, and so was the Fontainebleau.

In the beginning of the 1970s Miami Beach had slid into a dark and dramatic decline. Its fall from favor was brutal. Tourism had dropped by 50 percent from the previous decade, and for the first time in thirty years the number of hotel rooms had declined—by 3,000, contrasted to Las Vegas, where they were adding 10,000 new hotel rooms a year. In a city that once had a heated competition for "Hotel of the Year," the last new hotel in Miami Beach, the Konover, had been built in 1967. "So rapidly has the seven-mile-long island degenerated," *Time* magazine declared in a 1977 article called "Ebb Tide for Miami Beach," "that it can be fairly described as a seedy backwater of debt-ridden hotels."

Said former Miami Beach mayor Neisen Kasdin, "Business was so bad in Miami Beach I was happy just to see prostitutes."

How did things go bad so quickly? Locals can tick off the common wisdom practically by rote: Jet travel made foreign destinations easier and more convenient; the Caribbean islands became as accessible as Miami Beach and offered hotel and airfare package tours and tax-free shopping; the cruise-line industry had modernized and become affordable to the middle class, and the giant ships became like floating hotels with the powerful lure of on-board gambling; in 1971 Disney World opened in Orlando, siphoning off family business that was the financial bread-and-butter of smaller hotels. Other theorists blame the popularity of Morris Landsburgh's "American plan" for killing local restaurant business. When Hank Meyer, the public-relations spokesman for greater Miami, was asked his opinion of why the city had been abandoned by tourists, he answered, "Product, product, product."

But Morris Landsburgh had a more outspoken assessment. "Maybe," he said, "we should bring back restricted hotels."

It was a nasty way to put it, but Landsburgh was voicing the general consensus that what hurt Miami Beach the most was the perception that the city had been co-opted by the Jews, both as a resort and as a place to retire, and if the handwriting was on the wall for Miami Beach, it was written in Yiddish. As sociologist

Deborah Dash Moore observed in her 1994 book *To the Golden Cities: Pursuing the American Jewish Dream in Miami and L.A.*, "Americans increasingly associated the vulgarity and flamboyance of Miami Beach with an image of Jewish nouveau riche."

Ironically, Jews were never welcomed in Miami Beach in the first place. In the 1930s and 1940s anti-Semitism in Miami Beach was unabashed and prevalent. As late as 1960 no beach or golf club on Miami Beach would accept a Jewish member, and until the end of World War II, Jews were ghettoized in hotels below 5th Street. Even *Time* magazine published a map of Miami Beach in 1940 that suspiciously labeled the area below Lincoln Road as "The Bronx." There were land covenants forbidding sales to Jews, specifying that potential landowners be white, Christian, and "non-felons" (which in Miami was probably the hardest part of the covenant to fulfill). Hotels displayed signs that read, "We have a restricted clientele regarding pets, children under 12 years of age, and the Hebrew religion" or, worse, "Gentiles Only, No Dogs" and "Every room with a view without a Jew." When the city's advertising slogan "It's always June in Miami" became popular in the Northeast, some Miami locals sported automobile bumper stickers that read "It's always Jew'n in Miami."

In 1945 a group of Miami Beach Jewish war veterans began a painstaking door-to-door campaign in an attempt to rid the Beach of offensive signs. In great part because of their work, the Miami Beach City Council passed an ordinance outlawing "Gentiles Only" signs in hotels in 1949. It was with the passage of this law, noted Deborah Dash Moore, that "the council hung out a welcome sign for Jews." At the start of World War II there were only 8,000 or so Jews living in the entire Miami area; twenty years later there were 140,000. By the 1960s, the height of the resort's Jewish popularity, 90 percent of all tourists were Jewish, which meant that the economic health of the resort depended on a pool of 6 percent of the U.S. population.

What was the great allure of Miami Beach for Jewish people? The city's appeal was deeply emotional and mysterious. Miami Beach was the quintessence of the collective dreams of a million European immigrants. The city had open skies with low horizons, soothing trade winds, and a cerulean sea that was never too cool for bathing. The weather was warm and restorative, the streets and beaches were clean, and on every corner there was the sweet smell of coconut and freshly squeezed citrus fruit for sale. And then there were the palm trees—especially the palm trees. The author Isaac Bashevis Singer wrote that the first time he saw a palm tree in Miami Beach, he was so entranced that he stared at it for hours. In a foreword he wrote for the book *My Love Affair with Miami Beach* by Richard Nagler, he explained, "I had a feeling I had come to Paradise. . . . Where would I ever see palm trees in my life? I told [my readers] my impressions about the palm trees, how they are like trees and not like trees, how different they are. They created a mood in me, and maybe in other people, too."

A more soulful reason why the Jews flocked to Miami Beach was that Jews traditionally migrated together. They were less interested in assimilation than they were in sharing the commonality of their Jewishness in a large Christian nation, a desire that was rekindled in many Jews after the atrocities of World War II. The impact of Jewish coherence on a resort community had already been apparent in the success of a cluster of kosher hotels in the Lakewood area of New Jersey, which still today caters to Orthodox Jews, and in the Catskill Mountains of Sullivan County, New York, a fabled summer resort of the 1950s nicknamed the "Borscht Belt," with hundreds of kosher hotels and bungalow colonies and an almost 100 percent Jewish clientele. In fact, several Catskill Mountains hotels opened southern outposts for the winter, most prominently Grossinger's Hotel, which operated under the same name in Miami Beach; the Tamarack Lodge, which operated as the Marlin in Miami Beach; Kutsher's Country Club from South

Fallsburg, which ran the Haddon Hall and the Beacon; and the Loch Sheldrake, which opened the Nautilus.

The patrons of those Catskill Mountains hotels—predominantly New York City garment-center workers—found tremendous appeal in Miami Beach as a retirement community. From 1960 to 1970 the percentage of the population over sixty-five doubled to 50 percent of the resort's 90,000 residents, bringing the average age to sixty-eight years old. That meant most of the citizens were older than most of the buildings. Miami Beach was one of the few cities in the world that had a negative birth/death ratio. The 1977 *Time* magazine article claimed that the "lifeguards spend more time assisting heart-attack victims on the sand than pulling foundering swimmers out of the surf." Many old people were hit by cars because they didn't watch the lights or traffic signs; eventually the traffic lights were slowed down to give people with walkers enough time to cross the street. Not everyone was tolerant of the aged either. Paul Brunn, who authored the "In My Opinion" column for the *Miami Beach Sun*, wrote, "You gave your youth and your best living years to some other city. What makes you think goose pimples should be mine because you have selected to honor my city with your dying years?"

It was no honor. Life was depressing and filled with despair for the elderly in Miami Beach. By the 1980s many of the retirees were solely dependent on Social Security, their savings used up years before. They lined the front porches of the hotels or watched TV in the lobbies and lived in small, warrenlike hotel rooms. Their children up north stopped visiting, rejecting Miami Beach as a geriatric resort. The old men and women in South Beach were lonely and sick and unwanted, and they killed themselves at a far greater rate than did the rest of the population; in 1978 Miami Beach had the highest suicide rate of any city in America, and by the early 1980s the suicide rate was three times the national average. In Isaac Bashevis Singer's story "A Party in Miami Beach," one of the characters comments, "Here you can forget about death as much as you can forget to breathe." Singer postulated that perhaps old people in Miami Beach wore such brightly colored clothing because they were trying to trick the angel of death into thinking they were young.

BEN NOVACK watched frantically as the city devolved around him. Through all the turbulence in his life, the lawsuits, feuds, rivalry from competing hotels, he managed to keep a firm hold on the rudder, but he couldn't control the waning popularity of Miami Beach. "Social business had declined terribly," said the hotel's publicist, Lenore Toby. "I would say the main account in those years was IBM; they had several meetings back to back during the height of the season and that kept the hotel afloat for the rest of the year."

Now in his mid-sixties, Ben Novack had become a sad parody of himself. His hair was dyed too dark, his false teeth were too obvious, and his nose had grown long with his years. He had the odd, stretched look of a man who had had a bad face-lift, or two, and his spiffy made-to-order clothing was beginning to look as worn as his grand hotel.

Novack's empire literally began to fall apart with the collapse of the west wall of the old Sorrento Hotel directly to the south of the Fontainebleau. Novack bought the Sorrento in 1970 to renovate into a spa in hopes of attracting more convention business. When the west wall collapsed, he discovered that the construction company he had hired never put up an insurance bond and it would cost him nearly $3 million to rebuild the wall—money he had to take out of the Fontainebleau's cash flow. At this time the Fontainebleau was losing customers to the Doral Hotel and Country Club, a huge setup that boasted a new twist to a vacation at the beach resort—its own golf course with lodging. So Novack decided to build a golf course and clubhouse for the

Fontainebleau, "the world's most majestic country club," according to his bombast. In 1971 he bought a tract of land not far from Miami International Airport, and with a $2 million construction loan he started to build a golf course and hotel, part of what he envisioned as "Fontainebleau Park," a $25 million development that would include a hotel, condominiums, private homes, parks, schools, and two golf courses. In 1972 he bought 180 acres more and refinanced his holdings with a $6 million mortgage. By the mid-1970s he owed a fortune in mortgages, including one with the Connecticut General Life Insurance Company for $13.3 million and one with the Kentucky Central National Bank for $4.3 million, plus $4 million he owed to his partners in Fontainebleau Park, Roland International. With his increasingly limited cash flow diverted to paying off mortgages, the Fontainebleau began to look dowdy and run-down. "The money wasn't there to keep the rooms in the condition they needed to be in," Ben Jr. said. "TV sets needed to be replaced, wallpaper, furniture, fixtures, and equipment needed to be modernized. We took all the French Provincial furniture to our shop and repaired it every day. Nobody wanted it, it was outdated."

As Novack got more desperate for money to keep afloat, he found oddball business partners and strange pals to hang around with. He'd wine and dine four-flushers and fakes, and he was the one who always picked up the check, and took out the next mortgage to keep going. Reportedly one of the potential investors Novack asked to stay at the hotel had a bathroom ceiling fall on his head.

In February of 1977 it came to light that the Fontainebleau hadn't paid its employees' health insurance for two months—it was behind $25,000 in payments—and then it started paying salaries irregularly. A surprising number of employees stayed on out of loyalty. "We were at death's door," Lenore Toby recalled. "The hotel went about its business every day, but there was no pay.

The creditors may have been lining up, but there were desk clerks and the hotel kept running. The maids continued to make up the rooms—mostly empty, and anyway, they couldn't afford to do the laundry so they would change the bottom sheets into top sheets. I could be an expert on running a hotel without any money," Toby said. "It was . . . around the time of the final days, and I went into Novack's office on the mezzanine and there was a huge antique conference table big enough to seat at least twelve or fourteen people and that table was piled with stacks of cash."

Novack told her to start counting.

"Excuse me? What am I counting?" Toby asked.

"Make piles of nine thousand nine hundred dollars in hundred-dollar bills," Novack answered.

"So after I counted about one-quarter of the table he said, 'Okay, okay. Take one pile.'"

"And what do you want me to do with it?"

He said, "Take it to the bank. Get a cashier's check in your name and bring it to me. Under ten thousand you don't have to report it to the IRS."

"That was the only way he could get cash," Toby explained. "He had no money. *He had no money.* He was stealing from himself now."*

The hotel, with liabilities of $25 million, went into state court receivership, and in April of 1977 Novack tried to stave off the wolves by filing for reorganization, but it was too late. In October of 1977 he was forced to declare personal bankruptcy. When Harold Gardner, Novack's marketing director, was asked by a

---

*Ben Jr. remembered a different, more heroic version of the last days of Novack's Fontainebleau. He remembered that his father always kept two safe-deposit boxes in the hotel with "a couple of hundred thousand dollars in them, and I personally was there with my father when he emptied the boxes and gave the money to the general cashiers."

reporter if Novack was falling apart, Gardner replied, "He can't come apart because he has no seams."

"Physically, he was thrown out of that hotel," Lenore Toby said. "They told him to vacate. He had to get out. It was a scene beyond scenes. He was a broken man. Even though he might have been mean to everyone through the years, and as difficult a boss as he could be, everyone was heartbroken for him." Toby and the other executives bought him a platinum pocket watch, which they had engraved "To Ben Novack, Mr. Fontainebleau, Always." On his last night in the hotel, Toby went up to his suite to give him the watch on behalf of the other executives. "He came to the door disheveled. He was in a bathrobe and his hair was flying all over the place. He had a scotch in his hand and he was wheezing. It was the most pathetic sight I had ever seen.

"I said, 'I have a gift for you,' and he said, 'Sit down, sit down.' He was on the telephone trying to make a deal to raise funds to buy the Fontainebleau out of bankruptcy. He had to leave the next morning, mind you, and he was telling the man on the phone that if he could get there by seven in the morning they would have a meeting. . . . He was trying to the last minute to make a deal, hoping against hope that he could save his hotel. So terrible. Terrible. I mean, this was the man who had Ann-Margret and Frank Sinatra and all the entertainers in the world in his hotel and all the presidents! I met five presidents of the United States at the Fontainebleau. The Who's Who of the world stayed there. It was just an incredible experience. And to imagine that this man could fall that easily."

When morning came the Fontainebleau staff lined up in the lobby to say good-bye to him. He shook hands glumly and then he walked to the front door and left the hotel for the last time. "I never walked into the Fontainebleau again," he said. "I couldn't stand to walk into what I created."

Novack claimed he was broke. "I didn't put away a penny," he said. "A lot of people think I put millions away. Let them think that." He moved to a townhouse development eighteen miles west of Miami Beach and became manager of the Racquet Club in North Bay Village, which had a cocktail lounge. In November of 1983, at age seventy-seven, Novack had his personal possessions auctioned off in a Santini Brothers warehouse on NW 119th Street in Miami. A few days before the auction he went to see a preview. He walked around with a cane looking at all the spoils of the hotel. "These are the shreds of an empire," he told a reporter. There was a cigar box from Cuban dictator Fulgencio Batista, a photo montage of him and Ann-Margret, silverware, paintings, swizzle sticks. "These are just things," he said. "Why should I be sad?" As for Miami Beach, "They got what they deserved—decline."

The following month Novack showed again how indomitable he was when he and a partner took over a former A&P grocery store on Federal Highway in Boynton Beach and opened up a nightclub called Alcatraz, where patrons were "booked in," had their mug shots taken, and were seated at tables behind bars. "We're here!" Novack boasted when the club opened. "We're full of ego and ready to go." It lasted only a year.

Toward the end of his life Novack enjoyed the part-time companionship of a thirty-year-old former Miss Uruguay named Juana M. Rodriquez, although Ben Jr. claims that for the last year and a half of his life his father was in and out of lucidity. "He would never want the world to know that's how he spent his last days," said Ben Jr.

A week before his father's death, Ben Jr. asked a judge to find his father mentally incompetent and appoint him as legal guardian, and to dismiss the attempt by his father's companion, Juana Rodriquez, to get control of Novack's remaining assets. Ben Jr. claimed that Rodriquez had stolen a $15,000 diamond pinkie ring and a gold bracelet, and that his father had loaned her $100,000 that she had never repaid. In May 1985 Rodriquez filed a $500,000 slander suit against Ben Jr. for claiming that she had provided Novack with companionship for cash. The suit was later dropped.

Ben Novack died of a heart attack and lung failure on April 6, 1985, at age seventy-eight. His final resting place is the family hotel—a mausoleum in Brooklyn, architect unknown.

Novack's longtime nemesis, Morris Lapidus, enjoyed a long and prestigious career. He died a wealthy man in 2001 at the age of ninety-eight, having collected $50 million in fees. He left a legacy around the world of more than two hundred hotels and public buildings, including the Americana Hotel in Miami Beach, in which he put a rainforest with live alligators in a forty-foot-high open-topped terrarium in the lobby. He originally wanted to install a huge cage filled with monkeys, but they wouldn't let him.

Eight

THE MOST POWERFUL MAN IN MIAMI BEACH

Stephen Muss: Miami Beach Moses?

—*MIAMI NEWS*

Like the repeating images of an infinity mirror in a fun house, the hallway of the Château building of the Fontainebleau Hilton hotel seemed like it would never end. Because of the forty-five-degree arc of the building, a visitor couldn't see more than thirty feet ahead, and just when he thought the hallway should stop, would stop, it continued; more industrial hotel wallpaper and carpeting and four more room doors, and then four more, some doors open with chambermaids changing sheets and exchanging fresh towels for used, the rooms back-to-back duplicates of one another, boilerplate Hilton hotel-chain furniture, sheer drapes turned luminous by the sun. The 440-foot-long hallway curved, some said, so that when guests emerged from the elevator they wouldn't look down a coldly intimidating hallways of doors, like a prison block. Others scoffed that the hallways curved at a forty-five-degree angle for no better reason than the building was designed as a quarter-crescent to begin with.

The corridor finally comes to an end at door number 754, beyond which there was another kind of ending taking place. This was the door not to a hotel suite but to the private offices of Stephen Muss, the seventy-seven-year-old real estate developer whom the *Miami Herald* and the *New York Times* had called "the most powerful man in Miami Beach." In 1977 Stephen Muss and his partners, the Roland Group, snatched the Fontainebleau out of bankruptcy for $27 million. "I bought the Fontainebleau out of civic duty," Muss said. "I knew nothing about running a hotel. . . . It was really a community gesture." The hotel, he believed, was a barometer of the city's fortunes. "As goes the Fontainebleau," he predicted, "so goes Miami Beach."

Muss gleefully held a "Destruction Party" to celebrate a $40 million renovation he was planning and invited guests to watch the demolition of the cabanas. He built a new, $8.5 million half-acre pool with an artificial island planted with palm trees and a grotto with a cocktail bar. To help attract families, he created a small children's water park called Cookie's World, which included a raft ride and a water-spraying octopus. The glorious French gardens where the Firestone estate had once stood were transformed into a Polynesian luau. "Without having a lot of respect for Lapidus's vision," Muss admitted, he covered over the white marble floors with the black bow-tie pattern in moss green carpeting, and he cut a hole into the lobby floor and installed an escalator to the shopping arcade. He also disposed of a lot of the ornamental work, such as the seven-foot-high Art Deco statue of a French maiden created for the ocean liner *La Normandie* in 1935 that stood in a fountain in the hotel's lobby. Morris Lapidus had paid $1,200 for it and Muss sold it to Celebrity Cruises for $170,000 cash and $250,000 worth of cruises and services. The hotel was outfitted with new carpeting, draperies, bedspreads, and dressers, and Muss hired the Hilton Hotels Corporation to run the hotel's day-to-day operations and fill it with conventions to bring in a steady stream of revenue. Finally, after twenty-five years of the hotel's never having a sign to identify itself, Muss put up a forty-four-foot-long sign that read FONTAINEBLEAU HILTON.

"When Hilton put up their name," said Novack before he died, "it should have been in the bathroom."

For better and for worse, through good times and bad, Stephen Muss owned the Fontainebleau for the next twenty-eight years while Miami Beach changed around it. Now Muss had reached the eve of a tumultuous passage. He and his partners had sold the Fontainebleau in January 2005 for $165 million to Turnberry Associates, the Aventura, Florida–based developers that already operated six hotels. Muss had teamed with them to build a 36-story, 462-room-condominium-hotel tower, the Fontainebleau II. Another 18-story condominium tower with 286 rooms, the Fontainebleau III, was starting construction, and in the works was a $400 million renovation of the original hotel. The refurbished Fontainebleau would have accommodations for 1,504 guests, a 40,000-square-foot spa, its own House of Blues nightclub, 11 dining rooms, and a Gotham Steak restaurant run by famed chef Alfred Portale. Beyond that, the new owners believed that the name Fontainebleau was an internationally recognized brand, and they intended to open a chain of Fontainebleau hotels around the world. The first was in Las Vegas, a $2.9 billion, 4,000-room hotel on twenty-five acres.

It was Muss's choice to sell the hotel along with its name—he certainly didn't need the money—but it was nevertheless an abdication. The contents of the suite of offices from which he once lorded over the Fontainebleau—and over the city—were being packed up and shipped out, as were the contents of the penthouse suite that he shared with his wife. Muss was leaving with no active projects on his schedule other than supporting a high school in Haifa, Israel, named in honor of his father, Alexander, and possibly writing a memoir about his starring role in the saga of Miami Beach.

Stephen Muss was a lion in winter in a city where there is no winter.

"I am going to throw you out of here in twenty minutes," he growled to his visitor, who, feeling much like a Christian being fed to a lion, had been ushered into his office by a secretary. The blinds were open and outside the office windows the sky was a milky blue and the scorching sun glinted blindingly off the ocean. Muss remained seated behind his desk with a tight look on his face. At six feet five inches tall and more than 250 pounds, even at the age of seventy-seven Muss was a physically imposing figure. He had a large head, thin lips, and cold blue eyes. His bulbous nose had a crease down the middle, and his trademark mane of thick hair had gone thin and white, his beard more grizzled than groomed. He was dressed casually, almost sloppily, in Bermuda shorts and a thin white T-shirt that pulled against his very large, elliptical belly. He could have been any *alter kocker* who strolled in off the beach in front of the Fontainebleau and stumbled into this office.

"Write this down!" he bullied. "Write this down in our notes." They had become "our" notes when Muss refused to be recorded, because, he explained with the logic of a Lewis Carroll character, "How do I know what I'm going to be asked?"

"Okay, write this down: 'No egomaniac!'" he instructed. "You got that? Don't make me sound like an egomaniac. Okay?"

Then he said, "I have done more for this town than any other person, any group of people, or any agency."

Probably. In his best years he possessed power unequaled by a private citizen in any other American city. He was a political king maker and a real estate power broker. His father, Alexander, built the Towers of Key Biscayne, the Towers of Quayside, and, most famously, the Seacoast Towers in Miami Beach, a groundbreaking luxury complex. It was the highest concentration of rental property on the Beach, with over a thousand units, which made Muss the single biggest landlord in the city—and the biggest taxpayer, too. (In 1994 he sold the Seacoast Towers buildings to a real estate consortium for $94 million.) He was also the implacable proponent of a 3 percent hotel visitor's "bed" tax that gave the city enough cash to rebuild its aging infrastructure and public buildings, including the modernization and expansion of the Miami Beach Convention Center, making it world-class in size, a crucial requirement to host the big-league conventions that poured billions into the local economy.

It only made sense that Muss would want the Convention Center to be named after him.

In February of 1988, without any prior announcement or public debate, the Miami Beach city commissioners inserted into the "consent agenda" that the brand-new Miami Beach Convention Center would be renamed the Stephen Muss Convention Center. This enraged the local citizenry, who rose up in arms and almost stormed City Hall. A "Committee to Rename the Stephen Muss Convention Center" was formed, and much to Muss's embarrassment 6,537 registered voters signed a petition demanding his name be removed. To save himself further embarrassment, he asked the City Commission to comply.

Why would anyone think he had a reputation as an egomaniac?

"I'm misunderstood because I'm perceived to be wealthy," he said. Most people believe he is worth close to a billion dollars, but he snorts at the suggestion. "One reason people think I'm wealthy is because I was in the original issue of the *Forbes Four Hundred* list," which estimated his wealth at $400 million twenty years ago. "They must have called somebody in Miami Beach who told them, 'Well, he owns one thousand apartments and the Fontainebleau.' Forbes did no figuring of mortgages or partners—they didn't take it into account. I'm still not worth four hundred million dollars."

Another reason he's misunderstood, Muss contends, is that he's "never been wily enough to co-opt the press."

It is true; a great majority of what has been written about him is critical, but, then, he makes himself an easy target. He doesn't seem to care what people make of his behavior. He has three modes—boastful, arrogant, and abrasive—and he is often all three. If his gruff exterior hides a soft heart, he keeps it well hidden; this is no morality tale where the bully turns out to have the heart of an angel. Petty things bother him. He once had a hot-dog-stand owner banished from his spot on Collins and 43rd Street in front of the Sovereign Hotel because he thought the stand was hurting his restaurant business next door at the Fontainebleau. He threatened to "make war" with the owner. The hapless concessionaire told the press, "He's a multibillionaire and he's worried about a guy selling hot dogs?" One time Muss woke the manager of one of the Seacoast Towers buildings at 1:00 a.m. to come down to the lobby and pick up a cigarette butt left on the floor. And of course there is the scandal that when Muss's pal CenTrust banker David Paul went to federal prison for over nine years and asked his close friend Stephen Muss to look after his wife, Muss did exactly that: He married her.

Of the hundreds of articles that have been written about him, he is particularly rankled by a 1978 cover story in the "Tropical Life" section of the *Miami Herald* entitled "I'm Steve Muss and You're Not." The very thought of the article still makes his cheeks puff out indignantly. "They made me pose on my little boat with the Fontainebleau behind me," he recounted, "and they made it sound like I had some kind of a yacht." His boat, which was called the *Minnie Moo*, was a thirty-two-footer with twin inboard motors. The writer described Muss speeding on the waterways between the Sunset Islands and being admonished by a teenager on a smaller boat to slow down. Muss yelled back, "Calm down! Calm down! Didn't you ever speed?" At one point Muss was so angry with the *Herald*'s coverage of him that he demanded a meeting with the editorial board. "John McMullen [the editor] accused me of having too much power," Muss said, "so I described to him what I did with my power and I described to him what the *Herald* did with their power negatively."

He also blames the *Herald* for the demise of the most important—and controversial—of all his endeavors, the South

Shore redevelopment plan, which tore the city apart. The failure of the South Shore redevelopment plan haunts him. Not only would it have been his major legacy, but it would have sustained Miami Beach a lot longer than a trendy Art Deco district. It would have taken Muss out of the realm of a mere real-estate mogul and into the role of a city planner on par with Robert Moses. Instead it made him into a villain.

IT STARTED in 1973—four years before he bought the Fontainebleau—when Muss saw that Miami Beach was skidding into an abyss: failing tourism business, hotels going bankrupt, aging population, and a stagnant tax base. Muss hosted a breakfast in his penthouse apartment at Seacoast Towers for twelve of Miami-Dade's über-mensch power brokers, members of the Non-Group, a portable smoke-filled back room. The Non-Group was the largest concentration of influential men in the state, and in Miami Beach, Muss was the center of it. This secretive conclave chose the name Non-Group because the men who started it didn't want to admit it was a group at all. Having a real name would force them to categorize or explain their mission, which was to act as a shadow government for Miami-Dade County and set and implement public policies they believed were for the common good—deus ex machina—without the public's acquiescence or sometimes their knowledge.* The understanding among the members was that once a chore was agreed upon, each would use his influence to get it done.

---

*The forerunner of the Non-Group was formed to help restore the battered city after the hurricane of 1926. It was called the Committee of One Hundred and nicknamed "The Lonesome Millionaires Club." Not much has been written about the Non-Group, in part because it was cofounded by Alvah H. Chapman Jr., who was publisher of the *Miami Herald* and who did not want the Non-Group

At Muss's breakfast he proposed that they rescue the most deteriorated part of South Beach, the southernmost tip below 6th
Street, which was then called the South Shore, 225 acres of one of
the worst slums in America. It was a district of decrepit hotels and
apartment buildings that were home to thousands of poor and
elderly Jews, many of them concentration camp survivors. Muss
proposed to raze the entire neighborhood, except for about ten
buildings, and reduce it to the barren landscape that Carl Fisher
had started with sixty years before. From this tabula rasa Muss and
a team of designers, builders, craftsmen, and visionaries would create not just a new community but a new topography, a task no
smaller in scope than building the pyramids. It would "change the
image of Miami Beach as a place for old people . . . and bring the
other people back," Muss told the press.

Under what the *New York Times* called Muss's "forceful leader-
ship," the first step was to have the sad old neighborhood declared
legally "blighted" so the land could be appropriated by the law of
eminent domain, the seizing of private land for public use. There
was no real legal definition of "blight," other than some HUD
indices, so to achieve the appropriate level of decay, in 1973 the
Miami Beach commissioners passed a moratorium on all new

---

mentioned in his newspaper. Chapman and Harry Hood Bassett, chairman of
Southeast Banking Corporation, together chose the first twelve members from the
cadre of the city's elite. Chapman claimed that the Non-Group was so powerful
that he once raised $3.5 million for a redevelopment project in Liberty City in
only seven phone calls. In 1985, according to the *Herald,* the Non-Group's members included the heads of Eastern Airlines, the Arvida Disney Corporation, the
Barnett Bank of South Florida, Amerifirst Federal Savings & Loan Association,
Ryder Systems, Florida Power and Light, and Burdines department stores. In
present-day Miami-Dade the Non-Group has little influence. "The Non-Group
was a factor for a number of years," member Bob Dickinson, the president of Carnival Cruise Lines, told the *Herald* in 1996. "Now try to get a Non-Group and
you'd need 150 people and there'd still be many who would feel left out."

building in the area below 6th Street, from bay to beach. It was what the *Miami Herald* called "the purposeful creation of a slum." Just as planned, within just two years the area began to collapse in on itself: Property became worthless, banks would not give loans or mortgages to property owners, shops closed up, and the tax base stagnated. The quality of life, already bleak by any standards, became hell for the aged. In 1976 Muss's South Shore Redevelopment Authority was invested by the city of Miami Beach with the broad powers to condemn buildings, buy properties, and evict the residents.

Muss hired a young architect and expert in large-scale city planning from San Francisco named Steven Siskind, and over the next six years fifty-four architects, ten developers, and five master builders were consulted in creating the new community. The scheme they came up with was wildly ambitious, at an estimated cost of $650 million (in 1979 dollars). The plan was for the entire tip of Miami Beach to be reconfigured with nearly three miles of man-made canals, a spectacular inland waterway that would wander through the community. This "new Venice," with gondola-like taxicabs, would turn the South Shore into as much of a water community as one of automobiles and pedestrians. The canals would access 2,696 garden apartments, 9 new hotels, a 30-story convention center, and a marina with room for 800 boats, the largest in the world. Muss had a model made of the proposed new community that included every small detail, from traffic lights to palm trees and little boats in the canals, to unveil to the press.

Public sentiment already ran high against Stephen Muss, and his grandiose scheme to build a "new Venice" was greeted with derision—yet it won a public referendum held to decide whether it should continue. The *Miami Herald* took a strong stance against the leveling of the neighborhood, and the newspaper became the project's unrelenting and powerful critic. There was a lot to critique. Muss failed five times to find a master developer to take on the project. The city had no financial mechanism in place to float bonds for public construction, and underwriters had to be found. By state law a lengthy vetting procedure had to be followed before the bonds could be offered. When the bonds were finally approved by the state attorney general's office, there was a cap of 14 percent interest, but bank rates had spiked to 17 percent, prohibiting the city of Miami Beach from a public offering. The Tropical Audubon Society contended that the new community would displace and kill birds, the Department of Environmental Regulations had concerns about waste disposal, and the Redevelopment Authority was sued by environmentalists over issues of water stagnation.

And what about displacing the elderly Jewish residents of South Shore, an area that to them was less like a neighborhood than a shtetl in Poland? Studies had already been commissioned that predicted that the elderly Jews would soon die off and not become an issue, and they were dying off, but evidently not quick enough. So another plan was hatched in which the South Shore Redevelopment Agency would "relocate" the elderly people into private housing developments with subsidies. The Redevelopment Agency formed a team to study the needs of the elderly—where they shopped, how they got to the doctor, and so forth—and incorporate them into the plans. "We devoted twenty-five percent of the new housing in perpetuity to homes for elderly people," Steven Siskind said. But every day on the local television stations there were heartbreaking interviews with frightened elderly men and women who had no idea where they would move or if the subsidies would cover the new rents. Siskind told the *New York Times*, "There is a lot of fear among these people—we have been getting a half dozen calls a day asking when the bulldozers are coming."

"They've been trying to sell the old people a bill of goods," one elderly resident told the *New York Times*. "They just want to push us away."

"And look," Muss said, reflecting back on it, "redevelopment didn't happen and there are no senior citizens south of Sixth Street anyway."

In December of 1982 the Miami Beach City Commission terminated the Redevelopment Agency. "Dead at last," gloated the *Miami Herald*. "It was allowed to live for too long."

"The *Herald* wanted to find something wrong," said Steven Siskind. "We were on a mission, but it was not their mission. Stephen Muss was never treated fairly."

"The *Herald* killed the redevelopment program," Muss agreed. "I don't call the press the Fourth Estate," he said. "I call it the Fifth Column."

THE PROBLEM with Muss mistrusting journalists was the possibility that he'd never get his story told, and telling his story haunted him. He longed to leave a testament to his life, and to that of his father, whom he revered, and to have his story of what he did for Miami Beach told his way, not by some writer at a newspaper or magazine with an ax to grind. And oh what a story, a grand shtetl-to-stardom bildungsroman of a Jewish boy from Bensonhurst, Brooklyn, New York, the oldest son in a third generation of a family of builders, who became a czar of Miami Beach. "I could tell you how I started in the business picking up loose nails so they would not go to waste," he told his visitor. His zaydeh, a Polish immigrant, built and sold houses in Brooklyn for $3,900, and his father, Alexander, made millions with Long Island strip malls and Brooklyn apartment buildings.

All this was part of the rich story for which he was searching for a ghostwriter, or an agent, or a publisher, but so far there'd been no interest. He couldn't understand why a reputable writer or publishing company would not be anxious to work with him and publish a book that could be titled *The World According to Muss*. Perhaps, he suggested, the focus of his visitor's book should be about

Stephen Muss and not Miami Beach. He pointed to a low cabinet behind him on which were stacked thick scrapbooks stuffed with clippings, a treasure trove of research material for the right collaborator. "If I had to write a book," he had said, "it would be the rise and fall, the rise and fall, and the rise of Miami Beach to its present zenith. The Fontainebleau would be a part of it. Only that story is the rise, the fall, and the rise again."

Muss felt a sense of urgency in getting his story down on paper because he didn't just worry about his mortality, he tormented himself. He wasn't just seventy-seven years old, he pointed out, he was "seventy-seven *and a half* years old." His conversation was peppered with references to aging. "The pains start at seventy," he intoned. His omnipresent cigars were gone now at the doctor's insistence. Once an aggressive tennis player, he said that he was staying seated behind his office desk because he was having problems with his legs, and if he hadn't been waylaid by his guest, at that very hour he would have been in a therapy session in the swimming pool of his 12,000-square-foot, nine-bedroom waterfront house on Sunset Island 2 that he'd bought from musician Lenny Kravitz for $14.5 million. He purchased the house a few weeks after he'd sold the Fontainebleau and was forced to give up the penthouse he'd lived in for a decade (although as part of the deal, when the Fontainebleau was renovated, he'd have a penthouse there too). Speaking of which, he told his visitor, he wasn't sleeping well in the new house. "I fell asleep watching the game on TV at ten thirty and then I was up for four hours until five a.m.," he groused.

It could be because breaking up is hard to do.

Nine

SAVING SOUTH BEACH

See this South Beach area? I figure we can buy it for a song.
See? About three, four million, maybe five million,
and we take it down and we build a Disneyland—
pretty big blockbuster idea!

—Frank Sinatra in *A Hole in the Head*, 1959
(filmed at the Cardozo Hotel)

It was five o'clock in the morning on a warm October night in 1988 and Gary Farmer, thirty-five, had just locked up his restaurant, The Strand, and decided to stroll up Collins Avenue on his way home, taking his time. He loved South Beach early in the morning, so quiet and still, hardly a soul on the street save for a hooker who had drifted over from Washington Avenue to smoke crack in a doorway. There was no moon that night, and all the buildings looked the color of bone. South Beach had an elegiac beauty to it, like a seaside village lost in time; it could have been 1988 or 1938. Almost nothing new had been built in forty years, and most of the buildings were peeling apart, layer by layer, time bombs of decay built of cement mixed with sand from the beach and salt water from the ocean. "It looked as if Disneyland had been left to rot," Farmer said.

Lining lower Collins Avenue were scores of two- or three-story apartment buildings and hotels. Like snowflakes, no two were alike. They were an improbable combination of styles—Bauhaus modern, Mediterranean, tropical, Mayan—that had somehow been alchemized into what preservationists were calling "Art Deco," but wasn't exactly. They were actually a little cheesy, but that didn't matter; that was part of the fun. What mattered was that all of them were a piece in time, fanciful works that were intended to bring pleasure to the eye. They shared a specific architectural vocabulary, a sense of speed, of *aeroplane moderne*, of ocean-liner mechanical. They had rounded corners that looked like the right angles had been worn smooth, and thin ledges above the windows called "eyebrows" that shielded the tropical sun. Porthole windows called "occuli" were popular and made some buildings look like they might set sail. Some of the buildings were topped with ziggurats and spires, and the Delano Hotel had an architectural headdress that looked like the tail end of Buck Rogers's rocket ship had sprouted feathers.

"South Beach was magic at night," Farmer said. "Just beautiful. Peaceful. It was a neighborhood that had been built before everyone drove there in cars and when everything was walkable. The scale of the place was so small that the UPS delivery man might pull up next to you at a red light and recognize you and hand off your package. You could walk everywhere and recognize the faces of your neighbors on the street."

But Farmer had a feeling that wouldn't last.

The cozy, dilapidated little neighborhood was about to be shaken awake from a 20-year nap. Everybody who lived there felt it. Over the last few years several of the old hotels along Ocean Drive had been bought up and renovated by developers, and new cafés and restaurants were beginning to attract customers from across the causeway who were brave enough to venture to South Beach. There was a nightclub called Club Nu on 21st Street named for the Egyptian god of the night that had wild go-go dancers and changed its interior every six weeks, and on weekends the Carlyle Hotel on Ocean Drive had live jazz and attracted high rollers from out of the neighborhood who arrived in stretch limousines with women who looked like gun molls. The Rolling Stones' guitarist Ron Wood, an early fan of South Beach, had opened a music club named Woody's on 4th and Ocean, and on Lincoln Road, all but abandoned except by the homeless who slept in the doorways of the vacant shops, a new cooperative called the Florida Arts Center, with over forty studios, had opened and become the hub of a growing artists' colony, with more artists and creative people moving to South Beach every week, attracted by good light and cheap rents.

Exactly what kindled this revivification of South Beach was a lucky confluence of events. A group of preservationists had succeeded in creating an Art Deco historic district. In 1983 the artists Christo and Jeanne-Claude surrounded eleven small islands in Biscayne Bay with 6.5 million square feet of pink polyurethane and brought worldwide photographic coverage to the metropolis, showing how beautiful Miami was, and for the first time in years the city got into the news for something other than being the murder capital of the United States. That same year the movie *Scarface*, directed by Brian De Palma and starring Al Pacino as Tony Montana, a ruthless Cuban cocaine dealer, virtually defined the Golden Age of Drug Dealing in Miami Beach and made the city seem scary yet exciting, like Casablanca in the 1940s. In September of 1984 the TV cops-and-drug dealers show *Miami Vice* premiered and became a national obsession, thrusting Miami Beach into the spotlight for four years and even sparking a fashion trend for men of unstructured sport jackets and pastel-colored T-shirts. About the time that *Miami Vice* debuted, the influential fashion photographer Bruce Weber introduced the fashion industry to Miami Beach, both by recommendation—he bought a house just north of Miami Beach—and through his prolific fashion layouts. Another piece of the puzzle fell in place in September of 1986, when fifty journalists were flown to Miami Beach from New York for a whirlwind weekend to promote a Miami/Vegas issue of Andy Warhol's

Interview magazine, sending the city's hipster quotient soaring with media taste-makers.

But for many, the most significant harbinger of change was Gary Farmer's restaurant, The Strand, which opened at the end of November 1986. Like Les Deux Magots in Paris, Max's Kansas City in New York, and the Odeon in Tribeca—where Gary Farmer worked behind the bar in the 1980s—The Strand became the quintessential hangout of its time and place. How it was that The Strand managed to embody the promise of a new South Beach is hard to explain, except that its pull was so ineluctable that the cognoscenti would get off a plane from New York at Miami International and take a taxi directly to the restaurant with their luggage. "The Strand was the beginning of the end of the old world order," Micky Wolfson Jr. remembered. "The Strand set the pace. It set the style. *Big time.*"

Among the restaurant's financial backers were the artists Donald Sultan and April Gornick; Kay Bearman, a curator of the Metropolitan Museum of Art; Lisa Phillips, an associate curator of the Whitney Museum; and New York cultural czar Henry Geldzahler. Most of all it had Gary Farmer himself, a charming and gracious host. Farmer and two partners had leased the shell of a defunct 12,000-square-foot kosher restaurant called The Famous, stripped the red and gold-flocked wallpaper and decades of linoleum on the floor, and transformed it into a low-key, open space, with roomy booths, mirrors, a glass-block bar, and comfortable beige sofas where patrons could sit and watch the array of people coming through the door: Lauren Hutton; Philip Glass; Paloma Picasso; Prince; Daryl Hannah and John F. Kennedy Jr.; and, as filler, all the gorgeous young model wannabes of South Beach. "When we started," said Farmer, "we put a lot more emphasis on the waiters than we did on the food. We wanted people to be the focus. I wanted people in bathing suits next to people in tuxedos."

At least a part of the attraction was that it was located in one of the most dangerous parts of town, the center of the crack-cocaine trade, and Farmer had to provide curbside valet service at The Strand and a secure parking lot because customers were afraid to park on the street and have their cars stolen—or the gas siphoned out. One night everyone in the dining room stood to watch as a drama played out on the street on the other side of the big glass windows—a drug dealers' gang fight, with men stabbing each other to death right on the sidewalk like a Jerome Robbins dance from *West Side Story*.

"BARBARA, is that you?"

Gary Farmer had reached the corner of 12th and Collins and saw what he thought was a homeless woman sitting in the shadows on the front steps of the boarded-up Senator Hotel. It was a shell, about to be demolished, the windows smashed, the neon signs that spelled POOL and SENATOR ripped from the front of the building and smashed on the ground, waiting for the garbage dumpster.

When Farmer got closer he realized the woman sitting on the hotel's steps wasn't a bag lady at all; it was Barbara Baer Capitman.

She peered at him in the darkness and warbled, "Who is that?"

"It's Gary Farmer," he answered, walking over to where she was sitting. She looked tired and a lot older than her sixty-eight years. A few months before, she had been hospitalized for pneumonia and she had never fully recovered. Her eyes had dark pouches under them, and her wavy gray hair didn't look like it had been recently combed. She was a big, ungainly woman, dressed in a shapeless peasant blouse with a large arts-and-crafts necklace of amber beads around her neck, a full skirt, and tennis sneakers. She was, as the journalist Tom Austin described her, "a glorious mess." Next to her on the steps was a huge pocketbook, her "magic" pocketbook and handy "portable filing cabinet," from which she seemingly could produce anything, from a slide show on an Art Deco building in Seattle to a portable typewriter.

"You shouldn't be out here all by yourself at five in the morning," Farmer said. "It's very dangerous."

"But I *have* to be here," Capitman answered in her odd, trilling voice. "I'm here for the hotel. When the sun comes up they're going to start tearing it down."

Strange lady. Here she was sitting *shivah* on the steps of a deserted hotel looking like a homeless person, and yet the *Miami Herald* had named her one of the most influential women in South Florida, the "mother of Art Deco." It was hard to explain the quiddity of Barbara Capitman without making her sound like a crank. A relative newcomer to the area, she managed to polarize the city and throw a wrench into the machinery that could have brought it into the twenty-first century. There were many respected real estate developers who believed that Barbara Baer Capitman and her meddling would end up killing Miami Beach. The city needed to grow and renew, not save the old buildings, symbols of the Beach's failure to keep up. If history was any judge, tourism on Miami Beach depended on the newness of hotels, not the oldness. Murray Gold, the executive director of the Miami Beach Resort Hotel Association, is famously quoted by local pundits: "No one in their right mind just walks around and looks at old buildings."

Yet nearly ten years before, in 1979, Capitman and her coterie of supporters had managed to have 1,200 buildings in South Beach, just north of the area Stephen Muss wanted to rebuild, declared a National Historic District by the federal government. Her idea was to create an Art Deco section called "Old Miami Beach" that would be a living theme park, along the lines of Williamsburg, Virginia, or something that Disney would create. She envisioned that the employees of the district would wear period costumes from the 1930s and 1940s, and there would be big bands and swing music and dancing in the ballrooms, and the Art Deco cinema on Washington Avenue would show movies with Fred Astaire and Ginger Rogers. "If you preserve the architecture and design of the Miami Beach Art Deco District, economic growth and welfare of the area will follow," was her dogma. "This is going to be the center of the arts for all of Florida, and Ocean Drive is going to be lined with sidewalk cafés."

But there was a catch.

Although the federal government recognized the district as historic,* the city of Miami Beach was not bound to protect it. The federal designation had no local effect on whether or not a building could be torn down by its owner. It took the city three years to pass a toothless historic-preservation ordinance that required the owner's consent for a building to be declared protected—hardly a preservation law at all.

"You have to understand the context under which all of this was happening," Micky Wolfson said. "The Art Deco preservationists came on the heels of the building moratorium and Stephen Muss's Redevelopment Agency fiasco, so the hardest thing for people to swallow was the idea of 'My God! I can't do with my property what I want to do with my property?' These poor people had so many times been promised—you know—the redevelopment plan promised them everything, and then all of a sudden nothing."

It wasn't until January 1988 that Miami Beach city commissioners voted to give the city's Historic Preservation Board real power to stop the demolition of buildings in South Beach's National Historic District. But the law passed too late to save the Senator Hotel, which had already been slated for oblivion. At first glance at the Senator it was hard to understand what all the fuss

---

*The buildings were on average forty-five years old and they didn't qualify for protection, according to federal guidelines for historic buildings, so an exception was made.

was about. It was a rather dinky, three-story building built in 1939 with rounded corners and wraparound windows, a porch, and a tall spire at the corner. It was an average, second-rate retirement hotel for Social Security pensioners who could not afford an ocean-front hotel one block east on Ocean Drive. Some elderly tenants paid as little as $10 a week for a tiny room. Capitman thought it was one of the city's best examples of Art Deco hotels, part of some four hundred hotels, apartment buildings, and private homes designed by architect L. Murray Dixon, whose prodigious work dominated the city in the 1930s and 1940s. Yet nobody paid much attention to the Senator before Capitman declared it her Rubicon.

But the hotel had a deeper, more emotional significance for Capitman. Her eldest son, Andrew, once owned it, and his wife, Margaret Doyle, had beautifully restored the exterior. It was one of several hotels Andrew Capitman bought in 1979 with a group of investors to show skeptics how the old hotels in South Beach could be affordably renovated, instead of being razed. Andrew took his entire savings of $50,000 and used it as a down payment to buy the run-down Cardozo Hotel at 1300 Ocean Drive for $800,000, and over the next two years he assembled sixty-eight limited partners in seven South Beach properties, including the Senator.

The Cardozo Hotel, called "a streamlined three-story modern gem" by Paul Goldberger in the *New York Times*, was the silent star of the 1959 Frank Capra movie *A Hole in the Head*, produced by and starring Frank Sinatra as the owner of a run-down hotel who can't make his mortgage payments and who has the prescient idea to turn the whole area into a Disneyland-like amusement park. Andrew Capitman renovated the Cardozo and opened it in December 1982, and for a brief time it became a seaside version of Manhattan's Chelsea Hotel, a curio cabinet with a Fellini-esque cast. "The combined effect of which," said the *Miami Herald*, "has been the transformation of a spooky neighborhood filled with shady characters into a . . . spooky neighborhood filled with shady characters. . . ." The colorful assortment of habitués included the Chilean painter Enrique Castro-Cid, artist Woody Von Drasek, the writer John Rothschild, and two elderly women named Zelda and Elizabeth who shared a room to save money and dressed up every morning as if they were going to a party. The hotel's regulars also included the smiling Scull sisters, Haydee and Sahara, primitive artists from Cuba who designed and sewed their matching clothing, and Marie Zimmer, a destitute old woman who wore turbans and flamboyant thrift-shop gowns. Barbara Capitman encouraged Zimmer to inhabit one of the tables on the terrazzo porch and read palms and tell fortunes that always had a happy ending. After Zimmer died it was discovered that she had a yearly income of $100,000 in interest from more than fifty savings accounts in different banks and brokerages.

Alas, the price tag for bringing the seven hotels up to code was astronomical and the banks weren't giving mortgages because the area had been "red-lined" as a slum. In 1984 Andrew Capitman was forced to sell his hotels to investors from Philadelphia called the Royale Group, who eventually decided that the Senator property could be put to better use as a parking garage.

Adding to Barbara's distress was that her best friend, Leonard Horowitz, had lived at the Senator for two years in the corner suite, filled with cartons and canvases and piles of fabrics. Leonard gave cocktail parties there for the members of the Miami Design Preservation League, and he and his friends had water fights in the pool and drifted around on floats looking up at the taller Art Deco buildings that surrounded them. It was Leonard who had painted the lovely mermaid bas-relief in the Senator's pool, and it was loyal Leonard who sat lonely vigils with her to save the hotel until he was too sick to stay any longer. Now Leonard was dead and so was the Senator.

When the Senator's demise was announced eighteen months before, Capitman declared the demolition the "most tragic, awful, crazy thing" that could happen. She went so far as to travel to Washington, D.C., to attend the National Trust for Historic Preservation conference, where she handed out hundreds of postcards with a photograph of the Senator to the surprised delegates, imploring them for intervention and help. A City Council meeting on the subject degenerated into "a shouting match fraught with frustration and fatigue," the *Miami Herald* reported. There were demonstrations, protests, reprieves, and setbacks. The city offered the Royale Group a land swap in exchange for the Senator Hotel, or to put a referendum on the ballot to issue a $5 million bond to build other parking facilities for the area that would benefit the Royale Group's hotels. But it only prolonged the agony. Miami Beach mayor Alex Daoud described the Senator's saga as "crisis to crisis," adding, "I feel like Custer at the Little Big Horn." Eventually Mayor Daoud got sick of mediating between the two recalcitrant parties. "The Senator has achieved more prominence since it was targeted for demolition than it ever had during its heyday," he said.

In August 1988, days before the demolition was scheduled to begin, Mayor Daoud made a dramatic appearance at a Miami Design Preservation League rally at The Strand restaurant, where he announced that the demolition had been rescheduled and the Senator had yet another reprieve until September 7. Capitman was not appeased. "We can't keep being poised on the edge of disaster," she told the *Miami Herald*. One morning not long after that meeting, graffiti appeared on the facade of the Senator with the words SAVE ME and the warning DEMOLITION IS FOREVER. It was under those words that Capitman was sitting on the October night that Gary Farmer found her, all appeals exhausted, the building she had fought so hard to save condemned to destruction at first light.

Farmer asked Capitman, "Why isn't anybody else here with you?"

"Because nobody else cares," Capitman said. "Somebody has to sit here."

Farmer knew better; it wasn't that nobody else cared, it was that nobody else cared as much as she did. Several of her colleagues had sat vigil with her, but she had worn out her friends and supporters, and pushed them away with her stubbornness.

"You go home, Gary," she warbled, shooing him away. "I'm okay here by myself." But Farmer said he would not leave her. "It's too dangerous for you to be sitting here alone," he insisted, and he stayed and talked with her until dawn and the street slowly came to life with people and cars. Farmer kissed Barbara good-bye on the cheek and went home to sleep.

An hour or two later, when the demolition crew and the TV cameras arrived along with a small crowd of people, Capitman produced from her bottomless pocketbook a black graduation gown that she occasionally wore to represent the "robes of justice" and put it on over her clothes. She held up a picture of the Senator Hotel as it had once looked in its glory days and tried to make a speech to the gathering crowd, but there was too much noise for her to be heard, and soon a Miami Beach uniformed policeman removed her from the property and led her off, unrepentant. She told supporters she was too upset to watch the actual demolition and left for home. When the 36½-ton backhoe began to tear into the walls of the hotel, people watching cried in one another's arms. Months after the rubble was carted away and the earth flattened, it turned out that the Royale Group couldn't afford to build a parking garage. Instead, asphalt was poured, creating an ugly parking lot with spaces for forty-four cars—which is what it remains to this very day.

The day after the police removed Barbara Capitman from the Senator's front porch, she had severe chest pains in her apartment and an ambulance took her to St. Francis Hospital. While she was waiting for the ambulance to arrive, she telephoned the hospital's director of public relations.

"This is Barbara Capitman," she told him, "and I'm checking in. You better tell the press."

ART DECO LEADER IS HOSPITALIZED

MIAMI HERALD
October 14, 1988

Art Deco preservationist Barbara Capitman was in stable condition Thursday night at St. Francis Hospital in Miami Beach after she complained of chest pains earlier in the afternoon. Capitman, who has a history of heart trouble, had been locked in a struggle to save the historic Senator Hotel from the wrecking ball.

On Wednesday the Royale Group, which owns the Senator, began to raze the Art Deco–style hotel at 1201 Collins Avenue to make room for a parking garage. The demolition will take eight days to complete.

"It's been enormously stressful," she said. "My phone is ringing all the time with people calling me and weeping and telling me how they feel."

◆　◆

FOR MOST of Barbara's life it had been about her husband, and that had been okay. Before Will Capitman, nobody thought she'd ever get married. She was shy around men and went through a year of psychotherapy—an unheard-of thing to do in the 1940s—to figure out why she couldn't fall in love. She was twenty-eight years old when they met, two years older than Will. They were introduced in New York City in 1948 at a May Day party given by friends in the Young Communist League, both supporters of the third-party candidate Henry Wallace, who had been smeared in the press as being a "pinko." On their first date they went to City Island and walked along the water and looked at the Manhattan skyline. Two months later they were married by a justice of the peace and took their wedding picture in a photo machine at Woolworth's. "I'd barely kissed him before we were married," she said.

Barbara was an only child of strict German Jewish parents—her father was an importer of children's sweaters and her mother a painter and sculptor. She attended New York University, where she received a bachelor's degree in English. Will was a strapping guy from Brooklyn who enjoyed the outdoors and camping and kayaking, alien activities to her. He had been a UPI correspondent who'd covered the Japanese war trials, and Barbara supported him while he went to New York University School of Law. When Will graduated in 1951, the character committee failed him for having been a member of the Young Communist League and barred him from becoming an attorney. For years he made a living teaching business and marketing at Harvard and Yale, and at the University of Pittsburgh, where they lived while Barbara went to Carnegie Mellon to get a master's in art history. They had two sons, Andrew, in 1949, and John, in 1954.

In New York they opened a marketing research business, which Barbara subsidized by doing public relations for industrial design groups. Together they published two dozen books and pamphlets about social issues under Will's name, including in 1973 a well-received précis about the social responsibility of corporations called *Panic in the Boardroom: New Social Realities Shake Old Corporate Structures*. Later that year Will got a job offer—a tenured position at Florida International University School of Business.

Barbara and Will packed their belongings and moved to a small rented house in the artists' colony of Coconut Grove, in Miami. They had little interest in moribund Miami Beach, but Will was fascinated by what he called the "reminiscent lifestyle" and one day drove Barbara to Ocean Drive to see the Plymouth Hotel. "Why are you showing me that ugly old thing?" she demanded. Barbara remembered Ocean Drive from when she went there at the age of twenty-two to see her father, whose sweater manufacturing business had failed, and who was recuperating from an illness in Miami Beach because his doctor prescribed that he "stick his feet in the sand."

For Barbara and Will Capitman the shores of Miami did not have such a salubrious effect. They had barely unpacked in Coconut Grove when Barbara was diagnosed with viral myocarditis, a progressive viral infection of the heart. She was bedridden for her first two years in her new home, during which time Will took care of her until she regained her strength. In the summer of 1975 the family rented a vacation cottage in Maine to get out of the tropical heat, and while there Will unexpectedly fell ill. His diagnosis was shocking—pancreatic cancer, and there was little time to prepare; he died in a Boston hospital just two weeks after being diagnosed, on July 28, 1975, at the age of fifty-four.

So much had happened to Barbara so quickly and unrelentingly—the move to Miami, her getting sick, Will's dying, then suddenly her being left alone in a city where she was practically a stranger—that her voice changed from the trauma. She began to speak in a high-pitched, fluttering whine that became the trademark of her plight. For the rest of her life people would make fun of her unusual voice and mimic her. But sometimes people would listen too.

After Will's funeral, Barbara's two sons, Andrew, then twenty-five and starting out in the banking business, and John, twenty, a senior at Yale, went with her to Martha's Vineyard, where a friend loaned them a small cabin, isolated on the beach with no electricity, only oil lamps and a woodstove. "We huddled together in our sadness," Andrew said. "And we talked a lot about the future." He and John told Barbara that she'd never have to worry about money, or feel the need to support herself, because together the boys would take care of her. She would be free to do anything she felt good about doing. And they weren't talking about a cruise to Martinique. "The idea," said Andrew, "was that she wanted to do some social good."

In the fall of 1975 Barbara returned to Miami alone and moved from Coconut Grove to a new apartment at 1198 Venetian Causeway in Miami Beach. At first she floundered. She started something called the Sea Institute, whose mission was to prevent the construction of high-rise apartment towers along the beaches from Miami to Key West, but the Sea Institute idea didn't last long before it petered out. She was stumped, more than a little restless, searching for something to do, something of significance, and somebody to do it with.

And that's when she met thirty-year-old Leonard Horowitz.

In 1975 Leonard Horowitz was a doorman at Seacoast Towers V, one of the complex of luxury condominium buildings on Collins Avenue that were built in the 1960s by the Muss family.

Leonard didn't make very much money holding open the doors for rich people at Seacoast Towers, and he wasn't a very good doorman anyway, he would happily admit. It was just a temporary way to make ends meet until he got a real job in design, or he sold one of his canvases. So instead of being formal with the residents and visitors like the other doormen, he was just himself—goofy, flamboyant, inappropriately chummy, and sometimes a little annoying. Most of all, he was demonstrative and loud; when Leonard sneezed, he made such a great production of it that people out by the pool could hear, and his sneeze was nowhere near as attention-getting as his high-pitched, staccato laugh. Years later, when Leonard was called "an outrageous faggot" in an article about him in an architectural magazine, one of his friends asked if he was angry, and Leonard said incredulously, "But I am an outrageous faggot."

He had full lips, big ears, a receding hairline, and never much success in love. His hobby was collecting business cards. His clothes were bought in thrift shops, redolent with turpentine and paints from his oil paintings, none of which he ever sold, yet which he continued to paint, undaunted. He didn't care much about fashion, but he did have a great sense of style. He sometimes wore rhinestone shoe buckles strung together as a necklace or clipped to the lapel of his jacket. He lived alone in a grungy apartment near the Venetian Causeway and pedaled to work every day on an orange bicycle.

There were days at Seacoast Towers when he hardly seemed to notice people walking by. Sometimes he was just stoned on pot, but there were also days when he was meditating. Even as people came in and out of the building and he was directing visitors to the elevators and ringing upstairs, he was on another plane, dimension, experiencing, picturing . . . color . . . in his mind. Solid color. Transparent color. The colors of South Beach, at sunset and sunrise. He saw tones that were subtle, soft, pinks and blues, the tropical air so moist that the colors had no edges; they seeped into one another so it seemed as if the ether itself was a watercolor wash. Sometimes Leonard would pick a section of sky—no horizon or sea for reference, just a rectangle of clouds and reflections—and make it his color field. Or at dawn, after a night trawling for sex in Lummus Park, he would smoke a joint and sit on the low stone wall facing Ocean Drive and study the pale beige hotels that seemed just like a canvas waiting to be colored in. "He was a very highly evolved spirit trapped in that body," one of his close friends, Jane Dee Gross, explained, "hooked into the gods of color and vibratory intimacy."

According to Leonard, one day he was adrift in his ruminations when BANG! he went down on the marble floor of the lobby and cracked his head. "All of a sudden I was on my back," he explained, "and all of these people are gathered around me like I'm unconscious, but I'm really flying around, astral-projecting." Leonard astral-projected himself into a liability lawsuit and received a small insurance settlement, which he used to open a furniture showroom in the Design District, which soon went kaput.

Leonard was brought up in Sheepshead Bay, Brooklyn, New York, and spent the summers living in the staff quarters of the Concord Hotel in Monticello, New York, where his father then ran a nightclub, according to Leonard, that served Chinese food and featured female impersonators. His parents divorced when he was seventeen years old, and he moved to Miami Beach with his mother and attended Beach High. At his father's behest he studied business at Morris Harvey College in West Virginia, but Leonard hated business and he returned to Brooklyn, where his father then owned an auto dealership in Sheepshead Bay. His father wanted Leonard and his older brother to take over the auto dealership, but Leonard's brother had already crushed his father's hopes when he showed up at the car dealership dressed as a woman. When Leonard told his dad that he'd rather be an interior decorator than work at the car dealership and, by the way, he was gay, he was banished from his father's house. Later he and a partner opened a modular wedge furniture company in New York, but it went bankrupt, and that's about the time Leonard moved back to Miami and became a doorman at Seacoast Towers.

He met Barbara Capitman at a cocktail party for one of the interior-design trades. She was fifty-six at the time and the southern editor of a small industrial design magazine, *The Designer*, and a press member of the American Society of Interior Design, credentials that she used mostly to network. Capitman was never the least bit fazed by Leonard's homosexuality. She had befriended many gay men over the years while writing and publicizing interior design. According to her son Andrew, "My mother was always comfortable with gay people, and from a very early time she had a strategy that she would use her warm relationship with the gay community to promote the idea of an Art Deco district." Although Leonard was something of a buffoon, he was available to be her packhorse, and she enlisted him. The oddness of their situations and ages made no difference to them. They became stalwart pals, bickering, complaining, bitching behind each other's back, yet fiercely loyal. "He adored her," remembered preservationist Nancy Liebman, "he was her puppy and he put up with all of it."

"There was no 'eureka' moment about saving the Art Deco buildings," said John Capitman, Barbara's younger son. She had been making extra money running focus groups for a water-purifying company, Brita Filters, and spent a lot of time driving around South Beach, interviewing the residents. The indignity of the lot of the elderly Jews irked her. One June day in 1976 Leonard and Barbara and John, who had just graduated from Yale, were driving around in her car, looking at all the old buildings and the even older tenants when Barbara said to Leonard, "Look at all these old people. I wonder how we can save them?" and Leonard answered, "Forget about the people, how can we save these buildings?"*

"THE PEOPLE who lived in Miami Beach had nothing to do with its revival," said David Leddick, a writer and performer who was Barbara's friend. "They were uneducated, unsophisticated, provincial people, they could not see what it could become."

---

*Although this sweet story has become part of the preservationists' dogma, John Capitman doesn't remember this exact exchange, but like everyone else, he thinks it's a good story.

Micky Wolfson agreed. "All the modern reinvention of Miami Beach was due to outsiders, people who saw from afar the potential. The locals were too resigned."

The Miami Design Preservation League—they called it "Miami" because they wanted to be more inclusive—held its first public meeting on December 1, 1976. Barbara and Leonard, who had taped signs to bulletin boards and store windows, were stunned when four hundred people showed up, a mixture of curious retirees and young people interested in art and design. This was the first time she spoke publicly about Art Deco. She was too shy to look at her audience, and her lack of grooming and her unusual quavering voice were distracting, but after a few minutes her compelling conviction took over and she spoke articulately and with passion about creating an Art Deco district. What was moments before peculiar became charming. She showed slides (with some slides upside-down and backward) and told her audience, "It's a miracle that all this is lying dormant and the fabric is still intact. It's fortunate that it can all be brought back."

Barbara organized with precision. She gathered teams of volunteers to canvass the proposed Art Deco neighborhood and compile an inventory. She had Carl Weinhardt Jr., the director of the 1917 former Deering estate, known as Villa Vizcaya, now a state trust and museum, unofficially declare the buildings in the district "Art Deco." She badgered the City of Miami Beach Planning Department to give the MDPL a $10,000 grant to develop a plan, and she wrote individual letters to senators, state senators, the U.S. House of Representatives, and the Florida House of Representatives extolling the virtues of the buildings. When it came time to submit the formal nomination for the state register, Barbara was so determined that she took the twenty-page document to Tallahassee herself. "People would run when they saw her coming," said her friend and supporter Jane Gross. "She was a combination of Eleanor Roosevelt and a bag lady. She was always in your face. She got right in your face, she talked close up but with her eyes down, almost shyly, but she was anything but shy. If she got a hold of you there would be no end to it."

Barbara deftly assembled a coterie of supporters that bordered on a cult, mostly gay men and senior citizens. She carried gold stars in her magic pocketbook, and if she liked you she gave you a printed commendation and pasted a star on it. Her cause was taken up by a lonely wealthy widow, Edith Siegal, who drove a black Rolls-Royce and chauffered Barbara around the city and to her appointments, lending Barbara a certain cachet.

In three years Barbara managed to have over half of South Beach declared the only federally protected historic district of twentieth-century buildings in the United States, and the largest concentration of so-called Art Deco architecture in the world. "She fought tooth and nail to convince the authorities and the towns-people," said Wolfson. "It was a great triumph of public relations, marketing, and salesmanship. Barbara was the new Carl Fisher."

Ten

LEONARD AND BARBARA

Did you ever think of buildings,
As a living thing.
Standing way up in the sky.
Looking up at birds upon the wing.
Looking down at life go flowing by.

—From "Buildings," a poem by Barbara Baer
Capitman, age twelve

"Leonard Horowitz was a sweetheart," Micky Wolfson remembered. "He was striving, energetic, and diligent, and very much influenced by Barbara, who would direct him."

Wherever Barbara went, Leonard was close behind. They were an odd sight, Barbara in her frowsy clothes, Leonard in his hand-me-downs; Barbara buttonholing people on the street to tell them about Art Deco preservation, Leonard spouting sexual come-ons to passing gay men like he had Tourette's syndrome. "They were like something out of *Alice in Wonderland*," said author and actor David Leddick. "They were such unusual people. They weren't exactly idiots savants, but they approached it. Both of them had a genius for what they did, and they were absolutely in the right place at the right time."

The members of the Miami Design Preservation League became "like a family to me," Leonard told the *Miami Herald*. "It's a way of life. Everyone in the league takes care of everyone else."

Eventually he and Barbara lived in the same building at 1211 Pennsylvania Avenue, designed by one of Leonard's favorite Art Deco architects, Henry Hohauser. Barbara lived in the top-floor apartment, crammed with books, framed photographs, mementos of her life and career, and pieces of her artist mother's ceramics and sculpture. A kidney-shaped desk served as Art Deco command central. Barbara was distracted and absentminded and Leonard watched out for her. One day Leonard discovered her ironing a blouse on top of her television, melting the plastic casement, and on another occasion Andrew Capitman got a call from Leonard saying that Barbara's apartment had been robbed, but all the thieves got were checkbooks, no cash. It turned out that Barbara never carried money around with her—none at all—and paid for everything by check, even if it was only a dollar.

It was from 1211 Pennsylvania Avenue that in June 1981 Barbara and Leonard set out on their 10,000-mile journey across the United States in a little Chevette to visit historic districts around the country. Barbara was going to write thirteen dispatches from the road for the *Miami News* titled "Travels with Barbara: 10,000 Miles in Search of Art Deco." Barbara called it "a modern-day expedition of discovery that for Art Deco people at least ranks with Lewis and Clark." There was a bon voyage party for them at the Cardozo Hotel and "everyone was laughing at the 'odd couple,'" Barbara remembered, "the thirty-five-year-old designer and the sixty-one-year-old writer." Only hours after they left, Leonard said to Barbara, "Now it's your turn to drive," and within fifteen minutes of taking the wheel she'd driven into a ditch.

It was during that 1981 trip that Leonard first saw painted terra-cotta ornaments on buildings in Tulsa and Kansas City that made the architectural details pop. Leonard realized that one of the aesthetic problems with the Art Deco district was that it was colorless and drab; the buildings were painted white or gray or tan and the lines and details disappeared into the general dullness of the buildings. South Beach needed color, but not just any colors; it needed a color *scheme* that would suit it. The moment when Leonard created the palette for South Beach was like the moment in the movie *The Wizard of Oz* when everything goes from black-and-white to color.

The folklore is that Leonard invented the colors sitting in a lawn chair on Ocean Drive, staring at the heliotropic sea and sky, smoking joints and watching the soft colors playing in the changing light: peppermint, magenta, seashell rose, peach, pale lilac, mint, powder blue, powder pink, and a touch of tangerine.

His breakthrough assignment was Friedman's Bakery on Washington Avenue, an elegant, one-story Art Deco building with clean lines and a stack of octagonal architectural shapes above the main entrance. Leonard had the building painted like creamy cake icing: pistachio mint, powder pink, and baby blue, turning the whole structure into a giant confection, like an outsize Claes Oldenburg sculpture. Friedman's Bakery struck a chord with the design world the same way the "painted lady" houses of San Francisco had started a trend ten years before, and in 1982 Friedman's Bakery made the cover of *Progressive Architecture* magazine. Almost overnight Leonard Horowitz gained a national reputation as the designer who invented the color scheme of the new South Beach. Painting the buildings pastel colors would turn out to be the last missing piece of the puzzle that would help catapult the resort into a phenomenon. Leonard Horowitz literally put the icing on the cake.

Commissions came flying in. He was so busy he hired eleven employees and opened offices on Lincoln Road. He painted the Park Central Hotel white and mauve with moldings of green, and he had the Carlyle Hotel painted buff and green on the inside and mauve on the outside. He chose the palette for a mansion on Star Island, and Stephen Muss asked his former doorman to select the colors for the Poodle Lounge at the Fontainebleau Hotel for him, which were pink and black. Leonard chose the colors and fabrics in the 1980s renovation of the Victor Hotel on Ocean Drive, and he created Art Deco interiors for the Water Club in Washington, D.C. When the city of Miami Beach put together a budget for the revitalization of Washington Avenue, Leonard practically repainted the whole street. Perhaps his smallest yet his most pleasing triumph was that he was commissioned by the TV show *Miami Vice* to choose the colors for the food carts on the beach that appeared in the opening credits of each episode.

"I feel vindicated," he said. "They called me crazy."

Leonard began to enjoy himself. He was no longer just Barbara Capitman's lapdog. The rent was paid and he treated himself to a trip on the Concorde to Paris with a return trip on the ocean liner *QE II*. He had a sometimes boyfriend he'd met at a gay bathhouse in Coral Gables.

In 1985 he began to have strange fevers and night sweats, and he tested positive for HIV. "I just ignored the whole thing," he said. "I didn't have sex anymore. I was feeling fine. I had thrush once in a while, and I developed insomnia, but I wasn't sick." In August 1987 he was hospitalized for pneumocystis pneumonia, and later Guillain-Barré syndrome, which paralyzed him from the waist down. "One day I was driving my car and the pedals got harder and harder to push," he said, "and then I couldn't walk." No matter how sick he felt, he insisted on going out to events, even in a wheelchair. He desperately wanted to go to Jane Dee and Saul Gross's wedding because he had introduced them. "Listen, I don't want to give things up," he told the *Miami Herald*. "I'm not going to stop everything just because I have AIDS. There's really no reason for living if you can't go out to restaurants and see people. Why bother?"

In the end the Miami Design Preservation League did act like a family, just as Leonard had said, and they raised money and helped plan his care. Tony Goldman, the owner of the Park Central Hotel, paid the rent on Leonard's apartment, and the MDPL paid for a full-time live-in attendant, his phone bills, even the dentist. Members took turns keeping him company or shopping for him at Lundy's Market, which pledged $50 a week free food. But he wasn't very hungry, or amusing company, and slowly people stopped coming to visit him.

He was so lonely that when he got a wrong number on the telephone he kept the caller on the line. In his last interview a reporter from the *Herald* found him in a hospital bed in his apartment, hugging a teddy bear. "I'm looking for somebody I can just hug or something," he explained. "You know, you just need that. Just somebody to love and hug. That's all we were really looking for in the first place. It wasn't all the sex and everything. We just wanted to find someone to be with, like everyone else."

At the very end one of Leonard's Medicaid caretakers, a woman whose own son had died of AIDS, took Leonard into her home and saw him through. He died on May 5, 1988, at age forty-three. The *Miami Herald* said, "He draped the city like a rainbow." There was a standing-room-only memorial service at a Unitarian Church on Biscayne Boulevard, and when Barbara Capitman tried to speak she broke down in tears. He didn't leave much behind, but he left his sometimes boyfriend a ring. He was cremated, and a group of his friends took his ashes out on a motorboat and slowly went up and down the length of Ocean Drive, the buildings alive with all the wonderful colors that Leonard had painted them, and they threw his ashes into the ocean opposite the Park Central Hotel.

In 1989, 11th Street between Ocean Drive and Collins Avenue was renamed Leonard Horowitz Place in his honor. Tens of millions of tourists have walked beneath the street sign bearing his name, but hardly a soul knows who he was or what his legacy is.

IRONICALLY, THE success of Barbara Capitman's dream rendered her obsolete. The fruits of her labors were everywhere. Property values were soaring and tourism was beginning to return. Although some significant buildings had been lost, for the most part the Art Deco district had survived intact and would be protected permanently. At the same time, smart businessmen saw a real estate boomtown coming and started buying up the neighborhood wholesale. The Miami Design Preservation League needed to redefine its goals to stay relevant. Barbara's everlasting credo was "Never Compromise," but the younger members of the league wanted to be more conciliatory with developers and city commissioners, not adversarial, and Barbara didn't like it. Barbara wanted to focus on senior housing, and to stop South Beach from becoming so trendy, and to stop the condominium towers that she feared would loom over the beaches from the tip of Miami northward. According to Andrew Capitman, "People wanted the MDPL to roll over, and my mother had absolutely nothing to fucking lose. My mother said, 'I'm old, I'm poor, I'm famous, and I did it because I was true. Why should I roll over?'"

Barbara Capitman became increasingly implacable about issues. The way she saw it, a person was either with her 100 percent or he was a traitor. If anyone disagreed with her, she would snap, "Dry up and blow away," and that's exactly what many of her supporters eventually did. She couldn't make up her mind whether she wanted to be on the board of the MDPL or a paid executive director. The league began to grow broke. "A lot of people who started the movement with her dropped out," said community activist Nancy Liebman, who met her in 1979. "She would use people and then step on them and move right on. She would walk out on meetings, frequently, if people disagreed with her. She hated me because I took the lead role."

By the time the Senator was demolished, Liebman had emerged as the standard-bearer of the MDPL. She became the executive director in 1988 and served until 1991. Liebman was the polar opposite of Barbara, practical and diplomatic. She was a former elementary school teacher and the wife of a successful doctor. She

and her husband also, not coincidentally, had invested in the Cardozo Hotel, in which they had lost $35,000 of their own money.

"Barbara would go to the City Commission meetings and be
nasty," Liebman recalled. "She showed the commissioners no
respect. She was strident and refused to compromise. By not listening to other people, she negated her ability to get anything done."
The MDPL needed to distance itself from Barbara to keep its
credibility. Noted her friend and league cofounder Michael Kinerk,
"Barbara fomented being thrown out of the league, which was trying to pull itself out of insolvency."

When Barbara was told that she could not act in the name of the
MDPL without consulting with the other members of the board of
directors, she was irate and decided to challenge their legitimacy.
"She called a big powwow," Liebman said. "It was a showdown."
Barbara sent out a flyer announcing a meeting in a courtyard of a
building on Lincoln Road, where she made a speech announcing
that she was dissolving the MDPL and that she was starting a new,
national group called the Art Deco Societies of America, and that
everyone was invited to follow her on her new quest. But hardly
anyone was interested, and anyway, she had no authority to dissolve
the Miami Design Preservation League. She might have created it,
but she didn't own it. "Dissolving the MDPL would have been a
catastrophe. So she quit," said Liebman.

The last time Gary Farmer saw Barbara was when she came into
The Strand one night, very disturbed. "They threw me out of the
league and they won't let me come to meetings anymore," she told
him. She said that she had decided to focus instead on saving Opa
Locka, a small city in northwest Miami-Dade, developed in the
1920s by aviation pioneer Glenn Curtiss with an *Arabian Nights*
theme. "They need me there," she told Farmer.

But she didn't save Opa Locka and they didn't need her. That
project fizzled before it hardly started. By the end of the 1980s she
was nearly broke. "I'm so desperately poor now," Capitman told

the *Herald*, probably not without some guile, "I'm a little old lady in tennis shoes." She began to write letters to various people she had fallen out with over the years, trying to resolve issues. She had been in bad health and had had several hospitalizations over the years for pneumonia and diabetes. She fell ill for a final time in March 1990, when MDPL member Dennis Wilhelm called her in the hospital to talk about a story in the newspaper that day noting all the progress the Art Deco district had made and how it had saved South Beach. Wilhelm said to her, "How about those headlines?"

She said, "If you think that's something, wait until you see tomorrow's headlines."

She was right. The front-page headline of the *Herald* the next day was FIRST LADY OF ART DECO BARBARA CAPITMAN DIES. Capitman died on March 29, 1990, a month short of her seventieth birthday. There was a press feeding frenzy for a week. She was lionized in every local newspaper and TV newscast, and even received an obituary in *Time* magazine.

When her family and friends went to her apartment, they found notes under every object, very systematically placed, explaining what the object was and what it meant to her.

Nancy Liebman and the Miami Design Preservation League asked the city commissioners to name a street after Barbara, and in January 1991, one block south of Leonard Horowitz Place, the street from Ocean Drive to Washington Avenue was renamed Barbara Capitman Way.

In 1991 Gary Farmer sold The Strand to new owners. For him its appeal had evaporated in the hurricane-strength winds of change. South Beach was on the cusp of its future self by 1991. "Gentrification was taking place," Farmer said, "and at The Strand what was once a room full of artists was now a room full of models and hookers."

Eleven

THE MAYOR OF SOUTH BEACH

Miami Beach is a non-place populated by rootless people.
—MAYOR ALEX DAOUD

I t was April, the sun was hot and bright—a harbinger of the brutality of the summer to come—and Alex Daoud, sixty-three, dressed in a T-shirt, workout pants, and flip-flops, was padding down a trellised path outside of his family-owned apartment building with a ponderous gait. He is a big man, six foot three and 270 pounds (to which he will admit), and his knees are bad from carrying around so much weight. He once took great pride in being in excellent shape—he was a talented amateur boxer and he boxed at the 5th Street Gym for exercise when he was younger—and being fat now pains him. He's tried all sorts of diets and supplements, and he regularly goes to a local gym to work out, or so he says, but the real problem is he can't stop filling himself up. He has always been a man of voracious appetite.

Then there is the other kind of weight he carries, incorporeal, but encasing him as surely as his girth. It's an aura of regret and expiation, the yoke of a proud man who endured public humiliation and lost almost everything. He bent over laboriously to pick up a candy wrapper on the walkway and muttered to himself.

He leased a few of the apartments to young women who were in town to try to break into the modeling business and he was constantly picking up after them. Daoud keeps the grounds spotless. This sleepy, four-story, twenty-three-unit apartment building hidden behind a thick wall of ficus on the corner of Michigan and 18th Street, named by Daoud "SoBe Gardens," was once owned by his mother, Evelyn, but it is now held in legal trust for his fifteen-year-old son, Alexander, a necessity to safeguard this remaining family asset.

It is also the very place where he grew up; the apartment building stands on the lot where his family's house once stood, a handsome five-bedroom home with marble floors and elegant furnishings, supplied by Daoud's father, an émigré from Lebanon and the owner of Daoud's Auction Gallery on Lincoln Road, the largest antique furniture and jewelry gallery on the Beach, gone now. Daoud's parents divorced when he was a child, and after his father died his mother tore down the family house and built in its stead this small apartment building for income, in which Daoud now lives and works as landlord, janitor, and handyman. Daoud's eyes tear up when he speaks of his mother, his guiding light. "She was the youngest woman to graduate from St. John's Law School in New York," he said proudly, "and the youngest woman to pass the New York bar exam."

The most striking thing about Daoud's cramped, messy, first-floor apartment—stacks of folded laundry on the built-in banquette in the living area, a cluttered kitchen, unused exercise equipment gathering dust in a corner—is the hundreds of bottles and containers, large and small, of supplements and vitamins, on countertops and tabletops, in stacks on shelves, and littering the desk on which his computer stands. The major part of the room is taken up by his desk and some bookshelves. There is a well-worn high-backed chair, a giant but aging computer screen, large speakers from an old stereo, and shelves whose contents are hidden by towels draped over them.

It is at this computer that Daoud spent fourteen years of his life in what he described as a "deep depression" re-creating and rationalizing his rise and fall in a book entitled *Sins of South Beach*. He thought that writing the book would be cathartic, but instead he ended up wanting to kill himself. He wrote it all down, reliving every wrenching moment of it, including details of his love affairs and sexual peccadilloes. In the world according to Daoud, all of the other people were the architects of his fate—heroes, villains, or lovers, and sometimes all three—but not him. When he was finished writing, no mainstream publisher was interested because the book contained many potentially libelous passages—bribes, drug addiction, wholesale corruption of public officials—and Daoud became determined to publish it himself. It is *his* story, told his own way, and nobody could stop him from telling it. "Let them sue me," he said defiantly.

He makes no bones that he wrote the book to settle scores, and he leaves no slight overlooked, but he also wrote it as an apologia for the city in which he grew up and which he managed and still loves so much. "If you read my book," he said, "I think you'll get an insight into what really transpired in Miami Beach. The true story of South Beach has never really been told," he maintained. "The true story is the sacrifice, the sorrow, and the suffering that the people of South Beach endured, that the police department endured, from the Marielito Cubans."

IT WAS not a happy thing to get Alex Daoud really angry. After years of amateur boxing he packed a punch that could shake a guy's brains loose. He packed another kind of wallop in a gun holster on his right calf, a five-shot Smith & Wesson .38-caliber snub-nosed revolver, and on his waist, in a nylon holster, a sleek, German-made, semiautomatic SIG Sauer with a fifteen-bullet clip that he called a "perfect killing machine."

He was also the mayor of Miami Beach.

In fact, Alex Daoud wasn't just the mayor, he was a superstar mayor. He and the raffish little city by the sea were a perfect match. He was charismatic, good-looking, a real man, who gave Miami Beach hope that it was going to find its way out of decline. His constituents loved him. He was the first mayor to serve three consecutive terms; the first mayor of Arab-American descent elected by a Jewish constituency; the first mayor to be elected with over 86 percent of the popular vote, the greatest plurality in Miami Beach history. He dashed around town in a candy apple red 442 Corvette with the top down, dressed in a T-shirt and sport jacket, stonewashed jeans, and a gold bracelet around his wrist, brokering the future of the city with the most powerful men in the United States. He was so cool that the producers of the TV show *Miami Vice* asked him to appear in two episodes, one playing himself and one playing a corrupt judge.

Practically the whole of Miami-Dade County watched *Miami Vice* the night Daoud made his national television debut, yet he still kept his phone number published in the phone book so the voters could find him if they needed his help in the middle of the night. He found people hospital beds when they were told there were none available, he kept desperate old ladies from being evicted by greedy landlords, and he was an easy touch for a personal loan. He was kind to people. He remembered everyone's name, from car valets to the janitors in City Hall, and he always had five minutes to stop and chat. He was a tactile guy who would put his huge arm around the shoulder of some needy soul and say, "Hey, give me a hug."

"I really wanted to be a good mayor," he said.

Here's what Mayor Daoud did after midnight for entertainment.

Daoud and a team of police officers rode around Miami Beach in an unmarked police car looking for trouble. "For felony offenders or recidivists of major crimes, we developed a special treatment," he wrote in *Sins of South Beach*. "We apprehended the criminals, handcuffed them, and drove them behind the [Miami Beach] Theater for the Performing Arts. Once there, we would drag them out of the backseat of the car, still handcuffed, and punish them. The treatment usually consisted of Mace to the eyes, a few jolts from a stun gun, and a terrible beating. Sometimes the beatings were so severe that we didn't know if the criminals would live or die. Worse, we really didn't care. We threw them in body bags so no trace of bodily fluids could be found in the police car and then dumped their unconscious bodies in the empty alleys and streets of Miami, inside 'the Hood,' or by the Miami River or in other obscure areas where they would never be found. We referred to these brutal beatings with the euphemistic phrase 'attitude-adjustment sessions.'"

Daoud's forays with the police began when he first became a city commissioner, on a midnight shift on September 26, 1980, for what turned out to be a melodramatic odyssey that he says changed his life. It was only five months since the Mariel boatlift refugees had engulfed South Beach, and the city was a slaughterhouse. "The streets were disgusting," Daoud remembered. "There were drug addicts and drunks lying in doorways, people dealing drugs openly in the streets, garbage in the gutters, gangs roaming around like dog packs. They didn't have shoes but they had guns. They waited in the shadows looking for defenseless people to attack." In the first four hours Daoud spent with the police, they answered twenty-six calls, all but a few dealing with Mariel refugees. Daoud was nearly killed on the second call of the evening, a report of a domestic dispute in a dilapidated building on Lenox Avenue, where a mentally ill man, whom the neighbors called El Loco, jumped out of a closet and tried to whack Daoud in the head with a stainless-steel machete. One of the night's most poignant police calls involved an elderly Jewish couple who lived at an old hotel on Ocean Drive called the Betsy Ross. When Daoud arrived with the police, they found the crumpled body of an old man in the alley who had jumped from a window above, out of sickness and desperation. His elderly wife stood in the same window, preparing to jump after him, until the police restrained her.

For Daoud the call that would change his life came toward the end of the shift when he and his cohorts responded to a battery and rape of an old woman on 17th Street. The three suspects were spotted on foot nearby. When Daoud and the police arrived, they found the old woman lying in the street, barely conscious, her face bruised and swollen, a torn brown grocery bag and a crushed carton of milk next to her. Apparently she had walked to an all-night convenience store to buy milk and she was attacked and raped on the way home. Daoud spotted the concentration-camp numbers tattooed on her forearm and instantly realized who it was: Elsie Cohen, a woman in her eighties who had campaigned for him for city council and who lived next door to his mother in the family apartment building. He had met Elsie Cohen years before when he was working as a paralegal in the city attorney's office while still attending law school, advising the elderly on landlord-tenant matters. Elsie was a widow and her landlord was trying to evict her from an apartment in which she had lived in for ten years. Daoud gave her some advice on how to stave off the landlord, and she returned to the city attorney's office a few days later to give him a babka she had baked for him in gratitude. But the landlord persisted, and when Elsie had to appear in landlord-tenant court, Daoud went along to represent her. Unfortunately, he lost the case and Elsie lost her apartment. Remorsefully, Daoud offered her an apartment next to his mother's in the family-owned building, and she had lived there ever since. Over the years he had grown terribly fond of her, and a day never went by when he didn't give her a hug.

"She had survived the horrors of the Holocaust only to lie beaten, raped, and discarded on the filthy streets of South Beach," Daoud wrote. He and the police chased down the suspects on foot and cornered them just a few blocks away. Daoud said that he punched one suspect so hard he knocked out his two front teeth and then grabbed the man by the throat, "determined to crush the rapist's Adam's apple—to choke him to death," Daoud wrote, "to kill him slowly and painfully." The police officers had to pull Daoud off. The three suspects were beaten nearly to a pulp and brought to the emergency room of Jackson Memorial Hospital. They were arrested and stood trial, and each received a ten-year sentence. Elsie Cohen never regained full capacity. She returned to Daoud's apartment building for a time and died six months later in a hospital.

"A sense of deep frustration welled within me," Daoud wrote, "a mixture of impotence and hatred. . . . How could the politicians in Washington allow these criminals to enter the United States freely? . . . A sense of hatred burned in every part of my being against these alien criminals and the dictator Fidel Castro. . . . I was able to analyze the genesis of crime with an eye toward extinguishing it. The solution wasn't pretty. The harsh reality was that on the streets of South Beach, violence could only be conquered by more violence. In one night, my entire outlook on crime changed. . . . I continued to fight crime with the vigilante cops," he wrote, "because I was so caught up in the mental and physical high of risking my life with my friends."

And thus, sayeth Alex Daoud, he was transformed into the vigilante mayor of Miami Beach.

THE MARIEL Cubans are everyone's favorite villain in the melodrama of Miami Beach. Most of the 125,000 Cubans who came to the United States through the port of Mariel, Cuba, in 1980 were hardworking people, thrilled to leave Castro's oppression and start a new life as U.S. citizens. But there were about 25,000 of them— some reports say 45,000—who were criminals, rapists, child predators, sexual deviates, drug addicts, mentally ill, and at least 100 convicted murderers, whom Castro intentionally sent to the United States.*

Up till the time Castro opened the port of Mariel, there were only two ways for citizens to leave Cuba. One was in a boat or a raft, with a prayer and a hope that it would keep afloat the ninety miles to the Florida shores, and not be picked up by the U.S. Coast Guard and its occupants sent back to Cuba, where they'd be labeled political dissidents and thrown in jail to rot for life. Or they could try to leave through one of the two foreign embassies in Havana—Venezuela's and Peru's—whose policy it was to give political asylum to Cubans. The trick to this was to get *into* the embassy, because Castro had barricaded the entrances and put the Cuban army on guard to stop defectors. Still, desperate people kept sneaking through or, more frequently, battering their way through the army barricades with vehicles.

In April 1980 a small group of determined men hijacked a bus, drove it through the barricades, engaged in a gunfight with the Cuban army guards, and got safely inside the Peruvian embassy grounds, where they were granted asylum. A Cuban soldier was killed in the crossfire and Castro demanded that the Peruvian government return the five men to stand trial for murder. When the Peruvian ambassador refused, Castro retaliated by bulldozing the fence protecting the embassy and calling off his soldiers. Over the next two days 10,000 Cuban men, women, and children who

---

*When the term "Mariel" or "Marielito" is used in this book, it refers to the criminal element.

wanted asylum swarmed to the Peruvian embassy, crawling over the building, camping out in its lush gardens, pounding on doors and windows, sleeping on the roof. Pictures of the embassy overrun by people desperate to leave Cuba were broadcast all over the world, and it became an international embarrassment to the Cuban dictator. In a moment of spite or stupidity he decided that if dissidents wanted to leave the country so badly he'd "let the bastards go." He announced that the port of Mariel, a picturesque fishing village about thirty miles from Havana, was open to anyone who wanted to leave by boat. "We don't want them! We don't need them!" he said. Along with those fleeing his regime, Castro diabolically flushed Cuba of its most troubled citizens, sending them, like ticking time bombs, to the United States to live.

By 1980 there was already a sizable Cuban population in the city of Miami of about 100,000, who organized with urgency, and within four days of Castro's announcement 1,700 boats were sent to Mariel from the United States—anything that could float, including shrimp boats, dinghies, and even a World War II submarine chaser—to pick up refugees and bring them to the United States before turning around and going back for more. The Mariel exodus turned into the largest sealift in history. From April 15 to October 31, 1980, some 125,000 people fled Cuba through Mariel until Castro closed the port and ended the hegira.

The impact of 125,000 jobless and homeless people arriving on Florida shores in little more than six months overwhelmed the Miami-Dade authorities. Many of the refugees had no identification or documentation at all. Some brought money and some had relatives with whom they could stay, but many were destitute and had nowhere to live. There were also those who were physically ill, or mentally incompetent, and needed immediate hospitalization. Detention centers were arranged and massive tent cities materialized. At one point 22,000 people were garrisoned/imprisoned in a tent city at Fort Chaffee, Florida, where they rioted and burned buildings. Some lived under highway bridges, and squatters took up residence in deserted buildings.

South Beach became a dumping ground for the poorest and most dangerous of the Mariels. Thousands were relocated in the many boarding houses, small apartment buildings, and cheap hotels. As Alex Daoud remembered, "Stephen Muss, who owned the Fontainebleau, and the so-called redevelopment board, had created a false slum in South Beach that forced the property owners to rent to anybody and everybody. So when the Mariel refugees came, that's where they were sent—to South Beach. The federal government paid for housing in South Beach for many of these rapists, murderers, child molesters, and kidnappers because it was cheap. So they took over."

South of 5th Street was suddenly a very scary place, a combination of modern day Wild West and a Jewish ghetto, the last resort of an estimated 3,000 eastern European Jews, many of them Holocaust survivors, who had ended up in another fight for survival amid the mayhem of the drug trade. The elderly didn't have much, but they had wristwatches and purses with a few dollars in them and they were easy to mug or kill, or rape, like Elsie Cohen. Daoud said that if an elderly woman was mugged wearing a gold ring that couldn't easily be slipped off, the muggers would cut off her finger to get it. The occupants of South Pointe Towers, the pioneer luxury apartment building in that area, would only venture outside of the building through the garage in a locked car, and at night drivers were afraid to stop at red lights on deserted street corners. Andrew Cockburn, a *Village Voice* columnist who visited South Beach at the time, wrote of the "trembling hatred" with which the local residents spoke of the "Mariel scum."

By November 1980 the *Washington Post* reported there was so much crime that the police blotter in the city of Miami "read like a script for [the TV show] *That's Incredible!*" In 1980 more than 77,000 emergency phone calls were placed to the police and fire

Loren, Amber, and James "JR" Ridinger at their mansion before Amber's bat mitzvah. The birthday girl is wearing a $26,000 Dolce & Gabbana gown. *(Courtesy of Tara Ink)*

Stephen Muss, "the most powerful man in Miami Beach," failed to rebuild South Beach as a new Venice. *(Miami Herald)*

Micky Wolfson, the scion of the resort's most prominent family, admonishes critics not to ask too much from Miami Beach. *(Courtesy of Micky Wolfson)*

A quiet moment on Lincoln Road, with its many cafés and mesmerizing parade of tourists and locals. *(Steven Gaines)*

Michael Aller, Mr. Miami Beach, out for a Sunday stroll on Lincoln Road. *(Steven Gaines)*

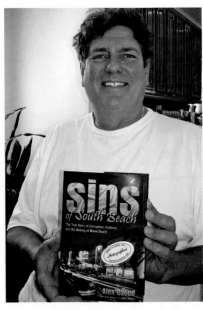

The amiable former mayor of Miami Beach, Alex Daoud, and his unexpurgated book, *Sins of South Beach.* *(Steven Gaines)*

Ben Novack under siege, always, sitting in his office chair explaining the way it is to a reporter from the *Herald*. *(Miami Herald)*

A Miami Beach police officer escorts crusading preservationist Barbara Capitman, dressed in her "robes of justice," off the steps of the Senator Hotel while news crews and photographers capture the moment. *(Miami Herald)*

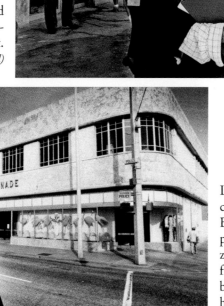

Leonard Horowitz, creator of the Beach's color palette, at his zenith, standing in front of an entire block of buildings he had painted in his trademark pastels. *(Miami Herald)*

Bernice Novack hated the lack of privacy living at the Fontainebleau Hotel as well as the expectation that she should be impeccably dressed at all times. *(Miami Herald)*

The architect Morris Lapidus wearing his trademark bow tie, a shape he claimed he incorporated into the marble floors of the Fontainebleau lobby. *(Miami Herald)*

The Fontainebleau's famous Spite Wall, said to have been erected to cast a shadow over the swimming pool of the Eden Roc next door. *(Steven Gaines)*

A computer-generated rendering of the twenty-first-century Fontainebleau complex with condominium towers. The iconic curved building remains— as does the controversy over who was responsible for its shape.
(Courtesy of the Fontainebleau)

Miami Beach's Bad Boy real estate developer Thomas Kramer enjoying a smoke in the swimming pool of his $60 million Star Island mansion.
(Courtesy of Thomas Kramer)

Ambika Marshall spent a season in South Beach trying to break into modeling before returning home to finish college.
(Courtesy of Marc Richards)

Ambika Marshall and fellow model Matt Loewen on the night before their romance came to an end.
(Steven Gaines)

The photo that earned Matt Loewen's ticket to Miami Beach. He subsequently decided to get rid of the eyebrow piercing and diamond earring.
(Courtesy of TJPhotography)

Michele Pommier, a former model, ran one of the highest profile modeling agencies in South Beach.
(Courtesy of Michele Pommier)

A night at The Forge: from left, Antonio Misuraca, Matthew McConaughey, Alonzo Mourning, Shareef Malnik, and Lance Armstrong. *(Courtesy of Tara Ink)*

The imposing faux French facade of The Forge restaurant and Glass nightclub on Arthur Godfrey Road. *(Steven Gaines)*

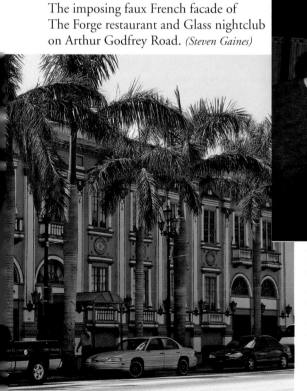

Brawny nightclub promoter Chris Paciello and one-time Madonna girlfriend Ingrid Casares, South Beach nightclub royalty, before the fall of their empire. *(Patrick McMullan)*

Michael Capponi, "SoBe prince of nightlife," on his boat with an assortment of new friends. Behind him is one of the many cruise ships that come in and out of the port. *(Steven Gaines)*

Erin Henry and Michael Capponi on their wedding day.
(Courtesy of Erin Henry)

department in Miami Beach alone, almost one call per person. In 1981 the Miami-Dade area led the country in murders with a record 623, and in Miami Beach itself statistics showed that Marielitos committed 70 percent of the murders—53 murders in Miami Beach in 1981 were attributed to Marielitos. The Marielitos themselves were murdered at five times the rate of the general population. The Miami Beach police force was so overwhelmed that a crime unit was formed specifically to study Mariel criminals and how they operated. By 1982, two years after their arrival, the Miami area was declared the "Murder Capital of the World" by the press and the Miami city morgue was so full of bodies that the medical examiner rented a refrigerated hamburger van for the overflow.

IT DIDN'T take long for the criminal element of the Mariels to notice that while they were busy robbing, raping, and pillaging for small change, the Colombian cocaine dealers were buying Rolls-Royce automobiles with cash out of shopping bags.

The Colombia-Miami connection had started twenty years before when Colombia became the number-one supplier of marijuana to the United States. Marijuana smuggling in South Florida became so profitable in the 1960s that many commercial fishermen were using their boats not to catch fish but to fetch bales of marijuana on the high seas. The problem with marijuana was that it was big and bulky to export, and there was competition from the Mexicans, who grew their own and began to cut in on the Colombian dealers' sales volume. So the Colombians moved from selling grass to selling cocaine, made from the coca leaves that were already plentiful in their climate, plus easier to smuggle and more profitable, too.

The smuggling and sale of illegal substances was not new or unusual in South Florida. Its 3,000 miles of coastline and untold hidden harbors have made South Florida a bootlegger's dream. Miami Beach was one of the wettest cities in the United States during Prohibition, when the local gentry, as if calling a liquor store, would order up alcohol from a bootlegger and have it delivered to their yachts. The contraband grew harder over the years, and in 1947 Miami was already recognized as a "possible dope capital," according to the *New York Times*. That year the police announced the biggest drug bust to date at Miami International Airport, where a smuggler was caught with $50,000 worth of cocaine strapped to his body.

The situation had changed drastically in 1978—and become more deadly as well—when one of the major drug dealers in Colombia, Carlos Lehder, formed a loosely knit association of drug lords known as the Medellín Cartel. Lehder bought an island called Norman's Cay off the coast of the Bahamas and made it the center of drug exportation. By 1981 the federal government estimated that every day some eighty planes carrying payloads of cocaine were landing surreptitiously in the Miami area. (This did not mean that marijuana smuggling was ignored by the cartel altogether. Of the 2.8 million pounds of marijuana seized by the Drug Enforcement Administration in 1982, 2.4 million pounds were seized in Florida.)

At first the Mariels were the petty street merchants of the Medellín Cartel, fighting between themselves over territory, but it wasn't long before they started to muscle in on the Colombians and then it was all-out intramural war, the era of the "Cocaine Cowboys" as it became known. The Cubans and Colombians were brutal enemies. As Miami crime reporter Edna Buchanan put it, "The Mafia would just shoot the person they were after, they wouldn't kill the whole family. But the cocaine cowboys . . . would go into a house, kill whomever they were after as well as the baby in the crib. Then they'd kill the next-door neighbors. If the Avon lady rang the doorbell, they'd kill her. . . ." By the mid-1980s, murder in the Miami area was up 53 percent and Miami-Dade had become a criminal armory and arms market that provided firepower to the new drug economy. There were as many federal cases for illegal firearms in Miami-Dade as there were in New York, Philadelphia, Chicago, and Los Angeles combined.

Miami Beach became a drug superbazaar, from which one-third of all the illegal drugs in the United States were distributed. The amount of cocaine seized in South Florida was double the total amount in the entire world. "There is so much coke it's unbelievable," said a member of the House Committee on Narcotics. The *Washington Post* called Miami "The Wall Street of Dope" and estimated that the street value of the drugs smuggled into the United States through South Florida was $7 billion a year, all in cash. About 350 full-time high-level drug dealers operated in the area, kingpins at the top of an organization that employed thousands of smaller distributors and dealers and made hundreds of millions of dollars.

Where did all this cash, known as "narcodollars," end up? The *Miami Herald* described the local banks as being "awash with money." Miami became the nation's capital of drug-money laundering activities, according to U.S. Customs and Justice Department officials heading Operation Greenback, a multiagency group aimed at detecting drug-money transactions in the 1980s. Cash was bulky, and Miami banks were forced to build additional safe-deposit boxes and vaults to store it all. In the 1980s there was twice as much cash in the Miami-Dade Federal Reserve Bank than in all the other Federal Reserve Banks put together, mostly in $100 bills, according to the Feds. Federal officials suspected that four banks were owned by drug dealers themselves, and authorities eventually froze $350 million of suspected drug money in 680 bank accounts linked to the Medellín Cartel.

Coincidental to all the illegal money pouring in, Miami became "a deposit gathering center," as the general manager of Credit Suisse called it, for an estimated $13 billion in legitimate foreign deposits of "flight capital" from wealthy Latin Americans and businesses who began to transfer funds to Miami banks after the Latin American debt crisis in 1982. More than 100 international bank offices opened in Miami, including the Bank of Tokyo, Banco do Brasil, and Vereins-Und Westbank of Hamburg. By 1990 there was $25 billion in foreign dollars in Miami banks.

The narcodollars bought Rolls-Royces, waterfront palaces, and condominiums overlooking the city. The drug dealers set the tone and style of Miami Beach in the 1980s, and it is the essence of the drug dealers' pimped-out style that prevails in Miami Beach today.

So it was that in November of 1985, after serving three terms as a city councilman, Alex Daoud became mayor to a city in turmoil. The job fit Daoud like a wet suit. He knew and loved his native city, he was passionate in his conviction that it could return to preeminence as a resort, and, most of all, he loved being mayor. He was reelected mayor for a second term in 1987 and for a third term in 1989.

The problem was the mayor of Miami Beach made only $10,000 a year, partly because aside from presiding over City Commission meetings and appointing committees, the mayor's job was only ceremonial. The man who actually ran the city of Miami Beach on a day-to-day basis, and had the power to hire and fire all employees, was the City Manager, who was paid $120,000 a year and hired by the mayor and a board of six commissioners. Being a commissioner was a power seat in the little city, but it too was regarded as a part-time public-service job, and commissioners were paid only a token $6,000 a year.

"How did they expect me to live on ten thousand dollars a

year?" Daoud asked plaintively. "I couldn't afford to buy a *suit* on ten thousand a year. I couldn't pay for my laundry bill on ten grand. You pay somebody ten grand a year, what do you expect? I was constantly surrounded by millionaires. I was surrounded by millionaires and *they were not the mayor*—I was! They were asking me for favors, so why shouldn't I have what they had? And why shouldn't they help me?"

One of the millionaires who asked Daoud for a favor was Abel Holtz, the chairman of the $2 billion Capital Bancorp empire and one of the more flamboyant figures of the new seat-of-your pants banking boom. They called Holtz the "Teflon Banker" in the press because he always seemed to be able to slip away from accusations made against him for banking improprieties, including two federal probes for money laundering and political extortion. He was tall and thin and had gray hair and piercing blue eyes, and he sat behind a desk in a chair with armrests of winged tigers that had once belonged to Haile Selassie, the emperor of Ethopia.

Holtz was a Cuban Jew who had been imprisoned four times by Fidel Castro. The last of his incarcerations ended when his wife bribed officials with $50,000 to let him go. Holtz arrived in Miami Beach in May of 1961, nearly destitute, and took a job as a waiter at Wolfie's restaurant on Collins Avenue, where he eventually worked his way up to maître d'. He later took a $75-a-week job at a mortgage company, then became a teller at a bank and immersed himself in the banking business until, voilà, in 1974 he created Capital Bank with $1 million. By the early 1980s Holtz and his wife and two sons held 51 percent of the stock in an umbrella organization that owned twenty-eight banks in Florida, California, and Washington, D.C., where his eldest son, Javier, became a director when he was only eighteen years old.

Holtz spent his money well, and conspicuously, too. He donated the Abel Holtz Capital Bank Tennis Stadium in South

Beach to the city. There was a street named after him in downtown Miami in honor of his philanthropic contributions. He kept a vacation home in Spain and he was driven everywhere in a black limousine, paid for by the bank. A fifty-foot yacht with a full crew was berthed at his sprawling waterfront estate on the ritzy Di Lido Island. He also fancied himself a good tennis player, which is how he met Alex Daoud, on his tennis courts. They played with two pros whom Holtz was paying, who quietly tipped off Daoud that if he wanted to be invited back, he had to lose the match; Holtz only played to win.

Daoud lost, he was invited back, and the men were sipping cold drinks on the patio when Holtz expressed concerns about all the mortgages his bank held in South Beach, where property values were nil. Then again, when and if the upturn came, those properties would be worth a fortune. According to Daoud, Holtz told him, "It's time for Capital Bank to become a player in Miami Beach. A lot of money is going to be made in real estate in South Beach in the near future. I need someone on the inside, someone who can control the flow of power. You're that person." Holtz flourished a white envelope with $1,000 in it and asked Daoud to arrange to have Holtz's twenty-four-year-old son, Daniel, appointed to one of the plum spots on the powerful Miami Beach Zoning Board of Adjustment. Daoud considered the request for a moment. He knew it would appear unusual for him to suddenly champion the appointment of the twenty-four-year-old son of a prominent banker to the zoning board. Daoud wrote of that moment, "Slowly, my eyes shifted to the attractive surroundings—the tennis courts, the custom swimming pool with the hot tub, and the large Italian custom-constructed boat moored to the expensive hand-built teak dock. I began to think I should have a home like his, that it was my right to live in luxury. After all, I was the one who had to run for political office and win elections and reelections."

Daoud took the envelope.

This was the start of a seven-year financial relationship and close friendship with Holtz. From here on in, it was arranged that a monthly retainer be paid to a local Miami Beach law firm where Daoud kept an office, so it would look as though Holtz was paying legal fees if it was ever questioned. This meant that Daoud would have to give a share of the fees to the law firm, but he felt it was worth it to be protected in case he ever had to explain what the money was for. Holtz's next request was a lot more difficult than a simple board appointment. He asked Daoud to arrange to have all of Miami Beach's financial accounts—over $100 million worth— moved to Capital Bank, according to Daoud. In 1979 Miami Beach had passed a law that the city's financial assets had to be deposited in a bank that had a branch in Miami Beach, and out of fairness the money had to be rotated to another bank every few years. Capital Bank had no branch in Miami Beach, but neither had the money been rotated. Holtz promised to look favorably on giving mortgages within South Beach, and after some political arm twisting on Daoud's part, it was done. Soon, Capital Bank had tens of millions of dollars' worth of mortgages on Miami Beach properties.

"I became what I thought of as an influence peddler," Daoud said. "No different than a lobbyist in D.C. or a senator who packs a bill with pork for his hometown." Daoud began to receive checks from Holtz to the tune of $20,000 a year. He became a regular vis- itor to Holtz's offices, sometimes two or three times a week. The two eventually became such close pals that Holtz paid for Daoud's wedding reception at The Forge restaurant, and Daoud named his first-born son Abel, after Holtz. "Although I expanded my horizons to take bribes from other parties," Daoud wrote, "Holtz's hold on me was enduring and almost absolute."

It was Holtz who introduced Daoud to Gilberto "Willy" Mar- tinez, a flamboyant drug runner and boxing promoter who lived in a waterfront mansion on Sunset Island and kept large amounts of cash in Capital Bank. Martinez needed Daoud's help. He claimed he had made a deal with boxing promoter Don King for the South Florida rights to the closed-circuit TV broadcast of the heavy-weight championship fight between Mike Tyson and Michael Spinks, and now King was trying to back out. The fight was taking place in Atlantic City at Donald Trump's hotel, and Martinez wanted Daoud to approach Trump on his behalf and ask Trump to use his influence with Don King in securing the TV rights for Martinez. Martinez offered Daoud $10,000 up front, just for trying, and if he wound up with the rights because of Daoud's interces-sion, he would pay Daoud an additional $90,000.

Daoud wasn't exactly pals with Donald Trump—he had met the developer once in his official capacity as mayor, but he agreed to contact him, and Martinez had a messenger deliver a $10,000 check to Daoud the next day. Daoud wrote a letter to Trump on his official Office of the Mayor of Miami Beach stationery about the prizefight, but Trump declined to get involved. True to his word Martinez never asked to recover his $10,000 down payment. But he did send Daoud another customer—a drug runner named Orlando Gonzalez who had illegally built an eight-foot wall around his Pine Tree Drive home to hide his smuggling activities. Daoud arranged for the city zoning board to give Gonza-lez's wall its approval, and the mayor was sent a $15,000 check. Daoud thanked Willy Martinez for the introduction by present-ing him with a key to the city of Miami Beach as an honored citizen—shortly before Martinez was arrested for trying to smuggle five hundred kilos of cocaine into the country from his backyard dock.

Daoud was an equal-opportunity influence peddler. Some bribes were large, such as the $50,000 Daoud claimed he was paid by a wealthy man to get his doctor son on the Florida Board of

Medical Examiners, or the $25,000 that Daoud took to swing the vote to license a topless club called Gold Club. Some were small, such as the $3,000 he received from broadcast media baron Egmont Sonderling and his wife after voting to allow them to build a driveway on city property in front of their Pine Tree Drive home.

At some point the line blurred between bribes and extortion. In 1987 Daoud paid $235,000 for a Mediterranean-style 6,000-square-foot house on Sunset Island 2 and began to persuade city contractors, plumbers, and electricians to work on the house for free, promising them cushy contracts with the city in exchange for their work. He was given free furniture, kitchen appliances, toilets, and Mexican floor tiles for the house, which he named the "Mayor's Mansion."

Daoud felt no guilt, no compunctions at all about his behavior. "I started feeling I was invincible," he said. "I thought I could fly."

It was the heat from David Paul's dock that brought Icarus crashing to earth.

David Paul was the most famous banker in Dade County, perhaps one of the most famous bankers in the United States. Abel Holtz was small fry in comparison.

Paul was a local boy, born in Miami, who disappeared from his hometown for a decade or two and turned up out of the blue in September of 1982 with a Harvard degree, a Ph.D., and a successful real estate company in Westport, Connecticut. He was like a ball of steel wool, short, stocky, balding, with a gravelly voice from smoking gold-tipped St. Moritz cigarettes. Although he had never been in the banking business before, in 1982 he made a breathtaking $53 million cash offer to buy Dade Savings, an ailing savings and loan that was losing $4 million a month. Dade Savings was a venerable local institution in which thousands of Florida retirees, in particular minorities, had put both their faith and their retirement savings. The depositors watched with apprehension when Paul changed the bank's name to CenTrust, and in a dazzling feat of financial conjuration, in just a few years he transformed the moribund thrift into one of the country's largest savings and loans, with $11 billion in assets, whose shares traded on the American Stock Exchange under Paul's initials, DLP.

Nobody asked how or why. The city was full of skyrockets like David Paul. Besides, he was good for Miami. CenTrust became a symbol of Miami's new prosperity and economic clout. The tangible proof was the glimmering, forty-seven-story CenTrust Tower in downtown Miami designed by I. M. Pei. Flat on one side like a sheet of glass, the other curved and steeped, the building was bathed in spotlights that made it glow colors at night. A massive parking garage took up the lower 10 stories, and on the eleventh floor there was a marble and gold "sky lobby" for pedestrians, with a reflecting pool in which all who looked saw the reflection of the Narcissus who had built it. David Paul ran his banking empire from the forty-fifth, forty-sixth, and forty-seventh floors in a 7,000-square-foot office, connected by a sixty-three-step, three-story white Italian marble and steel staircase that was so large and heavy it had to be airlifted to the forty-fifth floor by helicopter. The faucets in Paul's private bathroom were made of gold, the shower door was bulletproof, and on his office walls hung $30 million worth of Old Masters. Peter Paul Rubens's *Portrait of Man as Mars*, for which David Paul paid $13.2 million of the bank's money, hung in the living room of his La Gorce Island compound.

Paul, who was cochairman of the Florida State Democratic Finance Committee, became famous for his extravagances, such as the dinner party he gave in 1988 when he flew in six top chefs from France to cook for friends at a cost of $122,000. When his next-door neighbor on La Gorce Island complained about the constant construction on Paul's four-building compound, Paul shut him up by buying his house, tearing it down, and building a house-size koi pond and twenty-foot waterfall in its stead.

It seemed that David Paul was a man who could have anything he wanted, but one thing eluded him—a dock big enough to moor his prized possession, a $7 million, 120-foot yacht named *Bodacious*. Of all his toys the *Bodacious* was his pride and joy—he paid $1 million a year just in maintenance—and Paul felt the boat deserved a dock as important as she was. So he had plans drawn up for a hand-built teak dock so large they'd have to sink sixteen pilings out into Biscayne Bay to anchor it, which meant he needed a zoning variance. This was, ironically, not even his first dock; the existing one was perfectly fine, just not large enough for the *Bodacious*. Only seventeen months before, the City Commission had refused to approve the larger dock, and after petulantly suing the city of Miami Beach, Paul presented a new application for a reduced-size dock that would extend only seventy-six feet into the waterway.

According to Daoud, in May 1988, shortly before the vote on Paul's reconfigured dock, Abel Holtz arranged a meeting between him and David Paul—at a tennis match at Paul's estate—after which Daoud gave Paul his assurance that this time the zoning variance for his dock would pass. Just as Daoud said, Paul's dock was approved, and a month later Daoud received the first payment toward his fee of $35,000 from a subsidiary of CenTrust Bank called the Old American Insurance Company.

It was at this juncture, as David Paul was becoming one of Daoud's regular benefactors, that the savings-and-loan industry began to come under scrutiny by federal regulators. These "thrifts," as they were known, deregulated in the early 1980s and run like private corporations, yet federally insured, were allowed to invest their depositors' money with little oversight. Banking regulators began to take a closer look at some of the more high-flying savings and loans, and David Paul's ostentatious lifestyle had called attention to him. One of the first things that federal investigators discovered was that Paul had invested over $1.4 billion of CenTrust's assets in high-yield "junk bonds" that he bought through Michael Milken's investment firm of Drexel Burnham Lambert. By 1989, with the country in a recession, the junk-bond market imploded and CenTrust became insolvent. In February 1990 federal regulators seized CenTrust and its books were scoured by a team of forensic accountants. It took them a while to notice the payments made to Alex Daoud, and on April 10, 1990, a front-page headline ran in the *Herald*: MIAMI BEACH MAYOR GOT CHECKS FROM CENTRUST AFTER DOCK VOTE.

By this time a grand jury had been convened to investigate Daoud, and every penny that went through his bank accounts was scrutinized. Federal agents subpoenaed the financial records of the law firm where he kept an office, his records from City Hall, even the blueprints of Daoud's Sunset Island house. Soon the payments from Abel Holtz and others were uncovered, and on October 29, 1991, Daoud was indicted on forty-one counts, including the most serious charge of racketeering, and he was released on $500,000 bail. He was immediately suspended as mayor of Miami Beach.

Daoud hired high-profile Miami defense attorney Roy Black to defend him. From this point on all his assets would be eaten up by legal fees. He turned to David Paul and Abel Holtz repeatedly for help and was surprised when they broke off contact with him and didn't return phone calls. "I thought these people were my friends and that they would be supportive," he said, rather naively. "I had no idea how selfish they were." Still, he was faithful to them—for a time. Daoud, who was eventually tried for only thirty-five counts, maintained at his trial that he had taken no bribes and that the money received from Abel Holtz and David Paul was for legitimate legal work.

In September of 1992 he was convicted on one count—for

bribery, the Willy Martinez bribe—but only because Martinez turned state's evidence against him. A mistrial was declared on the other twenty-four counts, and a new trial was scheduled for the following year. By this point Daoud was disheartened and broke. He had a long talk with his closest confidante—his mother—and her advice was for him to plead guilty and get a lesser sentence. Just a few months later, after a brief illness, his beloved mother died, and it crushed him. By then he was an outcast, and only a few of his old friends showed up at her funeral or called to give him their sympathies. Nothing hurt him more. He was particularly angry that Abel Holtz didn't bother to send a note. Perhaps that was because the noose was already tightening around Holtz's neck. In November 1992 several of Capital Bank's board of directors sued Holtz, claiming that he had used $355,000 of bank funds to pay off two female employees who had accused him of sexual harassment.

Daoud decided he was changing his son's name from Abel to Alex Jr.

On April 6, 1993, Daoud admitted he was guilty of bribery and tax evasion, and he offered to help the federal agents snare Abel Holtz. "I just wanted to get him. I was really pissed," Daoud said. But he couldn't get Holtz on the phone, and he wasn't easy to corner. So five months later, one morning in September of 1993, he met with federal agents at a Howard Johnson motel in Miami Beach and was outfitted with a tape recorder that was taped to the inside of his left thigh with two microphones that ran up into his clothing. Daoud went to a phone booth and called Holtz's office and got his secretary on the phone. He told her that federal agents would be his next phone call if Holtz didn't call him back at the pay phone. The call was returned by one of Holtz's minions, who said that Holtz would meet him late that afternoon at The Forge restaurant. "If he doesn't show up he's going to jail, do not pass go," Daoud threatened. "I'm sending the guy to jail."

When Daoud arrived at the dark restaurant, several hours before it was open, a big bodyguard greeted him and then said, "Mr. Holtz is waiting for you at the back booth." Daoud found his way to where Holtz was sitting and slid into the booth across from him.

With the tape recorder turning, Holtz hissed, "How dare you call and threaten me?"*

"I'm glad you agreed to meet with me," Daoud said. "We have a lot to talk about, Abel." Daoud told him that the Feds were going to call a grand jury and indict him.

"Indict me?" Holtz asked. "What have the Feds got on me? Everything has been covered up or explained. The Feds have been trying to get me for a long time. I'm too smart to get caught."

Daoud said that even though he had stated otherwise at his trial, "The Feds know about the money you gave me."

Holtz replied, "Oh, but that's legitimate stuff."

"They're not that stupid," Daoud said.

"No one will believe you," Holtz told him. "You'll never be able to prove all this."

Famous last words. A grand jury was impaneled, and over the next year and a half Holtz spent millions of dollars in legal fees trying to thwart its investigation. Eventually, in October 1994, Holtz caved in and pleaded guilty to one count of obstruction of justice, ironically not for banking improprieties but for lying to the grand jury about his association with Alex Daoud. Holtz was sentenced to forty-five days behind bars, four-and-a-half months under house arrest, and three thousand hours of community service. Alex Daoud later testified against Holtz for a second time at closed-door hearings of the Florida Department of Banking and Finance, and

---

*This dialogue appears in Daoud's book and from his recollection of it in direct interview. Federal investigators never released a transcript of the tape recording made at The Forge.

in 1996 Holtz and his family were forced to divest their ownership in Capital Bank, which was sold to the Union Planters Bank for $300 million. Holtz lives quietly in the Miami area, and his name remains on both the Miami street and the Miami Beach tennis stadium named in his honor. In 2000 Holtz applied to the office of Bill Clinton for a presidential pardon, but he was denied.

David Paul was next on Daoud's hit list. Paul was brought to trial in October of 1993 on a hundred-count indictment in the collapse of CenTrust, which cost taxpayers $1.7 billion, making it the fourth-largest banking failure in history. In the course of the trial it turned out that David Paul didn't have a Harvard degree or a Ph.D. He admitted that the Rubens painting that he had bought with the bank's money didn't hang in the bank's offices but in his living room, and that all the money he spent on his beautiful house and 6,000-square-foot guest cottage, and on the koi pond that replaced his annoying neighbor's house, didn't come from his handsome salary and bonuses; the cost was buried in the CenTrust books. On top of that, he admitted that he had stashed away $200,000 in Israel on which he never paid taxes.

In October of 1993 Alex Daoud testified for two days at David Paul's trial reversing his previous position, swearing that he had never done any legitimate work for the banker and that all payments to him had been bribes. David Paul counterclaimed that Daoud had been paid only as a lobbyist who brought in deposits for the bank. "He did a terrific job lobbying for us," Paul told a reporter. By the end of his second day of testimony, Daoud had incriminated Paul and so many other powerful people that he was taken into protective custody and hidden in a motel in Deerfield Beach for three weeks by federal agents who feared for his safety until he could be taken to jail to serve his sentence.

The following month David Paul, fifty-five, was convicted of stealing $24 million from the bank's funds as well as ninety-seven other crimes, including banking fraud and security violations. He was sentenced to eleven years with no chance of parole before nine years and four months. The Feds seized everything he owned. The CenTrust Tower was sold for $44 million to the Bank of America. David Paul was stripped bare.

A year after Paul went to prison his wife, Sandra, divorced him and married Stephen Muss. "I was devastated," he told the *Miami Herald*. He pined for Sandra while serving nine years and three months of his sentence. Paul was released in 2004 and spent three years of supervised release. He told the *Herald* that one day he hoped to go back into the financial field, in venture capital. "I'm not saying what I did was right," Holtz said. "Never in a million years did I think I'd go to jail."

Alex Daoud was fined $75,000, and in 1993 he was sentenced to sixty-three months in federal prison, which was reduced to eighteen months for his cooperation with federal officials in their investigations of Holtz and Paul. A federal investigator even spoke on his behalf at his sentencing. Daoud lost everything—his house on Sunset Island, his savings, his mayor's pension. When he got out of jail in 1995, nearly broke, he took a job delivering flowers for a florist before he became caretaker of SoBe Gardens and settled in to write his book.

Sins of South Beach was self-published in 2007. His accusation of lawbreaking and drug-taking by public figures still living in Miami Beach was unsparing, yet to date no one in the book has come forward to sue him. Nor has Daoud ever been charged with a crime for his vigilante activities, and none of the policemen named in his book who accompanied him on his nocturnal adventures had any action taken against them.

Daoud gave well-attended book readings at the Books & Books stores in Miami Beach and Coral Gables, but, oddly, there was little local press. The *Miami Herald* assigned a reporter who followed him around and went to one of his book signings, but no articles or review of *Sins of South Beach* ever appeared in the local newspaper of record, only an item in a gossip column.

Since the publication of *Sins of South Beach* many of his old fans and constituency have rallied around him, which pleases him greatly. When he walks down Lincoln Road, people recognize him and stop to shake his hand and ask for advice, or sometimes they just want to tell them how much they loved him as a mayor.

Twelve

INTO THE NIGHT

*Wear enough makeup, show enough skin, and your
photo will wind up on michaelcapponi.com. Come
prepared to make out with strangers.*

— "Seven Days of Miami Parties,"
New York magazine, 2006

Michael Capponi was chimping again. It was a Thursday night
and he was sitting in a roll-backed chair at his usual table at
the Vix, the swanky restaurant at the Hotel Victor on Ocean Drive,
intently typing away at the miniature keyboard of his handheld
BlackBerry with his thumbs. It had been raining on and off all day
and he was text-messaging the tribe, trying to round up a crowd for
tonight's party upstairs at the rooftop nightclub. He seemed oblivi-
ous to everything around him, the buzz of the busy restaurant, the
loud music, and all the beautiful young women sitting at his table,
one more exquisite than the next, all of whom were trying to flirt
with him. If he would only look up.

One thing finally did get his attention away from his Black-
Berry. A young Hispanic busboy tried to remove a large oval platter
of chipped ice on which huge piles of stone-crab-claw appetizers—
several thousand dollars' worth—had just been served, and the ice
slurped off the side in a slushy sheet and onto Michael Capponi's
lap. Michael jumped to his feet, but too late; his pants and sport
jacket were drenched in fishy-smelling ice water. Diners at other

tables turned to watch while the manager rushed over to Capponi to dispense cloth napkins and help blot his pants. The mortified busboy, who had the hangdog expression of someone who was just about to get fired, kept his distance from behind one of the diaphanous white curtains that billowed between tables.

"Please don't get the busboy into trouble," Michael said to the manager with a hint of weary forbearance. "It was an accident." But the manager only nodded halfheartedly, so Capponi repeated a bit more firmly, "*Okay?* Don't get the busboy into trouble?"

The manager finally agreed, "Okay."

Satisfied, Capponi sat back down at the table and grinned at his dinner guests with a kind of goofy, just-my-luck expression on his face. He was a nice-looking man with neatly combed dark hair and a strong jawline. It was typical of him to be gallant and try to protect the busboy. The first thing people in Miami Beach say about Michael Capponi is that he's a nice guy with a good heart, charming and sweet-natured, and isn't that amazing considering that at age thirty-four he's the biggest nightclub promoter in the city—maybe the biggest nightclub promoter in the whole country, for that matter—and nice and nightclub don't often go together.

The second thing people say about Capponi (and he will be more than happy to affirm) is that he used to be a bad-ass heroin addict who practically came back from the dead, which makes him a folk hero in Miami Beach. His story is the recipe for greatness South Beach–style—notoriety, drugs, public flameout, and, always, forgiveness and redemption—but not necessarily in that order. He went from being the Prince of SoBe nightlife, as the *Miami Herald* crowned him at the tender age of twenty-one, to a homeless junkie who dropped out of the scene, as good as dead. A few years later he reappeared, full of humility and ambition, with a good haircut and a ready smile, clean of smack, seemingly even a nicer guy after all he'd been through.

In Miami Beach, Capponi's imprimatur on an invitation, or on the marquee above a nightclub's entrance, can materialize thousands of revelers at $20 a head admission. His parties deliver what his name has come to promise: a sexy young crowd under age thirty ready to party, 70 percent women, 30 percent men, and a sprinkling of gay men and a drag queen or two for a dash of diversity. Capponi's followers are so loyal to him that when he announced he intended to celebrate his thirty-first birthday at Nygard Cay in the Bahamas, more than two thousand people flew to the island to celebrate with him, most of whom he didn't personally know.

As for his drug habit, Capponi has been clean of drugs for seven years. "And I've never gone to an AA meeting," he said. "Never! Not once! And I've never relapsed. I'll never touch a drug again and I'm completely in the heart of nightlife. I'm surrounded by people who do drugs, and it doesn't affect me."

Yet he enjoys drinking. Having an omnipresent flute of Moët nearby helps him get through the long nights of meaningless chitchat with the thousands of strangers who want to talk to him. "You know what Jim Morrison said?" Capponi asked. Jim Morrison is his muse—not a great role model, but nevertheless. "Morrison said, 'I drink so I can talk to assholes. And I include myself in that.'" For Capponi, who is at heart a rather shy person, talking can also be hard because he's deaf in his right ear, the consequence of having a tumor removed from his brain while he was on his 1990s tricontinent odyssey to kick heroin. All night long Capponi is besieged by a procession of characters who want his attention and pump his hand, or touch his shoulder, or ask if he remembers them (he always says yes but he remembers no one's name). He treats everyone with equanimity and seems bemused and bored at the same time. On most nights at a club, he buys more than a hundred drinks for people whose names he doesn't know. That night at the Vix a woman wearing a red bustier interrupted him while he was eating and mistook him for his nemesis competitor, promoter

Tommy Pooch, and went on for a time about Pooch's success, but Capponi didn't flinch or correct the woman, he just nodded his head pleasantly and let her move on.

Aside from Capponi's good nature, there was another, simpler reason why he might have been so gracious about having ice water poured in his lap, and that was because at the moment he was being studied with great fascination by a dozen young women sitting at his table, none older than nineteen. They were part of this year's pick of the crop of freshman models from the Wilhelmina modeling agency. A week or two ago many of them were living at home with their parents, or in a college dormitory, or working as waitresses in their hometowns. Tonight they were decked out in their best finery, showing lots of tanned skin and cleavage, looking overwhelmed by their surroundings. Why were they invited to this dinner? What was expected of them? And was this expensive meal *really* free?

Michael Capponi's watchful girlfriend, Erin Henry, twenty-four, who was sitting to his left, could have told the young women that although not much in Miami Beach comes without a price, yes, this meal was free, and so would a lot of other meals and drinks be free to them in Miami Beach, in exchange for serving as ornaments. Models were coin of the realm in Miami Beach—the sizzle that helped sell the brand—and models went almost everywhere for free, because where models went, money followed. The top boutique hotels of South Beach were so eager to have models as guests and be seen in the lobby or lounging around the pool that a model could rent a room at the Raleigh Hotel for only $95 a night—$250 off the high-season price. Models also get free admission and drinks at nightclubs, even though it is illegal to admit anyone under twenty-one years of age into a nightclub in Miami Beach, except for what the *Miami SunPost* called the "young, beautiful, and famous law."

Erin could have explained a lot about life in South Beach to this neophyte class of beauties because three years ago she was sitting where they were, figuratively. Like most of them she came to Miami Beach from her hometown—in her case Portland, Oregon—to break into modeling. She signed with a top local agency, Michele Pommier, and went out on "castings." But she didn't get much work, because she was six feet tall and she had the athletic build of a volleyball player, not the long, lithe frame of a high-fashion model. To compensate she began to starve herself to look gaunt, and it worked: "I started to get booked a lot," Erin said. "I was what they called a 'money girl,' which meant that I had a dependable stream of income from catalogs, not high fashion. I'm the kind of girl that when you open a JCPenney catalog the customer feels comfortable looking at me. It wasn't glamorous, but it was a great job; six shots and you get paid three thousand dollars a day." The only problem was she couldn't eat.

In January of 2003, Erin went to a Super Bowl Sunday party at the Ritz-Carlton Hotel on Collins Avenue and a mutual friend introduced her to Michael Capponi. After chatting with her for just a minute Capponi took his friend aside and whispered, "That's the kind of girl I'm going to marry." He searched Erin out later in the afternoon and found her sitting on the grass out back, watching the ocean, and he sat next to her and they talked for an hour. She was shocked when she later found out he was promoting the party. "He pretended he had nothing to do," Erin said. "He was such a mystery. I had no idea about the heroin. I didn't know a thing about him. After that Sunday he called me for a couple of weeks and I kept putting him off, not making a date, and then one day he called and said, '*Last try.*' And so I went out with him."

Just a few weeks after they began dating, Erin fell seriously ill. She had been taking diet pills, not eating, and she was working out six hours a day to stay modeling-thin. Capponi called his physician-to-the-fast-lane-crowd, Jeff Kamlet, and Erin was whisked away to a room in Miami Heart Institute, where they discovered she had a kidney infection exacerbated by dehydration and lack of nutrients. Michael slept on the floor of her room for three days until she was discharged, and then he chartered a plane and took her to a hotel in the Bahamas to recuperate for three weeks. "I will always adore him for rescuing me like that," she said. She also loves him because he cries so easily, suddenly, unexpectedly. He'll remember something, some little moment from his past, and his eyes will fill up. And she'll always love him, she said, because he is barking crazy, quite literally—he often barks, just like a dog, to relieve tension, in the house, or out of the car window, or just that day, in the Publix supermarket, just the two of them alone in an aisle.

It was at the Publix market, in the yogurt department, that a beautiful young woman came up to her and asked if Erin wanted to ditch her shopping cart and go home with "me and my boyfriend," as the young woman put it, who was available for inspection in line at the checkout counter. The "me and my boyfriend" invitation had stopped surprising Erin. It was part of the ethos of the Beach. "Threesomes were in fashion," Erin said. "It was expected"—although not her personal cup of tea. In fact, she wasn't so certain that Miami Beach was the right place for her to begin with. "I grew up in West Linn, a suburb of Portland. My mother was a microbiologist and my father was a sales executive. I lived in a safe community where you didn't have to lock your doors at night. People talked to each other in the street."

There was no small amount of adjustment when Erin threw her lot in with Michael Capponi. She gave up her apartment and moved into his handsome house on Sunset Island 1, and she stopped modeling and started eating. She got her real estate license and a job at Sotheby's that would allow her to make her own hours. At night she went to a parade of restaurants, parties, and night-clubs with Michael, and she learned to tolerate the flirtations of other women. Three years of Miami Beach nightlife had passed and it had become more lonely than tedious, mostly because there was no one to talk to, and it was hard to make friends in the night crowd. It was hard to make friends in Miami Beach because people never stayed, they kept coming and going. Michael promised her that eventually he was going to give up nightclub promoting and get into real estate and design, but it was impossible for him to let go at the top of his game. He always said, "If you're the king of nightlife, you're the king of the city."

A photographer who worked for Capponi arrived at the Vix restaurant and took photos of all the guests at the table hugging and smiling, which would appear on Capponi's website at michael capponi.com the following week, archived along with thousands of other photographs taken at Capponi-promoted events, an effective marketing tool that drew 3 million hits a month. Erin posed for a photograph with a writer who was profiling Michael, smiling her professional smile but thinking to herself that she wasn't going to attend one of these promotional dinners again.

It is the promise of nighttime hedonism, according to the city of Miami Beach's Economic Development Office, that is the third most important draw for tourism, next to the natural gifts of climate and surf. Just as Mickey Mouse makes Orlando the number-one tourist attraction in the United States, and the slot machines and Barry Manilow bring millions of tourists to Las Vegas, in Miami Beach, in order of importance, it is the beach, big tits, and the probability of getting laid that feed the tourist engine and pack its hotels. There are more nightclubs per capita in Miami Beach than in any other city in America, and the consumption of alcohol adds $800 million yearly to the city's coffers. As for the famed Art Deco district drawing tourists, although 70 percent of the people polled by the chamber of commerce said they came to see the old buildings, "Let's face it," said former Miami Beach mayor Neisen

Kasdin, "we like to talk about the Art Deco district and preservation, but to the rest of the world Miami Beach is sex."

During high season, the nightclubs in South Beach vie to monopolize a particular night of the week and make their club that night's prime destination. At that particular moment Capponi promoted the most "nights" on the Beach. On Monday nights he promoted a party at B.E.D., a club on Washington Avenue where customers reclined on the floor on linen-covered futons and pillows while they drank Pussy Galore cocktails and ate dinner served to them on rattan trays. On Wednesday nights he promoted the wildest party of the week, the Mardi Gras–like celebration at The Forge restaurant and Glass discotheque that attracted a slightly older crowd. On Friday nights he promoted the party at Prive, the ultramodern "überlounge," as it was billed, with upholstered sofas, low hassocks, low tables, and high liquor prices. (A "setup" of an ice bucket and glasses can run anywhere from $500 to $1,000 without liquor.) On Saturday nights Capponi promoted the biggest, most bacchanalian party on the Beach at the 11,000-square-foot Mansion, which was also his biggest paycheck.

Thursday nights Capponi was at the trendy Hotel Victor. The seven-story hotel, designed in 1937 by architect L. Murray Dixon, had been treated to a gutting and reconstruction by the Hyatt Corporation in 2005, and lavishly decorated by Parisian designer Jacques Garcia in over-the-top 1930s Miami Beach style. The hip hotel also has a "vibe" manager whose job it is to program the mood music in the six different "sound areas" and burn scented candles to create the right sensual atmosphere. Rooms start at $750 a night in season.

Part of Capponi's perks (or trials) for his Thursday night promotion at the Hotel Victor was a gratis 10:00 p.m. dinner, to which he would invite a dozen young models to dress up the party at the rooftop club that would begin around midnight.

◆ ◆

IT WAS at another of those Thursday night promotional dinners that Capponi invited the girls who were living at the Karin Models agency's "models' apartment" at the Mirador condominiums. A "models' apartment" is a dormitory in which modeling agencies warehouse out-of-town recruits—typically, six vain, immature, and highly competitive young women age eighteen to twenty years old. Each pays $1,000 a month to sleep in bunk beds and share two bathrooms and all the neuroses that go with selling your beauty for validation.

"It was, in one word, hell," said Ambika Marshall, at age nineteen the oldest girl in the Mirador apartment at the beginning of that season. "All the girls talked about was the modeling business, photographers, and guys," she continued. They compared bookings and agencies and worried about what they were eating. None read anything but fashion magazines in the two weeks Ambika had been there. And unlike her roommates, Ambika hadn't been out on the town every night since she arrived a fortnight before from her hometown of Richmond, Virginia—"being the good girl that I am," she said.

She wouldn't have even gone to dinner that night at the Vix except that she was in a celebratory mood because she had finally landed her first modeling job—a runway gig at a fashion show for Roberto Cavalli—booked for the next day. She had no idea who Michael Capponi was or where she was going for certain, except that it was free, and that's how she wound up at the Hotel Victor.

Ambika was five foot ten, leggy and gamine. She was wearing a simple black dress with a V-shaped neckline, dangling earrings, and her dark hair piled up on her head. She had a warm smile and calm presence as she walked across the room to Capponi's table. Ambika—the name is Hindu for "nurturing mother"—was born in London, England, to West Indian parents from New Delhi. She was three years old when her mother took her to Richmond, Virginia, and remarried a well-to-do attorney. Ambika attended private schools and led a relatively sheltered life, and she spoke to her mother on the phone every day. She had been toying with a career in modeling since high school, and had no problem getting representation with an agency in Washington, D.C. But after a brief foray in the fashion jungle of New York City, where she was told she had a better chance for a successful career as a runway model than as a photographer's model, she headed to Miami Beach for the winter season to give it one more try in a fresh place.

"As soon as I got to the Hotel Victor," Ambika said, "I made a beeline for Erin Henry, Michael Capponi's girlfriend, because just looking at her I knew that Erin was the kind of girl I would know at home." Within an hour they felt as if they were old friends. After dinner they went up to the rooftop nightclub overlooking Ocean Drive and the beach. It had been pouring in sheets all day, and the air still felt wet and cool. The club had teak floors, striped canvas tenting, and wicker bucket chairs with canopies. The adjoining wall of the hotel's main building had been covered with a white stretch fabric, and a slide show of the revelers from previous Thursday night parties was projected on the wall.

Below them Ocean Drive stretched out like a neon-rimmed midway, a gauntlet of tourist restaurants, boozy nightclubs, and Art Deco hotels painted pastel colors like in a children's book. Architect and designer Philippe Starck called the Art Deco district "a pink fluorescent machine to pick money from tourists." There was a river of people on the street, a high-spirited carnival of gawking tourists with an occasional local sideshow freak thrown in—a man with a yellow snake draped over his shoulders, a Rastafarian hawking counterfeit CDs, a happy drunk in a Santa Claus hat. Across the street was a low stone wall with a wide grass park with benches and palm trees, and beyond that the white beach and the lapis-colored ocean under a cloudy sky.

Ambika stayed a long time, drinking and dancing, until about 2:30 a.m., when Michael and Erin asked her to go on to another party with them—insisting that it was still early, that it was *always* early in Miami Beach. But Ambika had her very first job the next day, and so they gave her a lift to the Mirador apartments and said good night. She figured chances were fifty-fifty that she would ever see them again.

The following morning at the Roberto Cavalli show, the stylist dressed Ambika in a long brown fur trench coat with only red panties on underneath. As Ambika strode from the wings onto the runway for the first time, the tent exploded with the harsh stop-action lightning of the photographers' strobes. It sent waves of adrenaline through her. The fifteen seconds she spent strutting up and down the runway in that long raincoat, flashing the red panties, thrilled her, as it did the audience. "I felt so hot," she remembered. "My heart was jumping out of my chest."

That night Erin and Michael surprised her by calling and asking her to celebrate her first job with them. Ambika was still wearing the professional hairdo and makeup from the runway show and she was glowingly beautiful. Michael and Erin took her to dinner at Casa Tua, an Italian restaurant with a clublike private dining room upstairs, and later to the nightclub Prive, where the security guards separated the crowds of people for Capponi like Moses parting the Red Sea and ushered him and his guests inside to the VIP area. Ambika danced until she was exhausted.

After that night Erin and Michael "took her up." She went out with them practically every night, everywhere, from one great party to another. During the day she went to an occasional audition, or to the beach with girlfriends, or met Erin for lunch on Lincoln Road. On Saturday afternoons she partook in the ritual of taking Michael's fifty-three-foot Sunseeker out to a sand bar about two miles south of Point Biscayne and anchoring to have lunch. Michael would show off for everybody by passionately waterskurfing behind the boat, and later they had a bottle of wine and Ambika and Erin stretched out in the sun on the back of the boat while Michael retreated into his BlackBerry.

The little city engulfed her with pleasure. The weather was always perfect, the trade winds intoxicated her, and she was golden tan from lolling on the beach. Everywhere she turned there were beautiful young people. As part of Michael Capponi's entourage she met a passel of celebrities. She went to so many glamorous parties in mansions and penthouses and nightclubs and hotels—two or three a night, all punctuated by the strobe lights of photographers, taking her picture as though she was a star—that it soon became an amalgam, undifferentiated pleasure, until one particular Saturday night when Michael and Erin called to say they were going to take her to a party at the estate of the notorious real estate developer Thomas Kramer, who owned the most expensive private house in Miami Beach, at the most expensive address, Star Island.*

LIKE SO many beautiful things in Miami Beach, Star Island is artificial. A scant 2,100 feet long and 1,000 feet wide, it was dredged up from the bottom of Biscayne Bay in 1917 by the real estate company of Carl Fisher, the first of nineteen man-made islands that were built to buttress the bay side of Miami Beach and increase waterfront real estate. Despite the island's evocative name, it is shaped not like a star but like an attenuated oval, to create as much waterfront footage as possible. At the northern end Fisher built an elegant yacht club and began selling waterfront lots for

---

*Another private island, Fisher Island, is reportedly the most expensive address in the Miami area—some say in the entire United States—but it's not a part of Miami Beach.

$200 a foot on what real estate brochures of the time called "The Isle of Enchantment."

A century later Star Island is still enchanted, perhaps even possessed. Its fifty-four mansions are the homes of some of the most famous personalities of our time, including TV host Rosie O'Donnell; entertainment entrepreneur Sean "Diddy" Combs; the singer Gloria Estefan and her husband, Emilio; recording industry executive Tommy Mottola and his wife, Mexican superstar Thalia; billionaire businessman Phillip Frost, the owner of IVAX pharmaceuticals; and Stuart A. Miller, president and CEO of Lennar, the largest builder of homes in America.

The island is accessible by land only from the MacArthur Causeway, over a two-lane bridge illuminated at night by white glass plinths, like a celestial runway. It has only one grand, elliptical street, Star Island Drive, with a wide, landscaped meridian studded by palm trees and ringed with the protective gates to fifty-four fantasy mansions of every style and architectural persuasion. Unfortunately for the prominent residents of Star Island, its greatest attraction—that it's an island—is also its greatest bane; all the backyards of all the houses are on Biscayne Bay, which is a public waterway. This means that from morning until dusk, tour boats circle the island like sharks around a rowboat while tour guides, in two languages, identify the houses of the rich and famous over piercing loudspeakers, frequently using the names of celebrities who don't even live there, such as Julio Iglesias and Madonna. The high-end shoe designer Donald J. Pliner got so frustrated hearing his Moorish mansion described as belonging to Sylvester Stallone that he personally called the tour-boat companies and corrected them, so now at least he hears his own name when the sightseeing boats go by.

Not every resident is as good humored about the attention as Donald Pliner. The constant scrutiny was misery for Star Island's biggest draw, Miami Heat center Shaquille O'Neal. Before O'Neal, the only other black person to live on Star Island, where deed restrictions prohibited the sale of property to blacks, was boxing promoter Don King. After he joined the Miami Heat, O'Neal paid $19 million for his eight-bedroom, ten-bath mansion, with a two-bedroom guest cottage, indoor racquetball court, three hundred feet of waterfront, and a swimming pool in which he had a Superman insignia tiled in the bottom. One big selling point for O'Neal was that the house had been built for another Miami Heat center, six-foot-eleven Rony Seikaly, who had the doors custom-built eight feet high, which meant that seven-foot-one O'Neal didn't have to duck. He did have to duck outside, though. O'Neal's three hundred feet of Biscayne Bay waterfront was packed with vessels of every description, like a boating convention, crammed with paparazzi and fans with binoculars and telescopes. Because the boaters were in public waterways, the authorities were unable to make them leave, even at night. O'Neal responded by erecting two colossal lighting poles with high-wattage floodlights focused into Biscayne Bay to blind prying eyes and foil cameras.

Unfortunately, the lights also blinded the residents of a huge condominium building on West Avenue in Miami Beach. The condo owners made a polite plea to O'Neal to have the lights extinguished or refocused, but O'Neal had little sympathy. "If they don't like it, tell them to pull the shades," he told a reporter, and he threatened to double his lights to four poles. In the end, the paparazzi and fans ruined the Star Island house for him, and in a little less than a year, O'Neal put the house on the market for $32 million, $13 million more than he had paid for it. He was so angry he threatened to leave Miami altogether and move to Fort Lauderdale. By the fall of 2007 O'Neal and his wife, Shaunie, were in the middle of a divorce and Shaq had moved out, leaving Shaunie, their four kids, his mother-in-law, a nanny, a chef, housekeepers, and estate managers behind. O'Neal almost had a buyer for the house in superstar baseball player Alex "A-Rod" Rodriguez, who signed a contract but backed out after a judge ruled Shaunie and the entourage were allowed to stay there until O'Neal found them another place to live. In 2008, with no buyer in sight, O'Neal reduced the price of the property to $29 million.

The island's lack of privacy was also the undoing of *Miami Vice* actor Don Johnson's brief romance with Star Island. The hit TV series had catapulted him to national stardom, and in February of 1986 Johnson purchased an undeveloped two-acre lot on Star Island for $800,000, intending to make Miami Beach his home. When his hapless real estate broker divulged the sale to the press, Johnson sued the man for $2 million for invasion of privacy, claiming that it was going to "cost a fortune," according to his lawyers, for extra security now that the public knew the nation's hippest TV cop was going to live on Star Island. Johnson not only won a settlement from the real estate broker for an undisclosed amount, but in August of 1987, claiming the city of Miami Beach was ungrateful to him for all he had done in uplifting its image, he sold his land for $1.39 million, a tidy profit, and quit Miami Beach altogether.

Ironically, although the island is exclusive, its main street is not legally private. The guard booth at the entrance is more of an amenity and psychological barrier because there is no authority to stop anyone from coming onto the grassy meridian, which is public ground. The residents were sharply reminded of this in 2006 when two hundred janitors from the University of Miami, on strike for higher pay, invaded the island and held a protest picnic because three board members of the university, including Gloria Estefan, owned homes on Star Island.

Security on the island is a problem. In 1998, while Estefan and her husband were away on vacation, $250,000 worth of watches were stolen from their home, and their compound has now become command central for a state-of-the-art security and surveillance system that blankets the island with discreetly positioned security cameras.

Although the island is not a chummy place—it's hardly the kind of community where you'd meet a neighbor walking a dog—for the most part people get along, even with high-strung personalities rubbing property and egos. The home of Rosie O'Donnell and her partner, Kelli Carpenter, and their brood of kids abuts the property of music impresario Sean "Diddy" Combs, not an auspicious pairing since O'Donnell is seriously into her children and a quiet home life and Combs is seriously into his party life. He has held huge promotional events at his house and blasts music at night over outdoor speakers. Once he set off a fireworks display that frightened O'Donnell's kids, and their dog "peed himself whimpering in terror," Rosie wrote in her blog.

The mansion in which the O'Donnells live was once the headquarters of the Ethiopian Zion Coptic Church, whose leaders paid $270,000 for the property in 1975. The Ethiopian Zion Coptic Church was unusual in that it had no Ethiopians, Zionists, or Coptics, but it did have an amenable leader named Thomas Francis Reilly Jr., otherwise known as Brother Louv. Brother Louv's teachings advocated smoking marijuana as part of the church's religious ritual, and he considered pot a sacrament protected by the law. The Ethiopian Zion Coptic Church generated huge amounts of publicity, including a segment on CBS TV's *60 Minutes*. Things came to a head when the Coptic children appeared on local TV news taking tokes on marijuana spliffs and the outraged state district attorney moved in. Eventually nine members of the church were indicted for distribution of marijuana, the church was disbanded, and the property was sold.

The island may have reached its apotheosis of silliness in the 1980s with the arrival of billionaire bad boy Mohammed al-Fassi, whose sister married Prince Turki bin Abdul Aziz, the son of the king of Saudi Arabia. That familial connection gave Mohammed royal status and nearly unlimited funds to buy toys, trinkets, and houses. He wandered the globe, spending lavishly, finally coming to national fame in the United States in 1978 when he built a thirty-eight-room mansion prominently situated on Sunset Boulevard in Los Angeles, which he had painted Day-Glo green. He also hired artists to paint the pubic hair of his statuary black.

In Miami Beach Prince Turki and his clan spent some $17 million on real estate, and Star Island residents were apprehensive when al-Fassi overpaid $1.5 million for two adjoining properties on the condition that the owners pack up and leave the very next day so he could have their houses torn down. A construction crew immediately began work on a four-building compound with its own artificial mountain and five waterfalls. There were plastic pyramids as well, a thirty-foot-high mosque with gold-leaf ceilings, a bowling alley, bathroom fixtures that cost $300,000, and a two-story clock tower with a computerized Swiss clock that would announce the time in twelve languages. Al-Fassi fled America in June of 1982 with a stack of bills, an unfinished estate, and an ex-wife after him. The property was abandoned, with tons of marble lying around, the doors open. The Miami Beach City Commission voted to demolish the estate in 1983.

Perhaps the most amusingly eccentric resident on Star Island was its very first, Edward R. Green, who bought the mansion that Fisher had built on the north end of the island as a yacht club and made it his home from 1925 until he died in 1936. Known as "Ned" Green, he was the son of the tightfisted "Witch of Wall Street," Hetty Green, who earned her nickname from the black clothes she wore when she visited her banker. Hetty Green amassed a $140 million fortune in the 1920s—$500 million in today's dollars. She was so cheap that she refused to light the candles on her birthday cake so they could be reused every year. When Ned was fourteen he dislocated his knee, and Hetty, refusing to pay for a doctor, took him to free clinics to be treated. Gangrene set in and his leg had to be amputated. Ned was fitted with a wooden leg, which didn't seem to hamper his many relationships with

women. He kept a virtual harem of pretty things in his house on
Star Island.

His mother might have been a miser, but Ned was not. He was
driven around Miami in a glass-roofed car, and he had a replica of a
Mississippi riverboat built on his dock with a 400-seat auditorium.
He once entertained by inviting the Ringling Brothers Circus to
perform. Since he had only one leg, he had all the toilets in his
house built very high, so his guests would find their feet dangling
in front of them when they sat down. This proved to be such an
amusement to him that he had secret peepholes cut into the bathroom walls so he could watch.

He wasn't the only Star Island resident who liked to watch.

There was also Thomas Kramer.

"To ANOTHER lousy day in Paradise!" Thomas Kramer toasted his
guests in a big booming voice, a schoolboy's mischievous grin on
his rosy lips. His huge Star Island estate stretched out behind
him—the tiled patio and royal palms, a floodlit swimming pool,
cabanas and a sauna on Biscayne Bay, and a yacht moored at the
private dock. The night smelled of lavender, sprayed into the air
like a fine mist by a machine to keep away mosquitoes.

"To Paradise!" the guests shouted in answer, raising their
glasses. One of the guests, a kittenish young woman with dark hair
and green eyes, was wearing a T-shirt that read "Good Girls Go to
Heaven, Bad Girls Go to 5 Star Island."

"I was mesmerized by Thomas Kramer's house," Ambika said,
yet from the start she felt something foreboding about its owner.
Kramer behaved like an out-of-control child in the body of a
6-foot 3-inch, strapping adult. He looked as though he might
have just stepped out of a beer garden during Oktoberfest, his face
flush from singing German marching songs and drinking beer,
only it was $300 bottles of champagne he was drinking. He had a

Lil' Abner shock of golden blond hair and a strong, Germanic nose and ice-blue eyes. He was wearing elaborately embroidered jeans with a white dress shirt opened one button too many.

Years ago, when South Beach was a slum, in one breathtaking $40 million splurge, Kramer bought up entire blocks of real estate like a man running up and down the aisles in a supermarket throwing groceries into a shopping cart, including thirteen waterfront acres, eighteen apartments in South Pointe Towers (the condominium building in which he then lived with his beautiful wife, Catrine Burda), the Ocean Haven Hotel, the Leonard Hotel, and the Diamond Apartments, all on Ocean Drive, and the Playhouse Bar on Collins Avenue, the Flagler Fidelity Building on Lincoln Road, and half a dozen rental properties. At one point he owned an estimated 20 percent of the southern tip of South Beach. That property today would be worth fifty times what he paid for it—that is, if he still owned all of it.

Kramer was a stockbroker from Frankfurt, Germany, who had earned and lost several fortunes. After he made $120 million in one day shorting gold prices, the German newspapers nicknamed him "Golden nose." In his twenties he dated Princess Yasmin Khan, who said that when she looked into Kramer's blue eyes she saw "dollar signs." Kramer had far-flung investments and kept offices in the World Trade Center in New York before he discovered Miami Beach and made it his home. He was instrumental in the revitalization of South Beach. He built the first of the new wave of luxury condominium towers in South Pointe called the Portofino Yacht Club that served to jump-start the deluge of upscale development in the area.

At it would turn out, the money that Kramer had been spending wasn't all his own. The money was from a German billionaire named Siegfried Otto, who owned the printing company that printed all official Federal Republic of Germany documents and legal tender, including passports, stock and bond certificates, and the German deutschmark. He was also Kramer's father-in-law, the stepfather of Catrine, whose mother had recently married the publishing billionaire. Otto allegedly gave his new stepson-in-law $145 million to invest in Miami real estate. When Otto died in 1994, his heirs wanted an accounting. Kramer claimed that the money was a loan and the Matisse painting he bought with it belonged to him. Otto's relatives—including Kramer's own mother-in-law—sued him for misappropriation, fraud, and for ownership of 5 Star Island, claiming he stole $60 million from them. Catrine, loyal to her mother, divorced Kramer in 1995. In 2000, under legal pressure from the heirs of Siegfried Otto, Kramer was forced to sell most of his real estate holdings to the Related Companies. But he remains an extraordinarily rich man. And a mischievous one.

Over the years Kramer has gotten himself into all sorts of trouble. He'd recently outraged the patrons at the steak house Prime 112 by having a big-buxomed woman crawl under his table and perform fellatio on him while he and his friends were having dinner. He has been sued at least twice for sexual harassment, and in London his secretary accused him of raping her, but she dropped the case before it went to court. More recently he was accused of touching a young boy in the bathroom of the Rainbow Room in Manhattan, which was settled out of court.

Kramer makes no apologies for his behavior. In fact, he revels in his reputation. He will be the first to tell you that he's got the devil in him. The devil—and the color red—is Kramer's theme. His short-lived South Beach discotheque was called Hell, and its sign is still evident hanging along the cobblestone patios of the outbuildings as one enters his estate. The red-toned Mediterranean main house is named "Casa el Diabilito"—the Little Devil's House, though there was nothing little about it—a compound of six buildings that included an office complex, a three-bedroom guesthouse, two staff quarters, and a nine-car garage with marble floors.

The interior decor was *Moulin Rouge* meets *The Damned*—red walls, upholstered sofas and chairs with gilt frames, marble busts, a taxidermied head of a giraffe, dragons painted on the ceiling, and floor-to-ceiling paintings of landscapes and still lifes. In the media room there was a huge red divan big enough for twenty people to lie down on and watch TV. The ceiling of the dining room was covered with a trompe l'oeil of gods and goddesses with big breasts throwing food down at the diners, and the dining room table was embedded with two gold "stripper poles" for what Kramer called "calorie-free dessert."

The estate displayed another motif: voyeurism. Prominent signs warned visitors that security cameras were photographing everything that happened in the house—including in all the bathrooms and the nine bedrooms of the main building. Kramer had been taping everything for years, and the British tabloids once ran a story about him headlined A SPY CAMERA IN EVERY ROOM. Kramer's penchant for kink was no secret. He had no secrets. He had much pride and little shame. His exploits and peccadilloes were extensively reported in the press, none of which seemed to particularly perturb him, and much of which evidently pleased him, since he posted most of his press on his personal website, thomaskramer.com, along with videos and party pictures.

Among the other guests that night at Kramer's party was the famed "breast man" in Miami, Dr. Leonard Roudner, also known as "Dr. Boobner." Dr. Roudner is the area's busiest breast-enhancement surgeon, a vocation he practices exclusive of all other plastic surgery: "I'm so inundated with clients." He is also so consumed with mammaries that the swimming pool of his house on Palm Island is shaped like a breast. In choosing his specialty, Dr. Roudner was no fool; breast-enhancement surgery was the number one type of plastic surgery performed in Miami. Roudner had a long waiting list of patients and charged an average of $7,000 for implants. He was so busy that he operated on five women every day of the week and squeezed in two more implants every other Saturday. "People are very exposed here," he said, "and South Americans love cosmetic surgery." He'd even shaped the breasts of three generations of women in the same family. Breast connoisseurs in Miami Beach claim they can tell a Boobner breast job from across the street. He called the trademark rounded, pert breasts he created "Goddess Breasts," which seemed to be in evidence on the attractive young women who arrived at the party with him.

Kramer offered to give Capponi and Erin and Ambika a tour of the house. "Everybody wants to see the bedroom," Kramer bellowed in his thick accent. He led them up a corkscrew poured-concrete staircase that spiraled three times to the gallery leading to the master bedroom. Outside the door there was a red light and a sign that read SEX. His bedroom was a large room with windows overlooking Biscayne Bay. It had a red ceiling, a red rug, and a king-size bed in an alcove. There was a red fire extinguisher disconcertingly mounted on the wall next to the bed, as if he expected pyrotechnics. Kramer also gleefully displayed a trunk of sex toys and referred to an adjoining room as the "recovery room." There was also a nearby "safe room" in case of a robbery, in which Kramer reportedly kept machines guns, handguns, and a bazooka. Kramer also showed his guests his walk-in closet. "There must have been fifty pairs of red pants," Erin said.

Ambika remembered the "straps on the ceiling right where the bed was," she said, "and he had all these photographs of orgies; it wasn't in secret or anything." Kramer also had photos on his cell phone that he showed everyone, taken in this bedroom, of a woman, his girlfriend he said, on the bed on her hands and knees, smiling at the camera with her ass up in the air, peeking out from under a flimsy negligee. Then the next photo was—Kramer in the same negligee in the same pose.

Ambika was speechless. Kramer seemed delighted she was shocked. He became even more animated and demonstrative, and as soon as they could break away, Capponi and the two young woman hurried back downstairs, where the party was getting boisterous. A woman with suntanned breasts wearing a crocheted top came up to Kramer and kissed him. He pinched her brown erect nipples poking through the yarn and everyone laughed. At a certain point it seemed as if some of the women were unbuttoning their blouses completely, and one of the men took off his shirt. "It got very weird," Ambika said, and Michael and Erin started giving each other nervous looks. The three bid Thomas Kramer adieu and got the hell out of there.

Thirteen
SOUTH BEACH STORY

Time? Oh don't ask me that. Here in Miami it's just light first and then it's dark and then it's light again.

—Robert Cummings in *Moon Over Miami*, 1941

A few moments after leaving Star Island, they were in Michael Capponi's car headed back over the causeway to the next stop of the evening, a birthday party for Madonna's brother, Christopher Ciccone. It was being held at the Paris, a former Art Deco movie theater on Washington Avenue that now operated as a nightclub. The atmosphere there was a whole lot lighter. And pinker. "It was really wonderful at the Paris," Ambika said. "Madonna's brother is gay, and there were lots of gay guys and drag queens everywhere with six-inch heels and big white hair and fake boobs. Erin seemed to know all of their names. There was also another model there that I knew," Ambika said, "this guy who was with Michele Pommier's agency, and he introduced me to another Pommier model, a guy named Matt Loewen, who was from Vancouver."

The club was noisy and Ambika had hardly said hello to Matt when her cell phone rang and she was buried in text-messaging. In another minute Michael and Erin wanted to move on to the next party, and Ambika and Matt never said another word to each other that night.

Matt Loewen doesn't remember meeting Ambika at the Paris, although he remembered Christopher Ciccone's birthday party well. It was a small but depressing moment of reckoning for the twenty-year-old. He kept wondering, "What the fuck did I get myself into?" He sat brooding on a banquette amid the flashing lights of the club, watching the drag queens and the muscle boys on the dance floor while Judy Garland in *The Wizard of Oz* played on a large screen over his head. He was disappointed to discover that Madonna's brother was gay because he'd hoped he was being taken to a straight club, but that didn't bother him as much as what had happened at the last party.

He'd just come from a publication celebration for the book *Lipstick Jungle,* written by Candace Bushnell, the author of the advice columns that were transformed into the hit television series *Sex and the City.* Bushnell was in Miami along with hundreds of other authors to participate in the Miami Book Fair International, the largest nonindustry book fair in the nation, and there were parties for authors and their books all over Miami Beach. This particular party was at an Italianate mansion with a piazza and beautiful fountains situated right on the water—Matt didn't know *which* water exactly because he didn't know where he was half the time in Miami Beach, everything was so new. He was there for two months before he realized that most of the time he'd "been walking around in circles."

When he walked in the door of the party, six foot two, with shaved head and blue eyes, in his skintight T-shirt and body-fitting jeans, he realized that all of the other guests were much older than he was, and more dressed up, although no one seemed offended by his jeans and T-shirt. In fact, in just a few minutes he was the cynosure of attention, sparking the interest of several photographers who were covering the party. Next to Candace Bushnell herself,

Matt was the most photographed person. That's when the two older women with Goddess Breasts asked him to dance.

Two weeks earlier Matt had been working as a shipping clerk at his father's auto-parts distributorship in Coquitlam, a suburb of Vancouver, British Columbia, after flunking out of his second semester in college, mostly from disinterest. He lived in his parents' basement and spent his days hanging out with friends, lifting weights at the gym, and dating a local girl who went to the University of Connecticut, whom he dumped the first week after arriving in Miami Beach. He was discovered by a Vancouver fitness photographer who saw Matt's photograph on a website called ratemybody.com, where, Matt said, one of his girlfriends had posted his shirtless picture. Among the thousands of muscled American youths whose pictures find their way onto the web, Matt's stood out. His head was shaved and he had a brooding, tough-but-sensitive-guy look. His body had almost no fat, and his musculature was so defined and well proportioned that it exempted him from the modeling prohibition against prominent tattoos like his, a stalking lion beautifully etched in muted colors, prowling over his left shoulder and down across his pectoral muscle. The fitness photographer offered to take a few headshots of him, and Matt figured he had nothing to lose. As fate would have it, the very first shot—Matt with his hand on his head, looking skyward, his blue eyes gentle and yearning—became his most important sales tool. The photographer showed the photograph to a local Vancouver agency named Richards, and Matt signed with them for representation, again as a laugh, expecting nothing.

It was this contemplative photograph of Matt that caught the attention of Christian Alexander Garces, twenty-seven, a booking agent at the Pommier agency in Miami Beach. Garces saw Matt's photo on the Richards agency website while trolling the Internet for new talent. Garces never got tired of looking at beautiful young men and women. A former fashion illustrator who grew up in

Brooklyn, New York, he'd moved to Miami Beach five years before and quickly become a connoisseur of beautiful people. "I'm stimulated by beauty, so I've always loved looking at pretty people," he said. The models loved him back. Garces was the top booker at the Pommier agency, where bookers made around $60,000 a year. A booker is the model's career lifeline, an adviser, booster, mother superior, and jealous older sister and/or brother. All of Garces's models called him "Crispy."

"Matt's body was gorgeously insane," Garces said, "and I showed his pictures around the booking table at the agency and basically everybody said, 'I wouldn't kick him out of bed, but . . . he'll never get work.'" Garces thought differently. "I looked at his photos and saw money. I knew he'd make a ton of money. So I said to Michele Pommier, 'Give me a month with him.'"

Pommier, one of the biggest names in the local modeling business, reluctantly agreed to front Matt's airfare from Vancouver to Miami Beach, as well as advancing him one month's rent at one of the models' apartments, all of which would be recovered by the company when he began to earn fees. Matt was on a plane to Miami one week later, and even before he arrived, on the basis of his photographs downloaded from the Internet, Garces was able to book him for a six-page bathing-suit layout in a local glossy in which he was featured in several photos wearing a tiny spandex swimsuit.

His second job was for superstar photographer Bruce Weber, a golden endorsement in the modeling world, like getting an affirmation from the pope. Weber photographed Matt for a bathing-suit layout in *VMAN, Vogue*'s men's fashion magazine, only Matt wasn't even wearing the bathing suit mentioned in the caption. Matt was naked, with his leg demurely positioned, the bathing suit resting on his shoulder as an excuse for the provocative photograph. When the shoot was over Weber wanted to work with Matt again. "You'd be very good for something I have coming up for

Abercrombie and Fitch," Weber told him. Matt did his second job for Weber the following week. "It felt like it was a reality show, or a game show," Matt said, "because Weber brought thirty of us from all over the world to Fort Lauderdale, and every day models would be eliminated from the shoot, until the last day there were just me and four guys left."

Christian Garces had found something. If Matt's career went on like this, and if Matt was as good on the runway as he was in front of a camera, he could break out, become the Next New Thing. If he played his cards right, by the end of the season, he could have made $75,000.

That Saturday night at Candace Bushnell's book party was another one of Matt's nights out on the town with Garces, who'd taken Matt to every gay bar in the city, which Matt benignly tolerated. That particular night Christian was entertaining an important client from a major department-store chain, a man who was in the position to give Matt a lot of catalog work if he desired. Matt was prompted by Garces to play up to the client and charm him, but he was distracted by the fun of Bushnell's party and drifted off by himself. There was a disc jockey and people were dancing, and Chinese food was being served in little take-out boxes. Matt hadn't eaten all day and he began to wolf down the food, and he knocked back several drinks. He was starting to feel good, standing around watching people dance, when, he said, "These older ladies came up to me and invited me to dance with them, so I started dancing." Matt was a pretty good dancer, comfortable with himself, and people began to take notice of him and a photographer took his picture. That's when Christian stepped in and asked Matt to stop dancing and pulled him aside.

"You can't do that," Garces said.

"Why not?" Matt asked, stunned that Garces had taken him off the dance floor.

"Because those older women were making you look bad."

"I guess I had to act suave," he said later. "I mean, I did kind of stick out a little bit, but I was just being myself. It wasn't as if I had an image to keep up. I was so taken aback, I didn't say anything for quite a while. I was kind of bummed out by that incident, like, what have I gotten myself into? And after, we went to the Paris, and it turned out that Madonna's brother was gay and that most of the guys at the party were gay. There was no one there I really wanted to talk to."

By the time they got back to Christian's apartment it was two-thirty in the morning. They smoked a joint and Matt did some lines of coke and sat back on the sofa, stoned, and Christian began to tell Matt that he better get comfortable around gay men if he was going to be successful in the modeling business. Christian told him that inevitably Matt was going to be put in a compromising position by a photographer or a client. Christian told him that he had a signal worked out with the models he represented, if a photographer or a client was pressuring them: "If you ever feel uncomfortable you text-message me '911.'" Christian explained that he would then call the photographer or client and stage a phony emergency to get the model out of there.

Matt was thinking, "Am I going to do this? *The hell no!*" He stood up and excused himself and headed out the door.

"Where are you going?" Garces shouted after him.

Matt started walking toward the one-bedroom apartment he shared with another model, Ricardo, who was from Brazil and also represented by the Pommier agency. He called Ricardo on his cell phone to see if he was at the apartment, a courtesy because he had already walked in on Ricardo in the shower with some girl, but when Ricardo answered his cell phone it turned out he wasn't in the apartment, he was at Snatch—the ideal name of any Miami Beach club—a club that had opened only a week before and was an instant smash. "Ricardo said it was still early and I should come over to Snatch and have a few drinks and I said to him, 'I'm broke. How am I going to get in to Snatch?' and Ricardo said, 'Just say you're a model with Michele Pommier.'"

Matt had never tried this "I'm a model" ploy before, but he was only a block away from Snatch, and nothing ventured nothing gained, so he walked over to the club, where there was a big crowd around the front door and a couple of bouncers as sentinels. Matt stepped up to one of the bouncers, and with all the assurance he could muster he said, "I'm a model with Michele Pommier" and sure enough, like Ali Baba saying "Open sesame" in front of the cave of the Forty Thieves, the bouncers stepped aside and allowed Matt to pass for free.

Inside the club it was a madhouse, noisy and fun and loose. Snatch was a rock-and-roll club with live music and a quasi-Western motif, with the waitresses dressed in frilly bustiers, a mechanical bull by the door, bar seats that were saddles, and "stripper" poles so customers could pole-dance. Matt was looking around for Ricardo when he accidentally stepped in the way of one of the waitresses who was carrying a tray full of drinks. "She was quite hot," Matt said. He was so taken with her that he just stood there and she had to grab his arm to move him out of the way, and he playfully grabbed her arm back and that started them talking. Her name was Hilly and she was twenty-six years old and she had the body of a *Penthouse* centerfold, not the slim, delicate look of the models Matt had met in South Beach. She began to give Matt free drinks whenever he ran dry. He told her that later that night he was hoping to go to Space, a huge nightclub in the city of Miami that was open all night, because Deep Dish, two disc jockeys whom Matt really liked, were playing there. Hilly liked Deep Dish too and they decided to go together when she got off from work at five in the morning. "I told her that I was going home to nap," Matt said, "and that she should call me on my cell phone when she was ready to go."

When Matt got back to his apartment, Ricardo told Matt that in a few minutes "some crazy rich Russian chick" was going to pick them up in a limousine and take them to a party in a mansion. Ricardo didn't really know who the girl was, or where the party was, but it didn't seem to matter. Matt felt like he had dropped down the rabbit hole in search of the tea party, or in search of *some* party.

Soon enough a limousine arrived and Matt and Ricardo piled into the backseat, where they found waiting a beautiful, blond, and evidently very rich Russian girl who didn't speak English well; Matt forgot her unpronounceable name almost instantly. Ricardo didn't speak English well either, so they spent the time in the rear of the limousine in a clumsy pantomime until they pulled up in front of a large, white, modern house with glass walls overlooking the bay. The door was unlocked and there didn't seem to be a host, or at least one who bothered to notice they had arrived. There were lots of drugs, and guests were smoking grass and doing discreet bumps of coke. Some people were on Ecstasy, which was available for the asking. The music was loud and guests were broken up into cliques, according to what drug they were on. Beyond the living room's glass walls there was a glistening infinity pool whose flat surface seemed to end in Biscayne Bay's dark reflection of the Miami skyline. "I ended up going upstairs and doing lines," Matt said. There were about ten people in a dimly lit bedroom, and when the group was stoned enough, "We played a game," Matt said, "where I did a line of coke off of some girl's body, and then a girl did a line off of me."

Matt was really buzzed by the time Hilly, the waitress from Snatch, called him on his cell phone around 5:00 a.m. and asked him to meet her at an apartment at the Flamingo, one of several large complexes filled with young singles along West Street. Matt had no idea how he was going to get to the Flamingo since he didn't have any money for a taxi, but before he could figure it out,

Ricardo told him that the party was shifting to yet another mansion where there were more drugs and more people, and the Russian girl, along with a group of brand-new friends, were piling into her waiting limousine and Matt followed. Ten minutes later the whole gang was dropped off at the new party in another neighborhood. Matt was in a daze, so instead of going inside the house he hung back and managed to convince the limo driver to take him to the Flamingo. Matt remembers with clarity the experience of being high in the back of a limousine by himself, the dark tinted windows up, gliding silently through the streets of South Beach.

At the Flamingo, Hilly called for a taxi—which she paid for—and they headed across the causeway. Space is immense, encompassing 25,000 square feet on two levels, with an open patio and a dozen or so bars. Dancing at Space is cultlike. The club is open only on Saturday nights and it holds a twenty-four-hour liquor license—unusual in Miami—which means that the booze never stops and the time of day is of no concern. The dance scene is hardcore and tribal, the music high-energy house/dub/techno, very loud, with one of the most powerful sound systems ever designed for a nightclub. The big moment at Space is sunrise, when dawn breaks behind the city of Miami Beach across the bay. "The morning sun was so bright," Matt said, "that everybody had to wear sunglasses with all the drugs in them." There is an indelible image in his mind of a thousand stoned people with sunglasses on dancing frantically in the orange dawn.

"We ended up leaving Space around noon on Sunday," Matt recalled, "and I went back to the Flamingo with Hilly. We smoked a joint and I was ready to go to bed, but Hilly pulled a tablet of Ecstasy from her pocket and crushed it up into two lines and snorted one. So I said to myself, 'Whatever . . . when in Rome,' and I did the other line. But even though I had just snorted Ecstasy, I was exhausted, mixed with the weed I was smoking, and the second my head hit the pillow I went to sleep."

Matt woke up at six on Sunday night. He and Hilly ordered a pizza—paid for by Hilly—and they watched a movie on TV, and Matt left at nine and walked back to the apartment he shared with Ricardo while around him the perpetual nightlife of Miami Beach was revving itself up again.

He never had sex with Hilly.

"I ran into that waitress once in a while," Matt remembered dreamily. He reflected on the evening. "I wouldn't call that a typical model story," he said. "But it could be a typical South Beach story."

Fourteen

WEDNESDAY NIGHT
AT THE FORGE

Miami Beach is its own reality.
—ALVIN MALNIK

It was nearing midnight on a Wednesday night at The Forge restaurant and Glass discotheque, and the atmosphere of giddy mayhem was gaining in momentum, just like the salsa/disco/conga music was getting louder decibel by decibel until the infectious beat had people dancing at their tables, beautiful women holding champagne glasses above their heads, the red-faced waiters in tuxedos bullying their way through the crush while balancing trays of lamb osso buco and $65 bone-in eighteen-ounce filets mignons under shiny silver domes.

Most of the women at The Forge were in their twenties and thirties, tanned and worked out, South Beach supernumeraries with white smiles, perfect veneers, Goddess Breasts, and tattoos on their breasts and ankles or at the bottom of their spines just above the cracks of their buttocks, which sometimes showed along with the straps of their thongs. There were also older women with Goddess Breasts, dressed in short tight dresses, accompanied by men with small bellies and pastel dress shirts who recognized each other from Delmar, New Jersey. Sitting on a small banquette in the bar area were two stunning young women in their twenties, expensively dressed, sharing a portion of French fries served in the Belgian manner in a waxed-paper cone with mayonnaise. Near them, standing at the bar, a zaftig woman in her forties sipped her margarita and shook her behind to the music while her companion showed the rest of the bar his territorial imperative by cupping her buttock in his palm, to which she responded by stepping up a bit, the anxious movements of a horse about to be hooved. A few of the women looked like professional escorts, but it was hard to tell; if they were escorts, they weren't $200 hookers, they were top of the line, Miami Beach Maserati call girls.

The Forge's owner, Shareef Malnik, a former attorney and professional speedboat racer, is bemused by stories of hookers at The Forge. "The high-class hookers these days don't look like hookers," he said. "In Miami Beach, where everybody is naked, it's hard to tell the difference."

Hookers or not, The Forge is decorated like a nineteenth-century New Orleans brothel, with more stained glass than the Vatican, including the main Dome Room, where a chandelier purported to be from the Paris Opéra house hangs from a backlit stained-glass ceiling purported to be from Trinity Church in New York, and on a brick wall purported to be from the Old Absinthe House in New Orleans are hung a set of fourteen-foot brass wall sconces purported to be from Napoléon's bedchamber at Waterloo. In each case, the provenance, like The Forge's clientele, is not easily verified.

That particular Wednesday night, the B-list comedian Pauly Shore was celebrating his birthday at a big round table with helium balloons tied to the backs of the chairs. Across the aisle the prize-fighter Lennox Lewis sat at a table that put him literally back to back with former Miami Dolphin Bernie Kosar, which in turn put Kosar a few feet to the right of Elaine Lancaster, the phenomenal female impersonator, who was having supper with *Miami Herald* nightclub columnist Lesley Abravanel. Tennis player Boris Becker, who lives in Miami Beach, was at a small side table with two friends. A magician in black tie managed to wend his way from table to table, trying to entertain. "I might be a magician," he said to a group of disinterested patrons, "but I'm not a mind reader. You have to tell me what card you were thinking of."

Although The Forge's food is good and the crowd is fun to watch, the thing that makes The Forge the most fascinating is not that last night John Travolta sat in the same place Michael Jordan is sitting now, but because in 1977 Meyer Lansky's stepson, Richard Schwartz, gunned down Craig Teriaca, reportedly a mobster, over a fight about $10, and Schwartz's body was later found in his Cadillac; and because Shareef's name was Mark when he was bar mitzvahed, before he converted to Islam and married into the family of Prince Turki bin Abdul Aziz, the son of the king of Saudi Arabia, who gave Shareef and his wife, Hoda, a $2 million wedding present; and most of all, because Shareef's father, the charming Alvin Malnik, seventy-four, was dubbed by the *Miami Herald* as the heir to Mob kingpin Meyer Lansky's throne—although most people don't think there's a throne anymore.

Malnik Sr. has always denied a close relationship with Lansky. One time he said he was Lansky's lawyer; then on another occasion he insisted that he'd only "met Lansky in an elevator once." Although Malnik Sr. has been under the scrutiny of federal and state prosecutors for decades—the U.S. Tax Court investigated him for twenty years—he's never been indicted for any wrongdoing, despite some rather suspicious things happening around him, such his yellow Rolls-Royce blowing up in the garage of a luxury building he once owned.

Alvin Malnik lives about thirty miles north of Miami Beach in a 35,000-square-foot waterfront Beaux Arts mansion with a white stretch limousine parked in the circular driveway. He has ten children from his multiple marriages—the last three, triplets with his present wife, Nancy, a former model whom he married in a $250,000 wedding in 1995 when he was sixty-one years old and she was twenty-five. Like his son Shareef, Alvin Malnik is pleasant and engaging. He is known in the business world as a clever deal maker and compelling negotiator, particularly for people with problems. His clients have included Frank Sinatra and Dean Martin, and Malnik recently represented the business interests of Michael Jackson. His son Shareef calls it "junk" and turns dark and angry if you ask him about his father's reported Mob ties, and polite people don't ask.

Alvin Malnik bought The Forge in 1968 so he and his friends "could have someplace to eat," and he ran it for twenty-three years before turning it over to his son in November of 1991. By the time Shareef took over the restaurant it was a relic. "The perception was that it was old, not relevant, staid," said Shareef. "I started Wednesday nights because Mickey Rourke said to me that he'd only take his mother to The Forge on Mother's Day. I thought, how can I get people there? Let me start a party one night a week." Shareef hired nightclub promoter Tommy Pooch to start Wednesday nights at The Forge, and Pooch deserves much of the credit for creating the wild mélange that Wednesday nights became.

"It's become such an overwhelming happening," said Alvin Malnik. "It's composed of so many elements that analytically you wouldn't think it could fit together."

WEDNESDAY night at The Forge, for fourteen years the longest-running "night" in Miami Beach, was now Michael Capponi's night. He was sitting at the head of a long table of twenty or so young women, keeping to himself as best he could, sipping a flute of champagne and working his BlackBerry. His girlfriend Erin, having lived through enough Wednesday nights at The Forge to last a lifetime, was happily at home. That particular night Capponi's dinner guests were an assortment of nymphets from a variety of modeling agencies on Miami Beach, much younger than the rest of the crowd, yet grown up enough to be primed for a Miami Beach adventure.

A short, nervous-looking man, with a five o'clock shadow, a gold ID bracelet on his wrist, and his expensive silk shirt hanging out of his pants, shyly approached Capponi. He bowed a little and began chattering away until Capponi shook his head no and the man backed off into the crowd looking disappointed

Capponi laughed. "That guy was telling me that he's a billionaire in telecommunications," he said. "He claims he met me before, years ago, at some club, when he was poor, and now he's very rich." The man indicated to Capponi that he was interested in meeting the girl with red hair sitting at Capponi's table and asked to be introduced. The twenty-year-old girl's name was Ronni, and even with the abundance of beautiful women in the room, she was a standout. Instead of the skimpy Miami underwear look, Ronni was wearing a tight Diane von Furstenberg cotton floral print dress that showed off her natural, full figure to great advantage. She had the winsome face of a 1930s movie star, and her magnetism was great enough that whoever walked by the table glanced in her direction for a better look. No girly cocktails for Ronni, she was knocking back Dewar's on the rocks.

In another minute a waiter appeared with a chilled bottle of Dom Pérignon in a bucket, a gift for Ronni, compliments of her admirer. Three seats down the table, Mandi Nadel, nineteen, was not amused. "That man," she said, pointing to the alleged telecommunications billionaire, "is trying to pick up my date by sending her champagne." Mandi meant her date, not her companion. To prove to everyone in the near vicinity—and the admirer who had sent the champagne—exactly what her claim to Ronni was, Mandi walked to where Ronni was sitting, pulled her out of her chair, and arched her pelvis against her. For a brief moment the two young women hugged and rubbed up against each other.

Mandi is 5 feet 9¾ inches tall, a willowy blonde, her green eyes flecked with yellow. She grew up in the Miami area and was enrolled in Florida State University, where she was taking poetry classes, and worked part-time at Brown's, a high-end shampoo and cosmetics shop on Lincoln Road. Mandi had been signed by the Irene Marie modeling agency, but her lithesome, innocent look hadn't gotten her many jobs. Her parents had paid for her apartment and college, and she wasn't supposed to be hanging out in nightclubs—back in her apartment at the Floridian there was a sign on the refrigerator door to remind her that she'd been grounded for a month—but Michael Capponi often invited her to his promotional dinners and she couldn't say no.

At first Mandi's parents had been "freaked out" when they heard their daughter was part of Capponi's entourage, but she convinced them he was a good guy. Although she'd been clubbing since she was sixteen years old, she was new to dating girls. She'd only recently acknowledged her attraction to other girls during her first ménage à trois. "It changed my sexual life," she said. "I was seeing this guy for about six months, and he was also dating this other girl, and we all ran into each other at a club. Later we went back to my apartment together. I was a wreck. She and I were cuddling and he was on the other side of the bed. I had this urge to take pictures." She didn't.

Mandi looked around the room at the crowd. "I feel like I'm too young for The Forge," she said.

Fifteen

MODELS

Moon over Miami
You know we've waiting for
A little love, a little kiss
On Miami shore.

—JOE BURKE AND EDGAR LESLIE,
"MOON OVER MIAMI," 1935

"The next time I saw Matt Loewen," Ambika Marshall said, "he was wearing surfing baggies on the beach at Fifth Street."

Matt went to the beach every day. If he was the Next Big Thing in male modeling, it certainly didn't feel like it. Instead of being filled with excitement and glamorous jobs, his days were listless. There were stretches when he had no casting calls at all, and he began sleeping until noon. When he finally crawled out of bed, he'd stare at himself in the mirror for twenty minutes and worry about every pimple on his face, or fret that he either wasn't tan enough or was too tan, and that his six-pack wasn't sufficiently ripped. He'd put on a bathing suit, brush his teeth, eat a bowl of cereal, and amble down to the beach at 5th Street, where he'd meet up with a group of other male models who didn't have any work either.

One afternoon the guys on the beach invited some of the models from the Karin Models agency to join them, and Ambika appeared. She was wearing a brand-new red-and-white gingham bikini, and as a joke somebody introduced her to Matt as a young "superstar" model.

"I believed it," Matt said, "because she was so tall and super thin and she had a beautiful body. I just assumed she worked as a model all the time."

Ambika worked less than Matt, and although she did have a beautiful body, she was also modest. While her gingham bikini might have looked small to the beholder, it was actually one size too big for her. The problem was that the top was so loose that one of her nipples kept popping out without her realizing it. Matt was so nonplussed, he didn't know what to do or say. The other male models saw the errant nipple as well, and they began communicating via text messages on their cell phones regarding the position of her aureole: "Is it in?" "Is it out?" When Matt told her about it weeks later, Ambika dissolved into shrieks of embarrassed laughter.

Late in the afternoon the group went to Matt's new apartment, a two-bedroom rental that he shared with some friends from Vancouver, and Ambika made sub sandwiches. Later they all went to a pool hall off Lincoln Road and shot pool, and after Matt and Ambika strolled over to the Sofi Lounge on 5th Street for a nightcap. "We had a really good talk on the way over," Ambika said, "and when we got to the bar I went a little crazy and started buying drinks for people on my credit card and Matt bought a round for everybody too."

Ambika found Matt unexpectedly soft for such a surly-looking guy, but he wasn't really her type. "The kind of men that I dated in Richmond didn't have tongue piercings and they didn't shave their heads. They all went to college and they wore chinos and blue blazers," she said. Yet, she figured, even if Matt wasn't right for her, he still might be right for her in South Beach. So she made a deal with herself: If she had an affair with this guy, it was going to end with the season. The relationship would have a beginning, middle, and end, neatly predetermined so nobody got hurt, and she wasn't going to fall in puppy love with him and break her heart or his.

After all, she was only nineteen years old.

Ambika had a modeling job the next day, but she was having

such a good time at the bar that she didn't want to go home. "So I said to Matt, 'I hope you don't mind, but I'm staying at your house tonight.'" Matt said he didn't mind.

"Nothing happened that night," Ambika continued. "Matt was such a gentleman—which blew me away about him—he only kissed me, he didn't try to have sex, and to me it made such a difference because since I arrived in South Beach, every guy I met had tried to get into my pants. If they're not gay, they're in your pants in five seconds in South Beach, or at least trying to. So it was really comforting to know Matt would respect that."

When she left the next morning, they made no plans to see each other again, which was disconcerting to her, and late that night she spotted him at Funksion, a bar and restaurant on Lincoln Road that was a models' hangout. Matt had been drinking and he seemed intent on picking up a young blonde model who'd recently arrived in South Beach from Poland and spoke only a few words of English. ("The model from Poland was more intent on picking me up!" Matt insisted later.) Ambika kept her distance and ordered a drink and watched out of the corner of her eye as Matt and the Polish girl flirted with each other, and she realized that Matt probably wasn't the right guy for her after all, and that he was turning out to be a one-night stand (even though they never actually had sex). She started to feel a little hurt watching them, so she finished her drink and headed for the door. She was just outside when her cell phone rang. It was a text message from Matt: "wait! where r u going?"

A minute later he came dashing out the door after her. They walked down Lincoln Road together, too shy to hold hands, gawking at the passing sideshow, feeling giddy in the balmy air. They turned off at Meridian Avenue, where tiny lizards skittering in the grass at the side of the street. On a dare they lay down in the road on the yellow line. "We were just being goofs," Matt said, "but she really impressed me that she did it." They giggled and rolled around on the asphalt and stared up at the moon, and Ambika impetuously rolled over next to Matt and they kissed lying in the street. Farther down Meridian they came to a magnolia tree with tangled branches, which Ambika said was her favorite tree in Miami Beach, and they decided to climb it, getting as far as the lower branches before they tumbled to the hard ground and had the wind knocked out of them.

Back in his apartment, they made love and Ambika fell asleep on top of him, curled up like a puppy dog. "He thought that was about the cutest thing," she said.

The following weekend Ambika's mother and father came to visit and stayed at the Raleigh Hotel. Ambika had told her mother about Matt on the phone, and she invited him to dinner to meet her parents. The next day her mother told her she disapproved of him. "This boy is not for you," she warned. But Ambika already knew that.

In another week or so, Matt went up to Michele Pommier's office and begged her to take on Ambika as a client, and after some reluctance, Ms. Pommier agreed.

"AMBIKA WAS taken on by this agency because of Matt. Okay?" Michele Pommier said. "Because that's the *real* story. I told the booking room, 'There's no way this girl is going to do very much.' I already knew. I said, 'If she can do catwalks it's wonderful and if she can do some TV it's wonderful. It was because she wanted to be near Matt that we took her, and it's very unusual for me to okay something like that."

That was true enough. Although she mothered some of the kids she signed, Michele Pommier, a former top model herself, wasn't known for coddling young models. At least not anymore, not after the lawsuit with Elsa Benítez, who was discovered in 1996 at a beauty pageant in Costa Rica when she was fourteen years old.

Pommier signed Benítez to a worldwide contract that earned the teenager $1.3 million in commissions in eleven months before she jumped ship to the Ford agency in New York. Pommier sued Benítez for defecting, but lost. "I gave up my life as a wife and a mother for two years for her," Pommier claimed. "I sent her mother two thousand dollars a month in Mexico. The loyalty factor really killed me."

Despite the fact that agencies in Miami Beach serve as farm teams where very young talent is groomed before shipping out for the major leagues, for Pommier modeling is a business, not a nursery. "The kids today whine and cry," she said. Still, she took on Ambika because keeping Matt Loewen happy was good business.

Pommier, looking cool, glamorous, and blonde on the day she greeted a visitor to her offices on Lincoln Road, was dressed in a tailored white pantsuit that coordinated with the minimalist, all-white decor of her modeling agency. The only jewelry she wore was a large, heart-shaped topaz ring on her right hand. Her trademark dark sunglasses, which completed her imperious look, were at the moment resting in front of her on the conference table, unmasking mesmerizing aquamarine eyes that were as businesslike and cool as the rest of her. Pommier mentioned in conversation that she'd turned fifty about two weeks earlier, making her seven years younger than had previously been reported. No matter, fifty or fifty-seven, her age was superfluous because her beauty seemed indestructible.

Pommier's long-suffering assistant, Penny, appeared at the door with Matt Loewen's composite card, which showed a headshot of Matt with his baby blue eyes looking up yearningly. Pommier held up the card and said proudly, "Here's our new star."

When Matt first arrived in Miami Beach, his booker, Christian Garces, tried to arrange for Pommier to have dinner with him, but before Christian could set a date, Pommier ran into Matt in the office. He was so intimidated by her that he turned unusually inarticulate and she lost interest in knowing him further. "Our dinner never materialized," Matt shrugged. His supposition is that she later changed her mind about him when she observed a brief interchange between Matt and his Brazilian roommate, Ricardo, who was at the agency using one of the computers to get his e-mail from home. Ricardo read some unexpected bad news about his younger sister and burst into tears in front of the computer. Although Matt couldn't figure out exactly what Ricardo was saying happened to his sister, Matt had a sister too, and suddenly *he* started crying and hugging Ricardo, and they had a good cry together under Pommier's watchful eye.

Pommier thinks Matt's appeal is not in the color of his eyes or his beautiful musculature but in that palpable body heat that makes a model alive on the page. "It's bullshit about models having to be beautiful," she said. "Attitude is much more important than beauty. Matt's got a lot more going for him than a good face. It's harder for a girl model because she has to have personality and be fun. Do you think a photographer wants to take a boring girl away to Alaska with him and a crew for a three-week photo shoot?"

Pommier, the daughter of a wealthy diamond dealer, grew up on a twenty-five-acre estate in Westport, Connecticut, and went to boarding school in Lausanne, Switzerland. She was discovered at age fifteen when the photographer Milton Green came to lunch at her father's house and was struck by her beauty. A photograph he took of her that day in a burlap-bag race, hopping down a green sloping lawn and laughing, originally published in *Life* magazine, captured the sweet abandon of a summer's day, and it became one of Green's most reproduced photos. By the time Pommier was out of college she'd been signed by the Eileen Ford agency in New York, and over the next dozen or so years she became one of the top ten brunette models in the business, with three fashion-magazine covers and a star turn as one of the most popular (and the only brunette) of the Virginia Slims "You've come a long way, baby" girls. In the mid-1970s she married a model and professional golfer/stockbroker named Peter Deil and moved to Coral Gables with him.

There was no modeling industry to speak of in Miami Beach in the 1970s, no local fashion industry or clothing manufacturing to feed it. "There were maybe five models in all of Miami that could do photography work," Pommier remembered. "There were only a few editorial jobs, mostly for the local newspapers." Because she was a big-time cover girl from New York, she worked a lot. "I was on page three of the *Herald* in a Bullocks ad every week for a year," she said.

Since there were so few models, Pommier became sort of a clearinghouse for photographers, and before long she started to book models herself, first from her own house, until the police stopped her from running a business from her residence, and then from a number of small offices in Coral Gables. Then in 1983 she discovered Christy Turlington, only thirteen years old, in South Miami, whose success thrust Pommier into prominence. Two years later, in 1985, the photographer Bruce Weber, whom Pommier knew from the New York modeling scene, asked her to find a nonprofessional male model, someone unpolished and natural, and Pommier suggested a young man named Tim Schnellenberger, who was the son of Howard Schnellenberger, the legendary football coach of the University of Miami. Weber posed him against the white Mayan-inspired concrete tower of the Breakwater Hotel, wearing only his Calvin Klein briefs, for an Obsession ad that ran all over the world. It started the word of mouth in the fashion industry that would transform South Beach into the photographic modeling destination of the world. It was cheap and easy to get to, and it had what seemed like inexhaustible locations for editorial shoots.

First came the Germans, who produced hundreds of big fashion catalogs. At one point Pommier estimates that her agency was doing 70 percent of its business with German clients. "The Germans would book ten and twenty girls a day, going all the time," Pommier said. "Once the Germans came, then the French started coming, and then the English. This place went off the wall. You'd see fourteen Winnebagos lined up on Ocean Drive every day, and modeling shoots on every street corner." A cottage industry sprang up. A dozen photographic laboratories for developing film opened; camera-equipment suppliers moved to Miami Beach; lighting technicians, stylists, makeup artists, hairstylists, and photographer's assistants arrived. All the flotsam that the fashion industry brings along with it migrated to South Beach. By 1995 the industry was generating $50 million a year. At its zenith there were twenty-two modeling agencies on the Beach, including Boss, Clique, Irene Marie, Next, Ford, Elite, and Karins, and an estimated 2,500 models lived within one square mile. "But Michele Pommier was the queen of everything," said Ford's Erin Lukas. To prove it, Pommier built a sprawling mansion and office at 81 Washington Avenue, a monument to her success, which people named the "White House of modeling."

"All of a sudden it started taking a nosedive," Pommier said. "Around 1998 there was a big drop-off when the Germans started to go to Cape Town, where they could get the models for half the price. And they'd used South Beach [locations] to death. After ten years they needed another location. Miami Beach was overused. Every single picture you'd see in all these catalogs had the same damn palm tree behind it. It was funny."

Her agency still does well, she said, but it isn't like it was. As for this year's crop of newcomers, she thinks Matt Loewen will emerge as a star. When the season ended, "He'll probably be on his way to Milan," she said. "But we'll get him back next season, when he'll have a better book and his rate will double. He's such a good kid, and there's a loyalty factor there."

When Pommier was told that Matt had second thoughts about

modeling and that he was disturbed that his self-worth was dependent on how he thrived in a meat market, Pommier shrugged. "Well, a few weeks ago," she observed, "he was sitting in Canada doing nothing."

In January Matt got himself into a little Miami Vice adventure.

Later, Matt would have only a sketchy grasp of the details, but it involved two of his buddies from Vancouver, who were enticed to come to Miami Beach by the stories of Matt's wild adventures that were filling his e-mails. His friends were two muscular guys in their early twenties with no regular jobs. They came to visit Matt for a week in early January, and they liked it so much they decided they'd move to Miami Beach for the rest of the season. At the same time, Matt wanted to get out of the models' apartment where he was staying because it was crowded and expensive. "So I said to my friends from Vancouver, 'Okay, I'll move in with you guys and we'll all pay rent together.' I found a place on Craigslist for two thousand dollars a month and I checked it out and it was okay, so I rented it and they moved in with me.

"They came down . . . I guess with the intention of selling drugs," he continued. "They had Ecstasy pills shipped from Vancouver. Among other things that these guys did wrong was to charge the Vancouver rate. They were going to sell them for twenty dollars a tab, way below the going price in Miami Beach.* Basically, they were selling Ecstasy in clubs all around Miami Beach, and they got caught by the police, selling it right outside our apartment building. The police brought them into the apartment and they were interviewing all of us, and searching the apartment, looking

---

*Ecstasy originates mostly in laboratories in the Benelux countries and is flown to Caribbean islands and from there smuggled to South Florida. Most X hits South Florida first, flooding it, at cheap prices.

for all the pills. There were thousands of Ecstasy pills hidden on top of the kitchen cabinets, and the police were searching and asking us questions and I was like '*Jesus!*'"

The police never found the Ecstasy, but they did find Matt's small personal stash, which included a few psychedelic mushrooms. When Matt saw the police holding up his stash and demanding "Whose drugs are these?" he knew that he was seeing his modeling career dematerializing and that he'd be deported back to British Columbia. He snuck a sideways glance at his friends and the police noticed it. One thing led to another, and the police arrested and handcuffed his two friends and took them away to jail. They let Matt go free.

"My friends blamed me for doing that one little thing," Matt said, "that one-second look because I was so scared I was going to be sent home to Vancouver. So I went to the jail and I bailed them out for one thousand dollars. Basically, they were supposed to sit tight and wait for their trial. But a few days later I went back to the apartment and they weren't there. They ran out. The rent was two thousand dollars a month, plus I'd given the landlord a two-thousand-dollar deposit. My friends owed me a thousand in bail money plus money for rent, and I started to worry what to do—I was by myself in a huge two-bedroom apartment. So I advertised it for rent on Craigslist, where I found it, and these guys from the Washington, D.C., area rented it from me. Which I guess wasn't very legal at the time either. Apparently one guy fell and broke a window. The man who checked the plumbing came to the apartment and saw all these guys there, and I wasn't there, and the window was broken, and he told the landlord, who said he was going to call the cops. I never got the deposit back."

With no place to live, Matt moved into Ambika's studio on Meridian Avenue with her.

On their first Saturday night living together, they decided to celebrate by dancing at Space, but when they arrived at the entrance Ambika realized she didn't have her fake ID with her. After seeing the look of disappointment on Matt's face, she graciously insisted he go ahead without her and promised she'd be waiting for him at the apartment when he got home. Matt reluctantly let her leave, but by the time she was in a taxi on the causeway he text-messaged her that he was miserable without her and that he'd meet her back at the apartment in ten minutes. They spent the night in bed, and when the horizon began to brighten they walked to the beach and watched the sun come up and Ocean Drive come alive. The homeless people began to materialize out of their hiding places, and the janitors and cleanup crews of the hotels and restaurants along Ocean Drive started hosing down the sidewalks and setting up chairs at the outdoor cafés. Ambika and Matt had breakfast at a small café and strolled back to the apartment and got back into bed. For the next three months they were rarely apart.

The biggest problem they faced was that there wasn't any work. Ambika hardly had any jobs, and Matt's bookings, although impressive, were only sporadic. The gossip among the models was that the season was a dud—there was no business and all the agencies were down from the previous year. Matt remembered the humiliation of the cattle call of "castings." "There were sometimes hundreds of guys lined up, and the casting directors would go down the line and go 'no, no, no, no, no.'

"Once for two whole weeks I didn't do one fucking thing. We went out to the clubs, we slept until noon, then we went to the beach, worked out—did a whole lot of nothing. There was one stretch when Ambika and I went out to the clubs eight nights in a row," he said. "This was the height of modeling season, and they said that in January and February business would pick up, but it never hit its stride. I worked better than most of the models at Pommier."

Without any money coming in, taxis were a luxury and they

walked a lot. They lived off of Ambika's credit card, which was charged to her parents, and it became a game for them to get free meals. Santos, a bar and restaurant on Lincoln Road, gave a free models' dinner every Tuesday night, and many of the promotional and fashion-industry parties served food, which made do for dinner. Also, Matt was asked out to dinners with his booker, Christian Garces, but Christian didn't want girls around, so Matt had to sneak Ambika to the dinners and pretend she was there by accident. Ambika was a little jealous of Matt's closeness with Christian, and one night she said to Matt, "I wouldn't be surprised if you two did it."

Matt said, "And what if I did?"

Ambika was shocked. "Did you?"

Matt teased, "Does making out count?"

At this Ambika burst into tears and Matt had to hug her and calm her down and promise her he was only joking.

On Valentine's Day the two of them decided they would buy each other new outfits as gifts and wear them out that night. The color theme was blue, they decided, and they went shopping together on Lincoln Road. Ambika bought Matt a cashmere sweater in a blue camouflage pattern, and he bought her a blue halter dress, short and flowery and sexy. They went to dinner at Santos because it was free, and later they went to the megaclub Mansion. They used the usual line "I'm a model with Michele Pommier," and not only did the velvet ropes part and they were let inside for free, but they were given a VIP table behind the DJ booth and complimentary bottles of vodka and champagne mysteriously arrived. They never found out who sent them or why. (Most likely Michael Capponi.) They do remember that they danced until the club shut down. It was the single best night of their time in Miami Beach.

The entire season they were in South Beach, they never worked together until the last show of the season during Miami Fashion

Week. By happy coincidence the show was timed so that they'd pass each other on the runway. Ambika was wearing jumper overalls with a gray T-shirt underneath that Matt quipped made her look like a sperm. Matt was in gray pants and a dark gray overcoat, and they strutted down the runway, having a great time, laughing as they brushed by each other midpoint. At the very last moment, when Matt hit the bottom of the catwalk, where the photographers with their cameras and strobe lights were waiting, he pulled out his own digital camera from his pocket and took a picture of all of the cameras facing him. It had been done dozens of times before by models on the runway, but everyone in the audience laughed loudly, and it was the last strobe flash of his stay in Miami Beach.

TWO NIGHTS before the end of the season, Matt and Ambika ate dinner at Miss Yip's, a popular Chinese restaurant just off Lincoln Road. Matt was dressed in jeans, a white shirt, and a white athletic jacket he'd been given as a gift from a modeling job for Fila, and he was drinking vodka martinis. Ambika was in a shiny beige top, with long dangling earrings and her hair loose, looking like she'd just arrived from Paris. Miami Fashion Week had ended and most of the models were leaving. There were lots of good-byes in the air, including Matt and Ambika's.

"We would never have moved in together," Ambika said in a sensible voice, "if we didn't know we were eventually going to separate." Matt agreed with a nod that didn't show much conviction. "I'm a strong woman," she continued, showing as much bravura as a nineteen-year-old could muster. "The whole time Matt and I dated, I told myself that we were leaving South Beach on March thirty-first and I didn't want to go home and be mopey about some boy. But I wanted some passion in my life while I was here."

How will they say good-bye? "We'll give each other a kiss and say good-bye," Ambika said.

This disturbed Matt. "That's really fucked up when you think of it."

"Yeah, but we knew . . ."

"Well, I always subliminally rejected the fact," he countered.

"We both changed," Ambika went on, "and however we changed, we changed in the same way."

"This season in South Beach has literally changed my life one hundred and eighty degrees," Matt said. "My life would never be the same if I had not come down here."

After the dishes were cleared, the waitress brought fortune cookies for desert. Ambika's fortune read "You have a strong desire for a home and your family interests come first."

"Well *that's* true," she said. "I want to have three or four kids and not work and take them to school and be with them all the time. I want to have dinner on the table when my husband gets home."

Matt's fortune read "It is very possible you will achieve greatness in your lifetime." Ambika smiled slyly, but Matt looked strange and his eyes brimmed with tears. He shielded his face with a trembling hand and sprang from the table, darting through the restaurant to a bathroom.

"He cries all the time," Ambika said, unmoved. "He cries over everything." She gave Matt a moment before she went after him and found him in the bathroom sobbing over the sink. Matt composed himself and they returned to the table a few minutes later.

"That fortune cookie—about achieving greatness?" he said. "Well, for months now I've been living in a shallow, delusional place. I've lived in a society with absolutely no culture and where money and fame are everything. I was immersed in it for so long that I began to wonder, 'Is this really *it*? Is it that simple? Am I really such an incredible guy because I look like this? Is that how I'm going to achieve greatness?' At the same time, I never thought . . . that I would do anything like this." He motioned to the bustle of South Beach outside the restaurant, to the hotels and the clubs and parties taking place all over Miami Beach, to all the seductive glamour of which he was but a grain of sand that year. Then he remembered that it was all over, the season was gone, and he felt even sadder, like that feeling when Color War ends at summer camp, or the end of the run of a show, or finishing a good book, the sweetness and sadness of going on and turning the page. That's why he cried.

Ambika and Matt walked out into the street and stood on the sidewalk in front of Miss Yip's and kissed. Lincoln Road was mobbed that final week of March, and hand in hand they made their way into the crowds of people who folded around them as they disappeared from sight.

At 4:00 a.m. they went to the beach and smoked a joint on a life-guard tower, and wrapped in each other's arms, they watched the dawn together one last time. When they could procrastinate no longer, they headed back to the apartment, crying in the streets. People looked at them like they were crazy, two beautiful young people holding hands and sobbing. The couple couldn't bear to say good-bye in the apartment, so they decided that Ambika should pack and go with Matt to the airport, even though her own plane didn't take off until six hours later in the day.

By the time they got to Miami International, Matt recalled, "Our eyes were so red from crying we wore sunglasses so people wouldn't stare." The two of them navigated through the terminal and security checks and finally went to the place where Matt was supposed to get on a shuttle train to take him to the gate. There was a bench nearby, and they sat on it for a few minutes in silence, staring straight ahead, exhausted from emotion. Suddenly Matt's cell phone began to play a melody and he flipped it open. The caller was a girl whom he'd met at a nightclub, or an audition, or a party, who represented models, and she thought she was reaching him in his apartment. She said that she realized it was early, but she'd been up all night and she was horny and she wanted to come over to his apartment and give him a blow job.

Matt said he was sorry, but he was at the airport on his way home, and he hung up.

"What was that?" Ambika asked when she saw the smile on his face. When he told her what the call was about they both started to laugh, and they couldn't stop laughing practically until Matt's shuttle train arrived.

He stood up and asked Ambika, "Do you have anything to say to me?"

Her heart was pounding. "Yes, I have something to say," she answered. "None of this makes any sense."

There was a pneumatic hissing as the doors to the shuttle train opened, and Ambika and Matt kissed and hugged and kissed, and then Matt got on the train with a stricken look on his face and turned his back to her. The doors lingered open for a moment and she expected him to turn around, but he couldn't bear to see her recede in the station, and Miami Beach recede with her, and he did not look at her again. When the doors finally slid shut with a thump, Ambika said, "It sounded like an explosion in my head."

MATT DID not become the Next Big Thing in male modeling, but he did become a success. That summer and fall he went on to photographic and runway work in Rome, Madrid, Berlin, Munich, Tel Aviv, Copenhagen, and Mykonos, and in Paris, where he did the spring fashion shows, including Yves St. Laurent, John Galliano, and Paul Smith. Matt was also booked heavily for the spring/summer shows in Milan for Dolce & Gabbana, Neil Barrett, Valentino, and Gianfranco Ferré. He became one of the top-earning American models in Europe. On his return to the United

States he worked for top fashion photographer Steven Meisel for Dolce & Gabbana, and he shot an Armani and Kenneth Cole fragrance campaign. He is now signed with DNA for representation, one of the most prestigious modeling agencies in New York.

Ambika is living at home in Richmond, Virginia, where she has happily returned to college to resume her studies. She is dating a handsome young stockbroker from New York and has no real interest in modeling again. Yet she is still too beautiful for photographers to resist: A full-page photograph of Ambika and her equally beautiful mother on vacation on the Caribbean island of St. Bartholomew appeared in the Decmber 2006 issue of *Town & Country* magazine.

The modeling industry in Miami Beach is greatly diminished from its heyday. The freshman class of wannabe models who show up every November is getting smaller each year. Many of the photographers, makeup artists, and tributary professionals associated with the modeling industry have left South Beach for more lucrative locations. From a peak of over twenty modeling agencies in the 1990s, there are now only half a dozen.

One unexpected casualty of the downturn was Michele Pommier. In late summer of 2006 her checks to employees began to be returned due to insufficient funds, and models and creditors stopped being paid. Although she maintains offices on Lincoln Road, the state license for Michele Pommier Management LLC expired at the end of May 2006 and has never been renewed.

Christian Alexander Garces quit after one of his paychecks bounced, he said, and he started his own agency down the street called Front Management. He still represents Matt Loewen in Miami Beach. Garces estimated that in his first season in South Beach, Matt Loewen generated over $45,000 in fees.

Matt Loewen claims that Michele Pommier Inc. still owes him over $15,000.

Sixteen

THE KING OF THE CITY

If you're the king of nightlife, you're the king of the city.
—Michael Capponi

When moist-eyed locals reminisce about the Golden Age of Chris Paciello in South Beach they never fail to say how handsome he was, how sexy, what heat he radiated, and that there wasn't any girl in Miami Beach he couldn't fuck—and didn't. But it wasn't his pretty face, or his big biceps, or other endowments that made him so seductive; it was his aura of mystery and his surprising thuggish charm.

When Chris Paciello showed up in South Beach on Labor Day weekend of 1994, he looked like just another *mook* in a wife-beater undershirt, a twenty-three-year-old tattooed muscle-head from Brooklyn, New York, wearing sweatpants and sneakers, casing out Ocean Drive and the bikini babes on Rollerblades. He had an impassive face, pouty cupid lips, amber eyes, and dark curly hair, pomaded and cut short. He was a big guy, six foot one, with a thickly muscled body, the rewards of a regimented two hours in the gym every morning and two hours again in the late afternoon.

That Labor Day weekend Paciello stayed at a friend's apartment off Washington Avenue and hung out with his buddies at the

Clevelander Hotel, then one of the cheesier places on Ocean Drive with a reputation as a party hotel—open room doors and all-night hookups. The Clevelander's big daytime draw was its wavy-shaped outdoor bar that was practically right on Ocean Drive, with girls in skimpy bathing suits and wet T-shirts drinking Fuzzy Navels, or lolling in a tiled swimming pool behind it. By weekend's end Paciello would have faded into memory along with every other sweaty guy looking for a piece of ass in South Beach. Except for one unusual thing.

By weekend's end, the unemployed twenty-three-year-old had made a deal to buy a nightclub. He agreed to pay $140,000 in cash for a fleabag club at 1203 Washington Avenue and promised to assume the club's $400,000 debt. It was the kind of place where regular customers passed the time pitching pennies up against the front wall. The joint was named Mickey's Place after one of the partners, actor Mickey Rourke, a Miami Beach High School graduate and local bad boy who reportedly was given a piece of his namesake club because he showed loyalty to Mafia don John Gotti in 1992 by showing up at Gotti's murder and racketeering trial in New York and sitting in the spectators' section. The principal owner of Mickey's Place was a man named Carlo Vaccarezza, who was once John Gotti's driver in New York. Gotti's presence was thick at Mickey's Place, where framed photographs of the Mafia don hung alongside autographed photos of famous Italian prize-fighters and sports figures. Carlo Vaccarezza migrated to Miami from New York in 1993 after his restaurant, Da Noi, was investigated as a possible front for money laundering. Coincidentally, the owner of Mickey's previous to Vaccarezza had been convicted of money laundering for the Genovese crime family.

Paciello and a cohort at the time, a Manhattan party promoter and Ecstasy dealer named Lord Michael Caruso, renamed the club Risk because that's what it was, risky business. It opened in late October 1994, less than two months after Paciello first hit town.

The doorman described the opening-night crowd as "mobster chic." Paciello had given the place a half-assed face-lift, with zebra print carpeting on the floors, an eighteen-foot bar with cheap mirrors behind it, and semicircular banquettes bought from another dive that had gone bankrupt. There was also a cheap smoke machine that coughed wisps of smoke onto the small dance floor, and toward the back of the club was a "public shower" under which go-go girls (or customers) could wet themselves down. There was also a separate "VIP" area for taking drugs, cordoned off with bamboo screens and an intimidating bouncer. Part of the gimmick of the club was that to get into the VIP room, customers had to use a password they could only get by dialing an unlisted phone number and listening to the word whispered on an answering machine.

"I was a big Guido from New York opening up a club," Paciello later said. "Everybody thought I'd be out of business in a week." The big surprise was what a good host Paciello turned out to be, smooth, charming, and accommodating. He was a quick study, and he soon lost the sweatpants and undershirts and bought himself a couple of pairs of good slacks and some tapered designer shirts. Paciello instituted some clever marketing ploys. In an attempt to attract Miami Beach's large gay population, one night a week he started a theme night called "Risk Your Anus," and on Monday nights he appealed to African Americans by reviving an R&B-themed night started by the bar's former ownership called "Fat Black Pussycat." "It kept Risk going and introduced me to all the locals," he said.

The club did okay; word of mouth among the Miami goons was good, and on any night there were a bunch of tough guys from New York lined up at the bar with the kind of ladies who love outlaws. Once in a while a big-time Gambino family member would stop in, such as Johnny Rizzo or John D'Amico, but in the main Risk was considered a local hoodlum den, small time and inconsequential on the lucrative Miami Beach nightlife scene. "Risk wasn't clicking at first," Paciello said. "I was successful, I was making money, but not a lot of money." There were lots of crappy little nightclubs like Risk all over Miami Beach, but only the top four or five big nightclubs were grossing real money—*very* real money, maybe $5 million a year—among them Glam Slam farther down Washington Avenue, owned by the rock star Prince. "I felt a New York–style nightclub would work in Miami," Paciello later said. "I didn't know if it was vision, brains, balls, or just plain stupidity, but I did it."

Paciello was ambitious, but he was young and an outsider, and the tough little Miami Beach nightlife community was wary of newcomers on their turf. If he wanted to play in the big league, he needed a way in. He was tipped off that there was a young guy about his own age who walked on water in Miami Beach as far as the nightclub business was concerned: Michael Capponi. But there was a catch. Capponi was a freak. He wore leather pants and flouncy shirts and did pirouettes on the street, pretending he was Jim Morrison. Everybody said what a nice guy he was, and that he was super-knowledgeable about the nightclub business, but also that he was a fucked-up heroin addict on his way to an overdose.

MICHAEL CAPPONI chokes up when he tells his story. It's his epic poem and he's the hero, pure of heart but tragically flawed and betrayed by circumstance. The way he tells the story the listener realizes that he has told this story many times, if not aloud to other people then inside his head, the kind of black-and-white movie that plays when you're nodding out on heroin.

He was sitting at the dining room table of his handsomely decorated waterfront house on Sunset Island 1, staring out the window as the setting sun created long amber shadows on Biscayne Bay. His girlfriend, Erin Henry, had just come home from a modeling audition and was puttering around in the kitchen behind him, putting things away in cabinets. When she was finished she came into the dining room, put her arms around his neck, and kissed him. She sat down at the table next to him and quietly listened to his story. Capponi was trying hard to explain how innocent and callow he was when he was nineteen years old, still doing wheelies on his bike or 360s on his skateboard along Ocean Drive, handing out party flyers from his leather shoulder bag to all the pretty young girls who were beginning to flood South Beach. Back in those days the surf rats and the models hung out on the beach together. "South Beach—there was nothing there," he said. "Half of the windows on Ocean Drive were knocked out. There was nothing—the Palace and the News Café, nothing else."

One afternoon out of a hundred sunny afternoons, he was surfing in the blue waters off Lummus Park, tripping out on the beautiful day, when Francesca Rayder, in a bikini, strutted out of the ocean nearby and he thought, "*Uh oh, this is the end, my friend.*" She would be the end of him because he would never be able to make her fall in love with him. He would never be able to make her understand that he would be forever true, that she would be Pamela to his Jim. "It happened that quick," he said. She was an instant obsession. Like a drug addiction.

She walked across the sand and gathered her belongings, and with the languid voice of Jim Morrison playing on the sound track inside his head, and his surfboard tucked under his arm, Capponi followed her up the beach onto Ocean Drive and down the street until she disappeared through the door of a modeling agency. He asked everyone in town who she was, and as soon as he mentioned her dark hair and green eyes, people said that must be Frankie Rayder, that he should leave her alone, she was just a kid (so was he), sixteen years old or so. She had been scouted one day in a local shopping mall in her hometown of River Falls, Wisconsin, by a local modeling agency, and she was whisked to New York, where photographer Steven Meisel fell in love with her boyish toughness and put her on the cover of Italian *Vogue*.

Capponi couldn't rest until she agreed to go out with him. "I literally thought about this girl one hundred times a day," he said. "I would go to the News Café and grab fifteen fashion magazines and just look through them to see pictures of her." But whenever he tried to catch her attention she seemed unimpressed and distant. So he embarked upon an elaborate scheme of romantic pursuit, filled with improbable coincidences and dramatic encounters as he tells it. Unable to stay away from her, he flew to Paris when she moved there to model, and not knowing where to find her, he wandered the streets and boulevards until one day a quirk of fate brought them face-to-face. When she saw him there on the Paris street, he said, Francesca wordlessly took his hand and led him to Jim Morrison's grave at Père Lachaise Cemetery, where they shared their first kiss. "I walked around until dawn," he said, "singing in the streets." On another occasion he broke into Francesca's apartment in New York and left the movie *Doctor Zhivago* playing on her VCR. "It was amazing how madly in love with her I was," he continued. "You can't even *imagine*. I would dance in the streets of Miami Beach out of pure joy. I would tell every single person who I ran into for a year how madly in love with her I was. I had a flower in my hand the whole time. I would do pirouettes and sing. It was so funny." He laughed sadly, "Ha ha ha."

By the time Capponi was twenty years old, he was like a rock star in South Beach. "I was making five or six thousand dollars a week," he remembered, "and I had not yet opened up a bank account under my name. The cash basically sat in a shoebox under the bed, and every night before I left I'd just grab a thousand bucks and spend it on drugs and alcohol." Just a few years before, he mused, he was eating cookies and drinking milk out of a carton sitting in front of the TV in his mother's apartment and now he was living in a condominium tower overlooking the ocean (he lied about his age on the lease). He had a brand-new 300 SL Mercedes, and he drank only Cristal champagne. His satin pants and chiffon shirts were hand tailored, and his hair was long and fashionably scraggly. He was mystical and deep and smoked clove cigarettes. The word TRUTH was tattooed on his arm in Japanese and the word LOVE written in ballpoint pen on his Filofax, which went everywhere with him, the forerunner to his omnipresent Black-Berry.

In March of 1993 journalist Tom Austin followed Capponi on his nightly rounds for *New Times* magazine and described him as "a nightlife star alternately attracted to and repelled by the world he inhabits." Austin observed that "women slithered around him like cats in heat," despite which Capponi was filled with "hopeless despair and aching lovesickness" for his girlfriend. "She's killing me, man," Capponi lamented about Francesca. "And this life is killing me more."

Six months later, on September 12, the *Miami Herald* crowned twenty-one-year-old Capponi the "SoBe Prince" of nightlife. But he didn't sound very princely. "I have to be out literally seven nights a week," he complained to the *Herald*. "I have to buy a hundred drinks a night for customers. I don't stop. I have to take people to dinner, I have to literally shake a thousand hands. People grab you, they shake you, 'Hey what's up?' They hit you on the head." The article noted that in his voice there was "a tinge of sadness—or is it plain weariness?" It was neither. It was heroin.

THE WIDESPREAD white-collar use of heroin in Miami Beach was the unexpected side effect of a federal Drug Enforcement Agency crackdown on Colombian cocaine smugglers. The DEA was putting pressure on the Medellín drug cartel through improved surveillance and monitoring of the Florida coastline, where most of the "go fast"–type, cigarette-boat drug smuggling took place. As more smugglers were being caught, the risk-versus-profits ratio increased. So the cartel decided to switch the drug they were peddling from cocaine to heroin. Cocaine was bringing only $25,000 to $30,000 a kilo, but heroin was selling for $400,000 a kilo, and heroin had the same legal risk as cocaine; both were considered Class A narcotics and carried the same prison sentence.

One of the problems with selling heroin in the U.S. was the deeply ingrained middle-class taboo against intravenous drug use, so the Colombians began to cultivate poppy fields that produced a much purer quality of heroin that could be inhaled. The cartel used Miami as an experimental model to decide whether the purer heroin could replace cocaine with regular users. Ground zero was the Miami Beach nightclub scene, where street-level drug dealers marketed the newer-quality heroin to Miami's cocaine set. The number of heroin-overdose patients seen in Miami-Dade emergency rooms rose by 300 percent in the early 1990s. Heroin soon began to filter into the modeling scene, and the brief fashion era of "heroin chic" was launched, a look that model Kate Moss made famous with her ashen skin and dark circles under her eyes, turning the ravages of addiction into a style in itself.

It wasn't difficult to get Michael Capponi interested in heroin. It was the drug that killed Jim Morrison, most likely, and smack, or "chasing the dragon" as Capponi romanticized smoking it, held great allure for him. A friend turned him on to the drug with a "bump," a little snort, which he took with the ironic self-awareness that heroin might someday kill him like Morrison. Then he tried smoking it, and four days later he was a heroin addict. "Within a month I was doing eight hundred dollars a day of one hundred percent high-grade heroin," Capponi said. "Imagine that. So my judgment, obviously, is not that good.

"I was super skinny. I had a three-hundred-and-fifty-dollar DuPont sterling silver lighter and a sterling silver straw with my name on it to snort the heroin. How stupid. I smoked heroin in front of everybody. I smoked it just like people smoke cigars. Even at Sly Stallone's house. I was at a party and I went into the wine cellar with some people I knew and smoked heroin. I thought it was cool." Stallone told him, "Get some new role models, kid."

Francesca Rayder didn't think smoking heroin was cool either. "Francesca was becoming a really big model, so it was harder on me," Capponi said. She was living in New York and Paris and he didn't get to see her much. "She was very famous. I was basically in competition with every guy on the planet for my girlfriend."

He still can't say exactly what it was that he did to lose her, yet memory of her loss fills him with remorse to this day. "It was a series of a hundred things—cheating, being mean to her, saying horrible things, and choosing heroin. Do you know the toll it takes to be with somebody who's addicted to heroin?"

The end came when "Francesca went to Australia on a weeklong job, and while she was away some young girl called me and I did heroin with her and had sex with her. When Francesca came home I told her and she cried and grabbed her bags and took off. I sat in a chair devastated for a week. Soon my addiction was so bad I had to smoke heroin every twenty-five minutes. One day I went to the bank to talk to my banker and I had to excuse myself after twenty minutes to go smoke heroin and come back and finish the conversation."

In November of 1994 he was arrested for possession of heroin outside of the Amnesia nightclub and released from jail with charges pending (this arrest was later expunged from his record). An hour after his release he was back on the street chasing the dragon, pursuing his fate.

PEOPLE JUST assumed Chris Paciello was "connected," but within his small circle of friends the Mob was never discussed. The intrigue was part of his allure. Clearly he knew a lot of gangsters from Brooklyn, but by not knowing the exact truth, you could imagine Paciello being as bad as you wanted him to be. Ironically, even with his Mob ties Paciello could never be a "made" man in the Mafia because he wasn't 100 percent Italian. His real surname was Ludwigsen, and his father, George, a small-time prizefighter and junkie who beat the crap out of Chris when he was a kid, was German. Paciello adopted his mother's maiden name to sound more Italian. He called Paciello his "stage name," and no doubt he thought of himself as the star of his own independent feature.

His mother, Marguerite, worked as a hairdresser in Bensonhurst, Brooklyn, where Paciello grew up in a lower-middle-class Italian/Jewish neighborhood of semidetached row houses with tomato gardens in the backyard, a church on every other corner, and an Orthodox synagogue on the others. His older brother was a convicted bank robber and his younger brother was a local tough. When he was sixteen years old he and his mother moved to a row house in Staten Island.

Paciello was a bad egg by the time he was a teenager—a car thief, bank robber, and apprentice hoodlum who enjoyed beating up people, and he was good at it, too. He was a natural boxer, coached by his father, and strong like an ox. Part of his legend was that one night at a New York nightclub, he got into an argument with the bouncer, a member of the Latin Kings gang, who came at Paciello with an ax handle. Paciello simply took the ax handle out of the guy's hand and cracked his skull open with it. He got the nickname "Binger" because once he went off on something—women, booze, violence, thievery—he could hardly stop himself.

Paciello was drawn to the New York nightlife scene, and he moved in on the Limelight nightclub in Manhattan, a veritable drug supermarket, where he set up shop protecting "franchised" drug dealers and beating up and stealing from others. He also enjoyed going to the all-night gay raves at Roseland, where he'd strip to his waist and be admired by two thousand gay men, and then ask around to find out who was dealing Ecstasy. Once he found the guy, he'd beat the crap out of him and take his drugs.

Paciello fell in with a gang of a dozen or so young hoods known as the "Bath Avenue Crew," led by Joseph Benante, a young gangster with financial ties to the Bonanno family, under whose protection they fell. Paciello was recruited as the group's muscle. He worked with another up-and-coming non-Italian hood named Thomas Reynolds, and together they robbed video stores and ripped off drug dealers. Occasionally they scored big; in December of 1992 they stole $300,000 in night-deposit bags in a "smash and grab" at a Chemical Bank in Staten Island.

Paciello visited Miami Beach several times before Labor Day of 1994 to have a good time, but this time he was there to lie low because of the accident with Judith Shemtov. In February of 1993, twenty-one-year-old Paciello was tipped off that Shemtov's husband, Sami, who owned a successful electrical supply company, kept a lot of cash at his home in Richmond Valley, Staten Island, as much as $300,000 locked in a safe in the basement. Paciello masterminded the heist—just ring the bell, a push-in, menace Shemtov with a gun to open the safe, tie him up, and leave. Paciello's job was to wait out front and drive the getaway car while the other guys did the dirty work. He was sitting behind the wheel of the car that night in February while the three other men rang the Shemtovs' doorbell. When forty-six-year-old Judith Shemtov answered the door, the men stormed in, guns drawn, and just a few seconds after they stepped inside the foyer the .45 automatic handgun that Thomas Reynolds was holding accidentally went off and a bullet entered Shemtov's right cheek and penetrated her brain. She collapsed, choking on her own blood, and Shemtov's husband, who was drinking tea in the kitchen, ran to the foyer to discover his wife dying on the floor as Reynolds and his accomplices panicked and fled.

When Paciello was told in the getaway car what had transpired, he was furious with Reynolds for turning a burglary into a homicide and making them all accomplices. Paciello was screaming uncontrollably when Reynolds took out the gun he had just killed

Judy Shemtov with, cocked it, and put it to Paciello's right temple, warning him to shut up, calm down, and not "rat" the others out.

Shemtov's death was such a random hit that it took the Staten Island police over a year to get a lead on it, but eventually somebody snitched. By the summer of 1994, homicide detectives were coming close to fingering Paciello and his pals for murder, so it seemed like a good time for him to leave New York and relocate, and what better place for a petty thug to hide than Miami Beach, where petty thugs are kings? Reportedly the money Paciello used to buy Mickey's Place was a loan from the Gambino family so they could have a front in Miami to launder money, but Paciello claimed he had his own stash of illegal funds into which he was able to dip. Whatever way he was bankrolled, within a year in Miami Beach, Paciello had two driver's licenses, two names, three birth dates, two Social Security numbers, and at least half a dozen addresses. One of which was Michael Capponi's.

"I MET Chris Paciello at a club on Washington and Espanola Way that I was promoting called Dune," Capponi remembered. "Paciello came into Dune dressed all in leather with a cheesy silver necklace. He was buying bottles of Cristal and he had a harem of girls with him. He was making an impression buying all that champagne, so I walked up to him and I shook his hand. I didn't know it at the time, but he had a mission to get to know everybody and infiltrate the market. His plan was to basically get to know everybody through me. But I didn't know that. So I was just cool with him and he started hanging out with me." At this point in time, Capponi continued, "I was probably making fifteen thousand dollars a week and everything I made I smoked. If I had bought real estate with that money, I would have been worth hundreds of millions of dollars today. I was constantly broke, but I was living large. I was two months behind on my forty-five-hundred-dollars-a-month rent for my apartment and the landlord had sent me an eviction notice. One night Chris Paciello mentioned in passing that he was looking for a place to live, so I invited him to move in with me. He got me out of my eviction by paying the rent."

Paciello hated drugs, it was said, because his estranged father was a heavy drug user. Apparently steroids were enough of a high for him. He was justifiably disturbed that Capponi openly used heroin. "Look at you, man," he said to Capponi one night as he was nodding out. "What's wrong with you? You got to get off that shit." Even though they had known each other for only a few months, in December of 1994 Paciello managed to talk Capponi into going to rehab, for which Capponi's mother agreed to pay. Capponi went to a clinic in Oklahoma for the first of what would be a cat's cradle of rehabs and treatments in Europe, Canada, and the United States. "They tried to detox me cold turkey with teas and they almost killed me," Capponi said. "I was strapped down and held. I was put in a bathtub screaming. If I could have punched the mirror and taken a piece of glass, I would have slit my throat."

Two months later he was back in Miami Beach. "I was sixty days clean and I was extremely skinny and so weak I could barely walk," Capponi said. One of the first things he did when he got back was call Francesca in New York and tell her he was clean. "She said to me, 'Do you have any fucking idea what you did to me?' And she hung up the phone."

When Paciello saw how serious Capponi was about his sobriety, he began to watch out for him. "I would be in a public bathroom and he would kick down the door just to see if I was in there doing drugs. So he did care. He was very protective of me. When I got back from rehab I was tired and weak, and I was walking down Washington Avenue and these three gangster guys with big muscles walked by in the opposite direction and brushed my shoulder. Chris came up to the biggest of the guys and said, 'What's up, man? Why don't you pick on somebody your own size?' Then he grabbed the guy by the neck and he hit him and the guy fell flat on the sidewalk, with one shot. Then one after another Paciello laid all three of them out. We laughed, '*heh heh heh heh heh*,' and just kept walking down the street. Basically, if the head of the crime family had someone to get beat up, he'd send Chris. He was a real tough guy."

Capponi hated the way he felt when he was clean of heroin. "I walked around for two and a half months with a dead body," he said. "Then one day I ran into somebody in a restaurant and they handed me a little bit of heroin and I smoked one puff, and all of a sudden I could walk and I looked amazing. I just did one hit of heroin and I was fine. That's when I understood that I couldn't function without it." He asked an addiction doctor who worked with rock stars why he felt so much better on the drug than clean, and the doctor told him, "You know, my advice to you is to just maintain your addiction. You'll never get off of it." Within a week Capponi was back doing $800 a day.

"Once I relapsed, Chris had no respect for me," Capponi said. "But he continued to live with me. When you're addicted to heroin, it's a very scary life. I had to knock myself out at night with roofies, and when I woke in the morning the bed was soaked through with a bucket of water. And I always needed dope. I would say, 'Chris, Chris, Chris, I need a thousand dollars.' And Chris would say, 'What can I hold on to?' I remember I had a real Louis the fourteenth chair that I sold to him, but Chris didn't know what it was. Little by little he inherited all my furniture and art and everything else. I pawned everything. I'd be holding my sound system sweating and shaking in the lobby of my building on my way to the pawnshop and I'm going to pawn it for two hundred dollars. I'd be walking down Lincoln Road with a painting of Francesca, the love of my life, and I'd be ready to sell it for five hundred dollars and I did."

What finished Capponi completely in South Beach was an April 1995 cover story in *New Times* magazine titled "Heroin Be the Death of Me." It was certainly the death of Capponi's career. "A reporter called me up," Capponi explained, "and she said, 'I know that you are a heroin addict and I'm writing a story to try to make people aware how bad a problem heroin is in Miami. Will you talk to me about it?'" Capponi agreed but only if the writer promised not to identify him. He asserted that he was going clean, this time for sure, and that the journalist could spend his "last night on heroin" with him. In Capponi's destructive vanity, he decided that for the sake of the article he'd throw a going-away party for himself, what the reporter called his "narcotic version of the Last Supper."

Capponi took the reporter along with him on his nocturnal peregrinations, including a visit to the apartment of a heroin dealer, where he shot up in front of the reporter. Capponi's tour included a frantic attempt to borrow money from friends at several bars, including Risk, which Chris Paciello then owned. Capponi ended up trying to sell his furniture at ten in the morning. The writer described his expression as having assumed "the beseeching aspect of an animal caught in a trap."

The article didn't name him, as the reporter had agreed, but it hardly disguised his identity. Capponi was described as "one of South Beach's best-known nightclub party promoters . . . fond of spouting stream-of-consciousness poetry and spontaneously breaking into dance." Soon things changed drastically for him; even his longtime friends, who'd tolerated his heroin use before, dropped him.

"After that article I didn't do any more 'nights,'" Michael said. "I couldn't get a job. I was in official free fall and no one would hire me. I was living on Biscayne Boulevard in twenty-dollar-a-night hotels. I was no longer involved in the scene; I was on the 'other side' already. I was shooting heroin because I couldn't afford to smoke it anymore, and it brought the cost down to three hundred dollars a day from five or eight."

That April, Capponi left the Miami area and moved to New York City, where he existed day to day, feeding his habit. The last anybody heard of him for a long time was that he was shivering on the street, living in a cardboard box (it wasn't true, but close). Then an item appeared in the newspapers that a man named Capponi had been murdered in Miami-Dade, and lots of people simply assumed that Michael Capponi was dead. But this was Miami Beach and life went on.

Anyway, there was a new king of nightlife in town.

THE SAME month that Capponi crawled out of town in April 1995, Chris Paciello's nightclub Risk burned to smoldering ruins. Paciello was reported to have cried when Risk burned to the ground. As the story went, he sat on a barstool out front in full view of people passing by, his head in his hands. When the possibility of arson was raised, Paciello hired high-powered criminal defense attorney Roy Black, who quoted the official fire report as saying "a cigarette fell in a couch cushion" and the fire was accidental. "Everyone thought I did it," Paciello said. "I did not." Federal authorities would later claim differently. The Feds claimed that three of Paciello's cronies had specifically come down from New York to South Beach to burn the place down. There was a handsome insurance payoff—$250,000—which Paciello was going to use to open up the biggest, hottest club South Beach had ever seen.

Seventeen

LIQUID

*This is paradise, I'm tellin' ya. This town is like
a great big pussy just waiting to get fucked.*

—Al Pacino as Tony Montana in *Scarface*, 1983

"The big question back then in South Beach," said Michael Capponi, "was 'How do I make Madonna a partner in my club?' Everybody wanted Madonna to invest, not for her money, but because of her fame. If Madonna owned a club, it would go through the roof, it would become the most famous nightclub of all time. That's what Chris Paciello did. He was smart because he made Ingrid Casares his partner, and that's how he got Madonna."

"Everyone knows [Madonna and I] are friends," Casares told a reporter. "I mean, M's a human being. She needs friends, right?"

Here is Madonna on Ingrid Casares from her book *sex* (which is narrated by a "fictional" character named Dita): They are at the Ritz-Carlton Hotel in Cannes and ". . . Ingrid is calling down to the sailors below while straddling the railing. I hope she's careful and doesn't slip and fall because her pussy is so wet right now it's dripping and she's kind of leaning over too far. Of course, I don't mind 'cause I get a perfect view of her ass, which is pretty fucking righteous. I wish I could stop playing with myself and thinking about sex. I'm going to have to go now because I have to finger fuck Ingrid or she's going to freak."

By the time Chris Paciello met Ingrid Casares at one of the Monday Fat Black Pussycat parties at Risk, she was no longer Madonna's girl-toy, but she still had easy and open access to the superstar singer, whom she pretentiously called "M." "I talked to her and we became friends," Paciello said. "We're a lot alike," he told *Details* magazine. "We think about the same things: money and women." Casares was petite, angular, and tightly coiled, like Holly Golightly on coke. An outcast private-Catholic-school girl who grew up in Miami, she was the daughter of a wealthy Cuban émigré who grossed a reported $20 million a year manufacturing windows and sliding glass doors for condominium buildings. Casares had once been romantically linked with the singer k.d. lang, who described Ingrid as "charming" and "childlike" and "trustworthy on a very deep level to people who have lost trust, people in the public eye."

But not too trustworthy. Sapphic lore is that in 1990, aimless and without a career, Casares met the actress and comedienne Sandra Bernhard backstage after she performed her one-woman show in Miami. Casares followed Bernhard to Los Angeles, where she worked as a booker for the men's division of the Wilhelmina modeling agency. It was in Los Angeles that Bernhard made the mistake of taking Casares as her date to Madonna's birthday party. It was evidently sex at first sight. Casares summarily dumped Bernhard, much to Bernhard's eternal wrath, and moved in with Madonna. Within weeks Cesares became Madonna's adoring best friend and confidante. It was Ingrid who brought Madonna to Miami, where the singer bought a $5 million mansion on Biscayne Bay and gave a party at which a hundred drag queens threw themselves into the pool.

Tales of Madonna and Ingrid's adventures became daily fodder for gossip columns and tabloids, and the women were happy to oblige with material, in particular Ingrid's starring role in one of the more pornographic passages of Madonna's fragmentary memoir *sex*, the photos for which were shot in Miami in 1991 by photographer Steven Meisel. In one photo Madonna is shown tongue-kissing

Casares. "I could find a cure for cancer," Casares is enduringly quoted as saying, "and I'd still only be known as Madonna's girlfriend."

The problem with Ingrid, simply put, was that she was an out-of-control cokehead, in and out of rehab. On a little bit of coke she was funny and upbeat; on a lot of coke she was a downer and nasty. In a 1995 interview Madonna recalled Ingrid as a "walking disaster," and in September of that year Paciello and Madonna joined together in a drug intervention that got Ingrid into a rehabilitation clinic. Her father, Raul Casares, later said, "Ingrid was a total disaster for many years until she met Chris. Our family thinks that Chris was the one responsible for stopping her from taking drugs."

With Casares turning over a new leaf, Paciello had a proposition for her. He was going to open a club with the $250,000 insurance money from the fire at Risk, and he wanted her to be the front woman. He would run the club; she would bring in the stars and book high-profile parties, fashion shows, and celebrity events.

But her most important job was to make her friend Madonna a frequent patron.

SEVEN MONTHS after Risk burned, Liquid opened.

"All that phony stuff started with Liquid," lamented Miami Beach socialite Merle Weiss, who'd moved to the city from Philadelphia twenty-five years before and once run a shop on Lincoln Road called Merle's Closet. "There used to be a great, arty, Bohemian vibe here. Paciello didn't make SoBe, he ruined it."

Weiss's observation is well taken, but by the time Liquid left its mark on South Beach, the "great, arty, Bohemian vibe" was already long gone. The prevailing vibe was already drug dealer–flashy, jet set–celebrity, played out in a city awash with new money and drugs. *That* was the Miami Beach that Liquid broke out of its chrysalis, and that was the zeitgeist that Liquid somehow managed to capture. For one white-hot moment Liquid became the international cynosure of celebrity, as close as Miami Beach would ever get to having its own Studio 54 (without the cultural resonance). "Liquid was an altar in the church of South Beach," said author Brian Antoni, "and every celebrity went there to worship." Its first year Liquid would gross $6 million, a small fortune for a Miami Beach club in 1995.

The nightclub's opening on Thanksgiving weekend of 1995 set the tone. The occasion was (again) a birthday party for Madonna's brother, Christopher Ciccone. Journalist Tom Austin described it as "the South Beach equivalent of Truman Capote's Black and White Ball. It was a watershed gathering that blended fame, beauty, talent, and shiny new money . . ." The guests were the A-list of pop society: Calvin Klein and his wife Kelly; singer Gloria Estefan and her manager/husband, Emilio Estefan; Shakira and Michael Caine, to whom Madonna sang "What's It All About, Alfie?"; businessman Barry Diller; film director John Schlesinger; Hollywood agent Bryan Lourde; Richard Johnson, the editor of the *New York Post*'s "Page Six"; Ian Schrager, a hotelier and the former owner of Studio 54; models Kate Moss and Naomi Campbell; New York–based photographer Patrick McMullan; and show business impresario David Geffen, whom Madonna was overheard scolding, "I'm a sensitive person and you were talking all that shit about me. I don't have a dick and I don't play that game."

Chris Paciello, the club's host, became an idol of the city. "This was the point in time when everybody in South Beach wanted to be a nightclub owner," said Gerry Kelly, himself one of the top promoters in Miami Beach. "Being a nightclub owner in South Beach is probably the nearest thing to being a rock star because you're treated like a celebrity and you're courted by celebrities because they're coming to your venue." The *Miami Herald* named Paciello the "King of Clubs," and *People* magazine christened him the "It" boy and Casares the "Queen of the Night."

As it turned out, Casares was a great partner and worked all the angles, giving interviews to the press promoting Liquid and keeping the flow of rich and famous coming through the doors. Paciello was also industrious, putting in sixteen-hour workdays in his new suite of offices at 407 Lincoln Road. He signed exclusives with two of the top "house music" DJs in the country, and he reinstituted the Monday night Fat Black Pussycat party from Risk, which became a hip, on-the-low-down hangout for celebrity athletes. "Madonna hosted our second-year anniversary," Paciello told a columnist. "She did it because of relationships. Back then you didn't have to pay celebrities to walk into nightclubs. Celebrities came because Liquid was fun. We didn't snitch them out to the press."

For a twenty-six-year-old guy from the sticks, Paciello wasn't the least bit intimidated by the famous who became his customers, who in turn seemed fascinated by him. He cleaned himself up, dressed in designer duds, got a manicure, and learned how to hold silverware and eat like a gentleman. He always stood up when a woman came into the room; it was sometimes clumsy, but the women loved it. The transformed Chris Paciello developed an interest in horseback riding and he flew to the Hamptons to attend polo matches. He drove expensive foreign cars, mostly BMWs, mostly stolen. Part of his legend is that he stole a car, got arrested for it, posted bail, then stole the car back from the police impoundment and set it on fire so there'd be no evidence. A real mark of his success was when he stopped stealing cars and started to buy them, including a Range Rover and a Mercedes.

With his riches Paciello bought a $1 million, six-bedroom, waterfront palazzo on Flamingo Drive and a fifty-foot yacht and named it *Liquid*. He sat in the front row at a Versace fashion show in Manhattan next to Madonna and Ingrid, and he owned courtside Miami Heat tickets. He was so prominent and respected that he was asked by the mayor of Miami Beach, Neisen Kasdin, to be on a community task force to monitor the nightclub business. In time Paciello and Casares opened a second money fount called Joia, an overpriced, perpetually booked Tuscan restaurant on Ocean Drive that became the equivalent of a dining-room extension of Liquid.

A great cocksman, Paciello dated supermodel Nikki Taylor, actress Daisy Fuentes, Univision TV personality Sofia Vergara, and former Miss USSR Julia Sukhanova. He also brazenly picked up Jennifer Lopez on the dance floor of his club, and he was her escort at the *Vanity Fair* magazine Oscar party in Los Angeles. "I was twenty-four years old and I owned the hottest clubs in the hottest place," he said. "I'm not that bad looking. It was the bad-boy mystique. I never had a problem getting girls, but the quality got better after opening Liquid."

All this would have been picture-perfect if it wasn't for his monster temper. The nightclub owner and promoter Gerry Kelly, who was hired to manage Liquid, shared an office with Paciello and remembered the "scary, crazy anger" in his face when he got angry. Observers chalked up Paciello's violent moods to steroid use, or "roid rage," but it was impossible to tell where that side of him came from. He was as solidly packed physically as he was emotionally loose. There are dozens of stories about him meting out sadistic beatings to helpless people. He once pummeled a doorman at Liquid for wising off at him and kept punching the guy even while he was unconscious on the ground. The next day Paciello paid for the man's doctors' bills and gave him a raise. When Michael Quinn, a former Mr. Universe, used the word "nigger in front of" Paciello, the young mobster split Quinn's head open with a beer bottle and knocked out his teeth. Paciello was so proud of his handiwork that he had pictures taken of Quinn all beat up and hung them in his office. When Quinn brought a civil suit against Paciello, the jury found that Paciello had acted in self-defense.

Michael Capponi remembered that "One night there was an argument in the VIP room of some club [not Liquid], and a real big guy got in Chris's face and said 'I'll fuck you up!' Chris went *whomp whomp!* The whole place turned into a brawl. Chris must've knocked out ten people." The club's security guards came after him, so Paciello climbed out a window and ran down the back alley to escape—but he was so pumped up and pissed off that he went back to the club through the front door, punched the guy who'd said "I'll fuck you up" one more time, and ran back out. "Man, it was like the Wild West when he was here," Capponi said.

Somehow Paciello got away with his violent behavior and illegal activities with impunity. He might still have managed to lead a charmed life if he hadn't tried to move Liquid to New York City in the spring of 1998. Casares and Paciello had been searching for over a year to find the right location for Liquid in New York. If Liquid was grossing $6 million a year in South Beach, a New York version could do $10 million, probably more. Not only that, it would make them famous and powerful. But New York wasn't Miami Beach. It was a more complicated place, where people were not willing to suspend belief and refrain from asking probing questions just because Chris Paciello was sexy or Ingrid Casares knew Madonna.

Casares and Paciello wanted to take over the lease of a 20,000-square-foot Latin music club at 16 West 22nd Street called Les Poulets in Manhattan's Flatiron District, a neighborhood filled with residential lofts and a few rowdy and troublesome nightclubs. Casares and Paciello hired a New York publicist and the "mega-club Liquid is coming" drums began to beat in the New York newspapers. But instead of creating anticipation, it made Liquid sound overwhelming and scary for the already nightclub-weary Community Board 5. Quality-of-life neighborhood activists lobbied the landlord of 16 West 22nd Street, David Yagoda, who was in his seventies, to refuse to assign Les Poulets' lease to Liquid, and Paciello and Casares countered by offering Yagoda a $100,000 signing bonus. It wasn't long before the story of the community versus Liquid ended up in the *New York Post*'s "Page Six," as well as in a few columns by Jack Newfeld, who defended the neighborhood's prerogative to a little peace and quiet. In the end the landlord withdrew the right to assign the lease, and shortly after, in what *New York* magazine termed a "bizarre" announcement, Rudy Washington, the deputy mayor of New York, came forward to declare that Liquid would never open in Manhattan.

The fuss put Chris Paciello under the scrutiny of William Bastone, an investigative reporter for the *Village Voice*, and in April 1998 an article appeared called "Thug Life: Wild Man Chris Paciello Has the Juice at Liquid." This was the first time that any serious journalist had looked into Paciello's background. The article revealed that Paciello's real name was Christian Ludwigsen, that he had been arrested three times for felony assault, and that he had a long police record, including car theft and grand larceny. The article claimed that FBI investigators believed that the Gambino family had owned a piece of the nightclub Risk and that the fire that destroyed it was caused by arson. It was also revealed that just recently, on a visit to New York, Paciello had been arrested for attempted murder after stabbing a paparazzo in the chest three times with a fork (the photographer mysteriously dropped the charges). The article also disclosed that three of Paciello's buddies, whom he employed at Liquid, were known Bonanno family associates and were brought down to Miami Beach from New York to be "cogs in a drug distribution network." As for the "quality of life" activists who didn't want Liquid in the Flatiron District, the *Voice* described Paciello as a "quality-of-life nightmare."

It was quite a mouthful, although it didn't mention the Judith Shemtov murder.

Casares was furious, not about the revelations but because her chances of opening a club in New York had been dashed and she'd been deprived of her shot at the major leagues. She saw herself as a victim of a conspiracy. "I just can't imagine those fuckers said no to me," she told *New York* magazine the day after the New York State Liquor Authority turned down her request for a liquor license. "There's some weird conspiracy going on between the other nightclubs—who don't want competition—the community board, and the press." She complained to *HX*, a New York gay magazine, "The whole thing left me with a really bad taste in my mouth."

Back in Miami Beach the reaction was singular.

People were enchanted with the news about Paciello. Their wildest fantasies were true. He was a bona fide bad boy, Mob connected. It was *Goodfellas* in South Beach. Ray Liotta as Chris Paciello. Lorraine Bracco as Madonna. "People will forgive anything for a good time," Michael Capponi observed.

On Paciello's twenty-seventh birthday Madonna called him on the phone and sang "Happy Birthday" to him, parodying Marilyn Monroe singing to John F. Kennedy, but she changed the lyrics to "Happy Birthday, dear *mobster*, Happy Birthday to you . . ."

IT WAS just about then that Michael Capponi returned to Miami Beach. In March 1998—after an odyssey of rehabs, relapses, and hospital stays, including one for a head tumor that left him deaf in his right ear—Capponi's mother found a drug rehabilitation facility for him in Montreal, Canada, where he somehow, finally, cleaned up. At that point he was addicted to high doses of methadone. "I went cold turkey to kick methadone," he said. "I sat in my room at the rehab and I had ten blankets and I screamed and sweated and went through all the possible nightmares and tortures." When it was over he met with a drug rehabilitation counselor. "He said that I needed to go to Narcotics Anonymous meetings and that I'd never be able to drink again," Capponi remembered. "He told me that I had to make all new friends, and that I'd never be able to be in the nightclub business again. He said that I'd never be able to go back to Miami. Never. Everything I am today is all the things the doctor told me that I had to give up. My attitude from that moment on was 'We'll see about that.'"

Did he ever figure out why he needed to obliterate himself with heroin in the first place? If he knows, he won't say. "It's a long, long debate," he offered uncomfortably. He was suddenly taciturn. "A bunch of different stuff. Mainly it was that once I was addicted, I couldn't get out of it. There's never a day when you're a heroin addict that you don't wish you weren't a heroin addict."

In the summer of 1998 Capponi slept on the couch at a friend's apartment in a run-down building on Collins Avenue and 71st Street. "It was pretty much of a shock for me to discover what a huge success Liquid had become and that Chris Paciello was now King of the City," he said. "He was at a level that I would never imagine. So my first night back in town, I dressed in the one outfit I owned and I went to Liquid." As it happened there was a party that night at Liquid celebrating a fashion spread in a local magazine and as soon as Capponi walked in the door people began to recognize him and the paparazzi took his picture.

"Chris almost died when he saw me," Capponi remembered. "He almost dropped dead. I could tell he wasn't happy to see me. He had an expression like 'Oh shit, the competition is back.' Everybody was super-skeptical about my recovery. The word on the street was 'Wow, Capponi's back, let's see how long he lasts—we'll give it a week.'"

Capponi worked hard to change that assumption. He was up early, he strolled on Lincoln Road so people could see he was not stoned, and he made an effort to eat breakfast every day at the Van Dyke Café at 9:30 a.m., "just to get waiters talking, 'Oh Michael Capponi is up in the morning...'" He deliberately wore only light, cheery colors, the opposite of his Jim Morrison persona. "I don't think I wore anything black for a long time." He would not go into a public bathroom, "even if I had to pee," he said. "I would not set foot in a public bathroom because I didn't want to give anybody the opportunity to say 'Yeah, I saw Capponi in the bathroom stall for fifteen minutes [doing drugs].'"

Although Paciello was cynical about Capponi's newfound

sobriety, he decided to give him a shot. Paciello bought Capponi some new clothes and offered him a job managing a $2.5 million lounge called Bar Room that Paciello and Ingrid Casares were going to open in January of 1999. Bar Room, with its bilevel VIP room, was designed to appeal to an older, more sophisticated crowd than the higher-energy Liquid.

Ingrid didn't like Capponi. "She had no real knowledge of who I was before I left," Capponi explained. "She had no idea that I'd been doing parties for seven years on this beach making ten thousand dollars a week. While I was gone Ingrid had a lot of press saying she was the Queen of the Night, and Queen Ingrid didn't understand why King Chris picked me to be the face of their new place. She thought he was making a bad choice. I demanded a three-thousand-a-week salary in the beginning and Ingrid came up to me and said, 'It'll be after I'm in my grave that you get three thousand dollars a week. I don't even make that.' I was bitter with her," but Paciello tried to smooth things over between them.

Once back in the saddle, Capponi showed that he hadn't lost his touch, and along with Ingrid's show-business contacts, Bar Room became another celebrity-packed nightclub and South Beach sensation, grossing $5.5 million in less than a year.

Since they'd been foiled in New York, the likely next step for Paciello and Casares was to open a branch of Liquid in Palm Beach, just ninety minutes away, a wealthy but sedate resort town ripe for a new, hipper kind of nightclub. Paciello found a property that was available in West Palm Beach, and he and Casares and Capponi set to work on creating the club. Capponi's idea was to have the grand opening on Thanksgiving weekend—the same weekend Liquid had opened in Miami Beach four years before. As part of his plan, on the Saturday before the official opening, they would throw a huge invitational party for the elite of Palm Beach. The goal was to show them what a night out on the town was really like. Capponi had a $100,000 budget and he pulled out all the stops. The night of the party "I loaded every single model that I could find in Miami Beach into rented buses to take them to Palm Beach," he said. "We had the modeling agencies' names on the sides of the buses. Three hundred people attended the party, and at the end of the night we handed every guest a CD that we'd created, which was an invitation inviting them back to the grand opening of Liquid Room the next weekend."

It was a heady moment. Capponi felt that he was back to full strength, as potent as before his downfall, and he was working well with Paciello, despite Ingrid's resentment. "We were set for the biggest opening ever in Palm Beach," Capponi laughed ruefully. "I went back to South Beach for a few days, and I was having lunch in a restaurant and the TV was tuned to CNN and suddenly I heard them say, '*Chris Paciello was arrested on murder charges*,' and I said, '*Oh my God!*'"

IN LATE November 1999, Paciello was charged with racketeering, felony murder, and bank robbery. Under advice from attorney Roy Black, Paciello pleaded not guilty and immediately paid the $250,000 in back taxes and penalties he owed.

As it would turn out, Paciello had been the subject of a two-year investigation by at least five different law-enforcement agencies, including the FBI, the U.S. Attorney's Office in Brooklyn, and the Miami Beach police. His fatal mistake was hiring a local cop-on-the-take named Andrew Dohler, who was working undercover. Paciello paid Dohler as a "security consultant" for Liquid, but his real value was in feeding Paciello information he could use against his competitors and cause trouble for them. He also gave Paciello advance warning about police raids conducted to find underage drinkers and drug sales at Liquid. To make Dohler's information seem authentic, the Miami Beach police staged planned raids so Dohler could tip off Paciello in advance and gain his trust. Paciello trusted Dohler enough to bring him along on the boat *Liquid* one day when Paciello went to have lunch north of Miami Beach with Colombo family Mob boss Alphonse Persico.

Dohler had been recording Paciello's phone conversations for months, including one in which Paciello made it clear that he didn't like snitches. "You know Sammy the Bull?" he asked Dohler about the man who ratted out his Mafia comrades and went into the Federal Witness Protection Program. "They should kill him and his whole family." The most damning phone call was one in which Paciello conspired with Dohler to kill his former employee Gerry Kelly, who'd jumped ship to work at a new club called Level. Kelly had been offered a piece of the action at Level, and he knew that Paciello would be furious if he went to work for the competition, so Kelly resigned by letter and left Miami Beach for a few weeks, hoping Paciello would have a chance to calm down by the time he got back. Paciello didn't calm down. Instead he told Andrew Dohler that he wanted to have drugs planted in Kelly's car and have him arrested by the police, or, failing that, "we got to get him beat up. I've got to get him whacked." Unknown to Kelly, an undercover police detail shadowed him for his own safety for several weeks after Paciello's phone call to Dohler.

Paciello's arrest made headlines, yet Liquid in West Palm Beach opened as scheduled that Saturday night. "Despite Chris's arrest," Capponi said, "or maybe because of it, the opening was a huge hit. There was tremendous media coverage. The next day, when I met with Ingrid to make up invitations for the coming weekend, I told her that I didn't think we should use Chris's name on the invitation, that it wasn't appropriate with Chris on TV and in the newspapers being accused of murder. Here I was trying to get the most conservative Palm Beach old-money people to come to this club. I thought the invitation should read 'Ingrid Casares and Michael Capponi invite you' and that we'd put Chris's name back on the invitations when he got out of jail. Ingrid lost it. She thought I was trying to take his place. She told Chris I wanted his name removed from the invitations, and he started threatening me with his thug brother—the brother who is in jail now on bank robbery charges. So I walked. I left. I didn't talk to Chris again for years after that. I really felt bad. Chris always perceived that I abandoned him. I was seen as the guy who left Chris hanging."

Paciello surrendered himself to federal authorities on December 1, 1999, facing up to thirty-three years in jail. His attorney, Roy Black, chalked up the accusations against his client as a result of Paciello's fame. "That's the way our society works," Black said. "When someone becomes a successful or high-profile person, they also become a target." Louis Canales, a promoter and publicist, told the press, "If Chris Paciello did everything the government said he did, he deserves an Oscar, because he fooled everybody down here. The Chris Paciello we're reading about in the newspapers is not the person we've come to know and love." Ingrid was still insisting, "He's innocent and everybody here knows that."

Paciello's bail was ultimately set at $15 million—$5 million more than John Gotti's bail when he was arrested—and his little kingdom was disassembled to pay off his debts, legal fees, and fines. The offices at 409 Lincoln Road were closed and Liquid, Bar Room, Liquid Palm Beach Room, the boat named *Liquid*, and the waterfront mansion were all sold. Paciello was placed under house arrest at his mother's home in Staten Island to await federal trial in October 2000. But on the eve of the legal spectacle he was picked up in the middle of the night by federal agents from the Witness Protection Program. He appeared briefly in court the next day and pleaded guilty to attempted robbery in the Judy Shemtov murder and to armed robbery in the Chemical Bank heist in Staten Island. The court agreed to reduce his sentence to only ten years—if he did the one thing he said he hated most: cooperate with the authorities and rat on his friends.

Paciello sent away a dozen guys. Among those he testified against were gangster Eddie Boyle of the Gambino family; Alphonse Persico, the acting boss of the Colombo crime family; Tommy Reynolds, the gunman in the Shemtov murder, who got thirty years; Fabrizio DeFrancisci, who got thirty-six; and Paciello's two pals from Brooklyn who came to work for him at Liquid, Rico Locasio, who was sentenced to five years, and Dom Dionisio, who was sent away for sixteen.

Paciello was remanded to a maximum penitentiary facility in Atlanta, Georgia, where he passed his time learning Spanish and earning his high school diploma. While he was in jail he and Casares reportedly sold the screen rights to the story of the golden age of Liquid to Dreamworks Pictures, which began to develop a script, until it became clear to the motion picture company that they were going into business with an accomplice to murder and the deal collapsed. A book called *Mob Over Miami,* authored by a New York *Daily News* reporter, was made into a 2007 roman à clef movie made for cable TV called *Kings of South Beach.* It starred actor Jason Gedrick as Paciello. "At least they got somebody good-looking to play me," Paciello commented.

After serving seven years of his prison sentence, Paciello was released on September 8, 2006, a date he has tattooed on his right wrist, and moved to Los Angeles. "Jail is humiliating and demeaning," he said. "Most of the people, including myself, deserved to be there. . . . I try not to be bitter. I have no right. I hurt people and I deserved to be there. Right now I'm looking forward to tomorrow." As for Judith Shemtov's murder: "So many times I've written letters to her family. What do you say? Sorry? I'm sorry. I'm very sorry. There's nothing I can do to change that."

Evidently living an anonymous life under an assumed identity was a worse punishment for Paciello than jail, because he soon dropped out of the Witness Protection Program and started living the high life again. "He's walking around Los Angeles like the cock of the walk," said a friend. In 2008 he attended the opening of a Beverly Hills clothing store along with Paris Hilton and Lindsay Lohan, and he's been out on the town with singer Natalie Imbruglia, supermodel Adriana Lima, and actress Sofia Vergara. In the summer of 2008 he became a consultant to a restaurant in West Hollywood called Murano, and he owns two pizzerias called Christoni's, one in Beverly Hills and another on Sunset Boulevard. He has told the press that Leonardo De Caprio is producing a film about his life, and there is an "Untitled Chris Paciello Project" feature film slated for production in 2009, with no producers listed.

He doesn't seem to have changed his old ways, either. In August 2008 he was arrested on felony assault charges for hunting down and beating up a man he got into an argument with in a West Hollywood nightclub. It was ruled self-defense. "I'm working with a psychiatrist to figure out how I can walk away from confrontation without feeling like a coward," he said. "I need to be able to walk away with my manhood intact." He isn't afraid of retribution for all the men he put away, either. "I'm not bragging that nobody could touch me," he told a columnist. "I could walk outside and get hit by a car. But I lived my life way worse in New York looking over my shoulder, carrying guns and robbing drug dealers. . . . I'm out all the time. If someone feels they want to come after me and get revenge, then that's going to happen. I don't live my life in fear."

As for Ingrid Casares, she lives in Miami and works sometimes as a club and party promoter, but the glow is gone. It seems she's squeezed every last ounce of value out of her friendship with Madonna; she recently promoted a Madonna look-alike contest on Miami Beach. In October 2000 she gave birth to a baby boy she conceived with a twenty-five-year-old German model named Dennis Schaller, and she devotes most of her time to being a mother.

Michael Capponi heard from Paciello after he got out of jail. He called to tell Capponi how proud he was of him and how happy he was for his success, and Capponi promised his old friend that they'd get together when he got out to Los Angeles. "Chris text-messaged me a few times to put people on the VIP list to some clubs," Capponi said, "but I haven't spoken to him again."

Eighteen

FOOL'S PARADISE

fool's paradise: n. a state of delusive
contentment or false hope.

— THE AMERICAN HERITAGE DICTIONARY, 2000

"The two great shocks of South Beach," said Brian Antoni, "was when Versace was killed, and when we found out that Chris Paciello was an accused killer."

The Italian designer Gianni Versace was killed the morning of July 15, 1997, as he was returning to his mansion on Ocean Drive from the News Café, where he went every day to buy the newspapers. A spree killer from San Diego named Andrew Cunanan, who had spent the night dancing at Liquid trying to pick up men, put two bullets in Versace's head on the front steps of the house, for no discernible reason other than for the notoriety and thrill of it. This particularly horrible murder cut close to the bone in South Beach; notoriety and thrill was partly what South Beach was selling.

Versace felt he was in some mystical way connected to South Beach. "Every happiness is a masterpiece, and that is what I think of Miami," he wrote in a book he published in 1993 called *South Beach Stories*. He had fallen in love with the city during a stopover at Miami International Airport on his way to Cuba. He had had a few hours to kill, so he got into a taxi and said to the driver, "Show me something fancy and fun," and the driver took him over the causeway to Ocean Drive. Versace sat at a table at the News Café and looked out at the beach and the Art Deco buildings, and watched tanned young people in their bikinis and Speedos on Rollerblades and bicycles, and before he could finish his Cuban coffee he had sand in his shoes.

In 1992 he paid $2.9 million for the old Amsterdam Palace apartment building on Ocean Drive and 11th Street and another $3.7 million for a ramshackle tenement next door, and lavished $30 million on the properties to create a dazzling 16,000-square-foot palazzo with a leitmotif of Medusa heads—some of them created out of the 5 million pieces of pebble tile used in the mosaics that sheathed the floors, walls, fountains and courtyards. The house had thirteen bedrooms, a Moorish gang shower for six, and a revolving observatory dome with a telescope from which Versace could watch the Cuban boys on the beach. Versace gave South Beach enormous cachet and attention, and his mansion came to embody all the glorious excess and overheated desire that was the pride of South Beach.

Three years after Versace's death, forty-two-year-old Peter Loftin, a drop-out from North Carolina State University who made $250 million buying and selling cell phone time, bought Casa Casuarina from the Versace family for $19 million and turned it into a venture more in line with the new Miami Beach— a private club, with membership starting at $30,000 a year, which included the opportunity of sleeping in Gianni Versace's baronial bedroom for $4,000 a night. Outside the locked gates of Casa Casuarina on Ocean Drive there is always a knot of people, mostly Japanese tourists, taking photographs of each other on the limestone front steps where Versace died, making it the single most photographed place in Miami Beach.

"Versace was excited about the exact same thing in South Beach that everyone was excited about," Antoni said. "There were a few brief years when all the creativity and beauty and wealth came together. Versace was living off the same energy we all felt, and when he was killed the whole thing changed. It became something else. It was like when Adam ate the apple."

South Beach may no longer be the Eden that Antoni remembered, but its beaches of mammon remain a powerful brand that sets cash registers ringing around the world. "Yes, South Beach is for sale now," Antoni lamented. "Back in the 1980s and early 1990s there were parties for the fun of parties; now there are only parties to sell something. Back then there was art for the fun of art; now there's Art Basel." Indeed, a Google search brings up over 3 million responses for products cashing in on the South Beach name, most with little to do with the resort, including perfumes, cosmetics, vitamin supplements, self-improvement tapes, and bed canopies. Among the more successful uses of the name are *The South Beach Diet* book, written by Arthur Agatston, a local cardiologist, which sold 23 million copies and launched a line of frozen diet foods, and the "healthy" South Beach Beverage company (located in Connecticut) that was sold to PepsiCo for $370 million.

It's no small irony that one South Beach product that isn't selling very well is South Beach condominiums. The building, selling, and buying of condominiums and homes is the second-biggest industry in the Miami area, next to tourism. One out of every seven hundred people has a real estate license. The *Wall Street Journal* reported that the housing inventory rose by 245 percent between 2005 and 2006, and that another 75,000 condominiums were scheduled to come on the market by 2008, a supply that would take five years for a healthy market to absorb. When giddy developers were forced to sober up in the real estate crash of 2008, Miami-Dade was left with a glut of condominiums second only to that in Las Vegas. In only one year, condominium prices declined by 30 percent—this in a state with a low population growth rate and a housing market wholly dependent on retirees and second-home buyers. It's what *Time* magazine called a real estate "pyramid scheme" that needs a thousand newcomers a day to keep it from crumbling. Equally as threatening to the real estate market is the fact that an estimated 40 percent of the new condominium apartments were purchased preconstruction by speculators, who bought up units with only a small deposit down and the balance due upon completion. Speculators were counting on the value of apartments to rise by the time of closing for a quick flip and fat profit, but by 2008 there were so many desperate speculators trying to get out of real estate deals for unsalable apartments that a cottage industry sprang up of lawyers specializing in breaking preconstruction contracts.

If history is any measure, Miami Beach's cycle of crash and recovery comes about every twenty years, which would mean the city is due for a rude awakening. It already suffers from the toxic syndrome of its own ubiquitous success. Its glamour has faded with its overweening popularity. Certainly it still attracts rap stars and tabloid queens for dirty weekends, but that's not what's happening on the streets and in the clubs. The experience of the average tourist is that two of the city's greatest attractions, Ocean Drive and Lincoln Road, have deteriorated into a Middle America mall, with drunken fraternity boys and tourists in velour sweatpants and undershirts on Ocean Drive, and purse snatchers and cross-dressers on Lincoln Road. If Miami Beach renews itself again, its future as a resort probably lies in more Las Vegas–like, self-contained mega hotels, like the new Fontainebleau, with myriad restaurants and an in-house nightclub to give the visitor an alternative to the two main streets. Perhaps Miami Beach's last best hope is to revisit the issue of legalizing gambling, which would lift the resort to a whole other level of appeal. Yet legalized gambling would be the end of the last vestiges of Miami Beach as a small community.

Brian Antoni is frustrated by what he sees happening to the city to which he is so dedicated. "I kind of want to kiss it and slap it at the same time," he said. He laments that many of the creative people who helped build the place into what it is today are fleeing South Beach for the city of Miami, where real estate is more reasonable and life is quieter. He can imagine a day soon when all the uniqueness and all the old-timers will be gone. "Will the last person who leaves South Beach," Antoni said, "please turn off the disco ball?"

ONE LAST piece of unfinished business.

Michael Capponi never stopped thinking about Francesca Rayder.

"I remembered that when we were living together she was paying my rent," he said, and in December 2003 he decided to send her a check for $5,000 along with a long letter of apology. "I said I knew she didn't need the money, but I felt that I owed it to her. I told her that I was finally content, and that I was extremely happy for her success, and that I would always love her and I hoped our paths would cross again."

A week later Francesca called him. "She was going to be in Miami Beach the next day on a photo shoot and she was staying at the Shore Club and she wanted to see me," Capponi said. He was thrilled to have the opportunity to show Francesca how successful and stable he'd become. He got a haircut and went to a tanning parlor and bought a new suit. He had his Range Rover washed and detailed. He rehearsed in his mind what he was going to say to her and how he was going to say it.

At seven the next night he drove his Rover up the driveway of Shore Club, and handed his keys to the valet, and just as he was entering the lobby he saw her. She was sitting on an upholstered white chair with her long tanned legs crossed, smoking a cigarette. She was still the most beautiful woman he had ever seen.

And he was over her.

He knew it just like that. The spell was broken. Released. Michael and Francesca had dinner and they reminisced about old times, and later they kissed good-night and he never saw her again.

The next year he met Erin Henry.

Erin loved Michael. He was kind and generous and full of ambition, and it certainly was exciting to be living with the King of Nightlife, but it was draining too. "He has people around him all the time," she said. "I don't know how he can bear it. Even on a Sunday there are twenty people there. I just can't be around people all the time. It's amazing that it doesn't suck all the energy out of him." She was also troubled that she hadn't made any close friends. Even people she felt a special bond with, like Ambika Marshall, were in and out of her life all the time. She had been trying to sell real estate and not done very well, yet in the two years she had lived with Michael his career had skyrocketed. His name had become such a recognizable brand in South Beach that he began to design and manufacture a line of upscale furniture, called Casa Capponi, and his real estate development company, Capponi Properties, had become one of the area's most successful builders and renovators of luxury homes. He sat on the boards of several charities, and every Thanksgiving he organized a drive to feed two thousand homeless people. Some days Erin hardly ever saw him.

In January 2007, tired of competing for his attention and disillusioned with life in South Beach, Erin broke up with Michael and moved to New York. She found an apartment in SoHo and resumed her modeling career full-time. It was bitter cold in New York that winter, and she wrote in an e-mail to a friend, "It's funny, because after all that complaining about Miami, I am getting a bit homesick. I could really use a weekend on the boat. It made me think of something funny I wanted to share with you. You may have witnessed it, I can't remember. Every weekend Michael *loved* to pack the boat and get on either his surfboard or a Jet Ski and show off for as long as he could last, spraying the biggest surf on the surfboard or jumping the highest boat wake much to the captain's annoyance. This was both his sole form of exercise and a little ego stroke to start the weekend off right. Michael would never say anything, but if everyone didn't watch he would be a little hurt. I always made sure everyone gave their full attention and acknowledged how much air he caught. We called this the Michael Capponi Show. I don't think he knows that, but it is kind of like his life. . . . The Michael Capponi Show on South Beach."

Six months later, unable to get the Michael Capponi Show out of her mind, Erin went back to Miami Beach and married him.

Bibliography

AMONG PUBLICATIONS, libraries, and sources that were consulted in the writing of this book were *Time; Look; Out; New York Times; New York Post; New York; People; Miami Herald; Miami New Times; Miami Sun Post;* Official Website of the City of Miami Beach; Miami Beach Visitor and Convention Authority; Miami Beach Economic Development; Florida Collection, Miami-Dade Library System; the Historical Museum of Southern Florida; the Wolfsonian Florida International University Museum; the Miami Design Preservation League.

TEXTS ABOUT Miami and Miami Beach that were consulted in the writing of this book include *Miami Beach* (Centennial Press, 1994) by Howard Kleinberg; *Miami: The Way We Were* (Surfside Publishing, 1989) by Howard Kleinberg; *South Beach: The Novel* (Black Cat, 2008) by Brian Antoni; *Fabulous Hoosier* (Robert M. McBride & Company, 1947) by Jane Fisher; *Dying in the Sun* (Charterhouse, 1974) by Donn Pearce; *City on the Edge: The Transformation of Miami* (University of California Press, 1993) by Alejandro Portes and Alex Stepick; *Going to Miami: Exiles, Tourists and Refugees in the New America* (University Press of Florida, 1987) by David Rieff; *Last Train to Paradise* (Three Rivers Press, 2002) by Les Standiford; *The Life and Times of Miami Beach* (Knopf, 1995) by Ann Armbruster; *Castles in the Sand: The Life and Times of Carl Graham Fisher* (University Press of Florida, 2000) by Mark S. Foster; *Miami, U.S.A.* (Henry Holt and Company, 1953) by Helen Muir; *To the Golden Cities: Pursuing the*

American Jewish Dream in Miami and L.A. (Harvard University Press, 1994) by Deborah Dash Moore; *The Last Resorts* (Harper & Brothers, 1948) by Cleveland Amory; *Miami: Then and Now* (Thunder Bay Press, 2002) by Arva Moore Parks and Carolyn Klepser; *Tropical Deco: The Architecture and Design of Old Miami Beach* (Rizzoli, 1981) by Laura Cerwinske; *My Love Affair with Miami Beach* (Simon & Schuster, 1991) by Richard Nagler; *Woggles and Cheese Holes: The History of Miami Beach's Hotels* (Greater Miami & The Beaches Hotel Association, 2005) by Howard Kleinberg; *The Most of Everything: The Story of Miami Beach* (Harcourt, Brace and Company, 1960) by Harold Mehling; *My Story* (Gove Press, 1977) by Judith Exner; *Catskill Culture* (Temple Univerity Press, 1998) by Phil Brown; *South Beach: America's Riviera, Miami Beach, Florida* (Arcade Publishing, 1995) by Bill Wisser; *Saving South Beach* (University Press of Florida, 2005) by M. Barron Stofik; *Sins of South Beach: The True Story of Corruption, Violence, and the Making of Miami Beach* (Pegasus Publishing House, Inc., 2006) by Alex Daoud; *Deco Delights: Preserving the Beauty and Joy of Miami Beach Architecture* (E. P. Dutton, 1988) by Barbara Baer Capitman and Steven Brooke; *Miami Beach Memories: A Nostalgic Chronicle of Days Gone By* (Insider's Guide, 2007) by Joann Biondi; *Clubland: The Fabulous Rise and Murderous Fall of Club Culture* (St. Martin's Press, 2003) by Frank Owen; *Miami: Hot and Cool* (Clarkson Potter, 1990) by Laura Cerwinske and Steven Brooke; *Old Miami Beach: A Case Study in Historic Preservation, July 1976–July 1980* (Miami Design Preservation League, 1980) by H. Michael Raley, Linda G. Polansky, and Aristides J. Millas; *Everything by Design; My Life As an Architect* (St. Martin's Press, 2007) by Alan Lapidus; *Too Much Is Never Enough: An Autobiography* (Rizzoli, 1996) by Morris Lapidus; *MiMo: Miami Modern Revealed* (Chronicle Books, 2004) by Eric P. Nash and Randall C. Robinson Jr.; *The Making of Miami Beach 1933–41: The Architecture of Lawrence Murray Dixon* (Rizzoli, 2001); *Rediscovering Art Deco U.S.A.: A Nationwide Tour of Architectural Delights* (Viking

Studio Books, 1994) by Barbara Capitman, Michael D. Kinerk, and Dennis W. Wilhelm; *Little Man: Meyer Lansky and the Gangster Life* (Little, Brown 1991) by Robert Lacey; *Miami: City of the Future* (Atlantic Monthly Press, 1987) by T. D. Allman; *Billion Dollar Sandbar* (E. P. Dutton, 1970) by Polly Redford; *Diary of a South Beach Party Girl* (Simon Spotlight Entertainment, 2007) by Gwen Cooper; *Morris Lapidus* (Assouline Press, 2004) by Deborah Desilets; *Life on Mars: Gangsters, Runaways, Exiles, Drag Queens and Other Aliens in Florida* (Doubleday, 1996) by Alexander Stuart; *Up for Grabs: A Trip Through Time and Space in the Sunshine State* (University Press of Florida, 1985) by John Rothchild; *Historical Sketches and Sidelights of Miami, Florida* (Privately Printed, 1921) by Isidor Cohen; *Miami: The Magic City* (Continental Heritage, 1981) by Arva Moore Parks; *Mob Over Miami* (Onyx, 2002) by Michele McPhee; *Moon Over Miami* (Random House, 1955) by Jack Kofoed; *Jackie Gleason: An Intimate Portrait of the Great One* (Pharos Books, 1992) by W. J. Weatherby; *Vulgar Favors: Andrew Cunanan, Versace, and the Largest Failed Manhunt in U.S. History* (Dell, 1999) by Maureen Orth; *Miami* (Vintage International, 1987) by Maureen Orth; *Miami Beach: Images of America* (Arcadia Publishing, 2005) by Seth Bramson; *Miami in Vintage Postcards* (Arcadia Publishing, 2000) by Patricia Kennedy; *His Way: The Unauthorized Biography of Frank Sinatra* (Bantam, 1986) by Kitty Kelley; *Miami Beach in 1920: The Making of a Winter Resort* (Arcadia, 2002) by Abraham D. Lavender.

THE FILMS *A Hole in the Head* (MGM, 1959) produced and directed by Frank Capra; *Moon Over Miami* (20th Century Fox, 1941) directed by Walter Lang; *The Bellboy* (Paramount Pictures, 1960) directed by Jerry Lewis; *8th & Ocean* (MTV television reality program, 2006); *Scarface* (Universal, 1983) directed by Brian De Palma; *Cocaine Cowboys* (Magnolia Pictures, 2006) directed by Billy Corben; *Tony Rome* (1967) directed by Gordon Douglas, were also viewed in the research for this book.

Acknowledgments

THE AUTHOR would like to thank Don and Katrina Peebles; Thomas Kramer; Michael Capponi; Erin Henry; Matt Loewen; Ambika Marshall; Michelle Pommier; Irene Marie; Rabbi Gary Glickstein; Rabbi Zev Katz; Stephen Muss; Melanie Muss; Michael Aller; Andrew Capitman; John Capitman; Esther Percal; Lina Barcelo; Neisen Kasdin; Brian Antoni; Lisa Cole; Lenore Toby; Tom Austin; Erin Lucas; Tara Solomon; Gary Farmer; Antonio Misuraca; Steven Siskind; David Leddick; Louis Canales; Saul Gross; Jane Gross; Elaine Lancaster; James Davis; Bonnie Smith; Leslie Abravanel; Dona Zemo; Daisy Olivera; Gary James; Peter Loftin; Beat Fornaro; Gerry Kelly; Matti Bower; John Streiff; Alex Daoud; Christian Garces; Shareef Malnik; Alvin Malnik; Richard Mufson; Leonard Roudner; Michele Pommier; Myra Farr; Mitch Kaplan; Philip Levine; David Granoff; Mandi Nadel; Tommy Pooch; Robert Maideski; Zachary Felter; Jill Hertzberg; Donald Pliner; Mark Shantzis; Merle Weiss; Eddie McIntyre; Buck Winthrop; Ariel Stein; Richard Hoberman; Michael Kinerk; Dennis Wilhelm; Brian Bilzin; Maria Beatriz Gutierrez; Susan Brustman; Margaret Doyle; Joann Biondi; Ricardo Tibet; Nancy and Norman Liebman; Ben Novack Jr; Bernice Novack; Michael Paul Dreiling; Lilla Hartai; Chapman Ducote; Jeff Kamlet; David Colby; Amy Zakarin; Sam Boldrick; Dawn Hugh; Shelly Acoca; and Joe Allen's restaurant.

My gratitude for the support of my friends Ellyn Jaffe; Linda Kamm; Carolyn Beegan; Diane and Alan Lieberman; Andrea

Ackerman; Paul Brennan; Susan Aarons; Sidney Butchkes; Frank Miller; Judith and Rudy Giuliani; David and Kathy Gelfand; Wally Smith; Ted Conklin; Brenda Landrum; Randy Quintal; Joseph Olshan; Debra Stein; Lynn Grossman, Bob Balaban, Hazel Balaban, Mariah Balaban; Sophia Tezel, Frank DiGiacomo, and Antony DiGiacomo who loves South Beach.

My thanks as well to Matthew Martin; Nathan Roberson; Martha Trachtenberg; Katie Wainwright; Sarah Breivogel; Lauren Dong; Kevin Garcia; Mark McCauslin; and Nancy J. Stabile.

No author could have received better creative guidance than I did from my patient editor at Crown, Rick Horgan, or have a finer agent, or know a nicer guy, than Richard Pine.

STEVEN GAINES
Wainscott, New York

Index

Abdul Aziz, Prince Turki bin, 181–82, 201

Abravanel, Lesley, 201

Agatston, Arthur, *The South Beach Diet*, 256

Aller, Michael, 14, 23–25, 27, 28, 32–33

Ameche, Don, 42

Amory, Cleveland, 12

Annenberg, Moe, 12

Anshen, Robert, 68

Anthony, Marc, 5

Antoni, Brian, 241, 254, 256, 258

Arafat, Yasser, 22

Arnstein, Danny, 47

Art Basel, 17, 256

Art Deco historic district:
  and Capitman, 113, 116, 129–30, 131, 136–37
  creation of, 113, 116
  and Horowitz, 131–34
  and MDPL, 129, 131, 136–38
  palette for, 132–34, 175
  and preservation law, 117
  promotion of, 128, 131–32, 173
  and South Beach renewal, 113, 128–29

Ashanti, 3

Astor, John Jacob, 66

Austin, Tom, 15, 228, 241

Bailey, Pearl, 76

Balazs, André, 7

Bass, Johanna and John, 19

Bassett, Harry Hood, 106n

Bastone, William, 245

Bath Avenue Crew, 232

Bearman, Kay, 114

Becker, Boris, 201

Beebe, Lucius, 38

Belafonte, Harry, 21

Benante, Joseph, 232

Benítez, Elsa, 208–9

Berle, Milton, 42

Bernhard, Sandra, 239

"Binder Boys," 31n

Black, Roy, 160, 237, 249, 251

Bonanno family, 232, 245

Boyle, Eddie, 251

Briggs, W. O., 12

Bruce, Lenny, 23

Brunn, Paul, 92

Buchanan, Edna, 150

Burda, Catrine, 184, 185

Busch, Clarence, 43

Bushnell, Candace, 190, 193

Caine, Michael and Shakira, 241

Calderin, Pepe, 7

Campbell, Naomi, 241

Canales, Louis, 251

Capitman, Andrew, 118–19, 123, 124, 128, 132, 136

Capitman, Barbara Baer, 115–16, 118, 119–25, 127–28, 129–30, 131–38

Capitman, John, 123, 124–25, 128
Capitman, Will, 122–24
Capone, Al, 42–44, 82
Capote, Truman, 241
Capponi, Michael:
  and Ambika, 174–77, 187, 216
  and Erin, 169–72, 175–76, 187,
    202, 225, 259, 260
  and Francesca, 226–27, 228, 230,
    234, 236, 258–59
  and heroin, 167, 168, 225, 229–30,
    234, 246–47
  Jim Morrison as muse of, 168, 225,
    227, 229, 247
  as nightclub promoter, 167–69,
    173–74, 176, 177, 189, 202–4,
    222, 228, 233, 236, 238, 250
  and Paciello, 225, 233–37,
    243–44, 246, 247–49, 250–51,
    253
  personality of, 167, 168, 225
  and Ridinger party, 3
  at Vix, 166–67, 168–69
Carlton, Vanessa, 3
Carpenter, Kelli, 181
Carrillo, Enrique, 7
Caruso, Lord Michael, 223
Casares, Ingrid, 238–40, 242–46, 248,
  250–51, 252, 253
Casares, Raul, 240
Castro, Fidel, 22, 83, 145–47, 153
Castro-Cid, Enrique, 119
Catskill Mountains:
  Borscht Belt in, 91–92
  hotels in, 39, 53, 92
Cavalli, Roberto, 174, 176
Chapman, Alvah H. Jr., 105–6n
Cherner, Joseph, 56
Christo, 113
Churchill, Winston, 41
Ciccone, Christopher, 189–90, 194,
  241
Cirque de Soleil, 18
Cockburn, Andrew, 148

Cohen, Elsie, 144–45, 148
Cohen, Sam, 45, 77, 78
Cole, Nat King, 21
Coles, Lisa, 35
Collins, John, 30
Colombian drug dealers, 149–52,
  228–29
Colombo family, 250, 252
Combs, Sean "Diddy," 178, 181
Committee of One Hundred,
  105–6n
Connery, Sean, 67
Costello, Frank, 82
Costner, Kevin, 67
Cowles, Jan, 7
Credit Suisse, 152
Cugat, Xavier, 42
Cummings, Robert, 189
Cunanan, Andrew, 254
Curtiss, Glenn, 137

D'Amico, John, 224
Daoud, Alex, 120, 139–45, 148,
  152–57, 159–65
Dash, Damon, 3
Davis, Kitty, 41
DeFrancisci, Fabrizio, 251
Deil, Peter, 211
De Milhau, Dolly, 40
Dempsey, Jack, 41
De Palma, Brian, 113
Dickinson, Bob, 106n
Diller, Barry, 241
Dionisio, Dom, 252
Dixie Highway, 30
Dixon, Lawrence Murray, 46, 118,
  173
DJ AM, 2
Dohler, Andrew, 249, 250
Donahue, Troy, 67
Doner, Michele Oka, 7, 10
Dorsey, Dana A., 21n
Doyle, Margaret, 118
Dreamworks Pictures, 252

Drug Enforcement Agency (DEA),
150, 228
Duchin, Peter, 9

Eden Roc, 72–80
Edison, Thomas, 54
Estefan, Gloria and Emilio, 178, 180,
241

Farmer, Gary, 111–12
and Capitman, 115–16, 120–21,
137
and The Strand, 114–15, 137, 138
Farrow, Mia, 36
Fassi, Mohammed al-, 181–82
Firestone, Harvey S., 54, 55
Fischetti, Joe "Stingy," 82, 83, 86n
Fisher, Carl, 11, 20, 28–32, 43, 54,
177
Fisher, Jane, 11, 29, 30, 32
Fisher Island, 21n, 177n
Fleischmann, Julius, 12
Florsheim, Leonard, 12
Fontainebleau Hotel, 33, 54–71
behind the scenes, 24–25, 35–37,
64–65
burglaries in, 67–68
construction of, 24, 58–62
design of, 56–58, 69
dining room, 65–66
dress code, 63–64
and Eden Roc, 72–76, 80
filming in, 66–67, 81
in financial difficulties, 88–89,
93–97
funding for, 55–56
hallway of, 99
home life in, 69–71
land acquisition for, 54
organized crime in, 81–87
ownership of, 85–87, 100–102
and postmodern architecture,
68–69
and Sinatra, 81–82

staircase to nowhere, 64, 74
and zoning, 55
Ford, Henry, 1, 54
Ford (modeling) Agency, 209, 210
Forge, The, 199–204
France, Roy F., 46, 48, 49–50
Frank, Howard and Mary, 7
Frazier, Brenda, 41
Friedman, Charles, 45
Friedman, Marvin Ross, 7
Friedman's Bakery, 133
Froman, Jane, 42
Frost, Phillip, 178
Fuentes, Daisy, 243

Gambino family, 224, 233, 245, 251
Garces, Christian Alexander, 191–94,
209, 216, 221
Garcia, Jacques, 173
Gardner, Harold, 95–96
Garfinkel, Howard, 78
Gedrick, Jason, 252
Geffen, David, 79, 241
Gehry, Frank, 18
Geldzahler, Henry, 114
Genovese crime family, 223
Gerry, Alex, 66
Giancana, Sam, 56, 82–83, 84, 87
Glassman, Herbert, 56
Glass, Philip, 114
Gleason, Jackie, 67
Godsrary, René de la Jousselinière de
Villermet de la, 65
Gold, Murray, 116
Goldberger, Paul, 118
Goldman, Irving, 80
Goldman, Tony, 134
Gonzalez, Orlando, 156
Gorlitz, Jules, 56
Gornick, April, 114
Gotti, Irv, 3
Gotti, John, 223, 251
Grable, Betty, 42
Green, Edward R. "Ned," 182–83

Green, Hetty, "the Witch of Wall Street," 182–83
Green, Milton, 210
Greene, Shecky, 42, 84
Griffin, W. M., 12
Gross, Jane, 129, 134
Guccione, Bob, 79

Haas, Richard, 33
Hannah, Daryl, 114
Harris, Julie, 72
Hawks, Howard, 41
Henry, Erin:
    and Ambika, 175–76, 187–88, 189, 259
    and Capponi, 169–72, 175–76, 187, 202, 225, 259–60
    and Ridinger party, 3
Heroin, 228–30, 234–37, 247
Hertz, John D., 12
Herzog, Jacques, 18
Hildegarde, 42
Hilly (waitress), 195, 196–98
Hilton, Paris, 252
Hohauser, Henry, 46, 132
Holden, Michael, 7
Hole in the Head, A (film), 81, 111, 118
Hollo, Tibor, 79
Holtz, Abel, 153–55, 159–63, 164
Holtz, Daniel, 154
Honeywell, Mark, 12
Hoover, William, 12
Horne, Lena, 21
Horowitz, Adam, 2
Horowitz, Leonard, 119, 125–28, 129, 131–35
Houston, Marques, 2
Houston, Whitney, 67
Hutton, Lauren, 114
Huxtable, Ada Louise, 68

Iglesias, Julio, 178
Imbruglia, Natalie, 252

Indianapolis Speedway, 29
Issa-Khan, Iran, 7

Jackson, Michael, 202
Jaffe, Ben, 85n
Ja Rule, 2, 3
Jeanne-Claude, 113
Jessel, Georgie, 32
Jewish population, 89–93, 108
Johansson, Ingemar, 77
Johnson, Don, 180
Johnson, Richard, 241
Jolson, Al, 41
Jones, Clarence, 85
Jordan, Michael, 201

Kamlet, Jeff, 3, 14, 170
Kaplan, Michael, 18
Karin Models, 174, 205
Kasdin, Neisen, 19, 89, 172–73, 242
Katz, Rabbi Zev, 6
Kefauver, Estes, 45
Kelly, Gerry, 241, 243, 250
Kelly, John Sims "Shipwreck," 41
Kennedy, John F., 36, 84, 246
Kennedy, John F. Jr., 114
Kennedy, Robert F., 85
Khan, Princess Yasmin, 184
Kinerk, Michael, 137
King, Don, 156, 179
Kleinberg, Howard, Woggles and Cheese Holes, 47n
Klein, Calvin and Kelly, 241
Koefed, Ted, 44
Kosar, Bernie, 200
Kramer, Thomas, 3, 177, 183–88
Kravitz, Lenny, 110
Kresge, Sebastian, 12

Lancaster, Elaine, 3, 20, 200
Landsburgh, Morris, 77, 78, 89
lang, k.d., 239
Lansky, Meyer, 77–78, 83, 85, 87, 201

Lapidus, Morris, 19, 34–37
    death of, 98
    and Eden Roc, 72–74
    and Fontainebleau, 37, 56–58, 59n,
        60–65, 68–69, 74n, 100
    and Sans Souci, 48–50
Leddick, David, 128, 131
Lehder, Carlos, 150
Levi, John, 39
Levitt, Jules, 45, 76
Lewis, Jerry, 66
Lewis, Lennox, 200
Liebman, Nancy, 128, 136–37, 138
Lima, Adriana, 252
Lincoln, Abraham, 29
Liquid, 240–46, 247–49, 250–51,
    252
Locasio, Rico, 252
Loewen, Matt, 189–98, 205–10,
    212–21
Loftin, Peter, 255
Lohan, Lindsay, 252
Lopez, Jennifer, 2, 5, 243
Lourde, Bryan, 241
Ludwigsen, Christian, 231, 245
Ludwigsen, George, 231
Ludwigsen, Marguerite, 231
Lukas, Erin, 212

MacArthur, Douglas, 41
Madonna, 178, 246
    and Casares, 238–40, 242, 244,
        253
    and Ciccone (brother), 189, 190,
        241
    and Ridinger party, 5
Maidique, Modesto A., 7
Mailer, Norman, 52
Malnik, Alvin, 201–2
Malnik, Shareef, 200, 201, 202
Mandela, Nelson, 22
Manilow, Barry, 172
Marden, Ben, 44, 47
Mariel refugees, 143, 145–49

Marshall, Ambika:
    and Capponi, 174–77, 187, 216
    and Erin Henry, 175–76, 187–88,
        189, 259
    and Kramer, 183, 187–88
    and Loewen, 189–90, 205–9,
        214–20
    in Virginia, 221
Martin, Dean, 202
Martinez, Gilberto "Willy," 155–56,
    161
Maugham, W. Somerset, 19
Maytag, Elmer, 12
McCulloch, C. A., 12
McMullan, Patrick, 241
McMullen, John, 104
McSwane, Floyd "Mac," 36, 63
Medellín Cartel, 150–51, 228–29
Mehling, Harold, 27n, 41
Meisel, Steven, 221, 226, 239
Meuron, Pierre de, 18
Meyer, Hank, 89
Miami Beach, crash and recovery
    cycles, 257
Miami Design Preservation League
    (MDPL):
    and Art Deco historic district, 129,
        131, 136–38
    and Capitman, 129, 136–37, 138
    and Horowitz, 119, 129, 131,
        134–35
    and Senator rally, 120
Miami Herald, 85–86, 104, 107, 120,
    122
Miami Vice (TV), 113
Mickey Mouse, 32, 172
Milken, Michael, 160
Miller, Stuart A., 178
Monroe, Marilyn, 36, 246
Montauk, New York, 31–32
Moon Over Miami (film), 42, 189, 205
Moore, Deborah Dash, To the Golden
    Cities, 90
Morgan, Swifty, 36

Morrison, Jim, 168, 225, 227, 229, 247
Moss, Kate, 229, 241
Mottola, Tommy and Thalia, 178
Mufson, Harry:
  death of, 77
  and Eden Roc, 72, 73, 74, 75, 76, 77
  and Fontainbleau, 55, 56, 58
  and Novack, 50, 53, 55, 58, 72, 74, 75, 76
  and Sans Souci, 47, 50, 77
Muir, Helen, 44
Muss, Alexander, 102
Muss, Stephen, 100–110, 116, 117, 133, 148, 164

Nadel, Mandi, 203–4
Nagler, Richard, 91
Newfeld, Jack, 244
Nichols, John, 80
Nolan, Margaret, 67
Non-Group, 105–6
Novack, Ben, 34–40
  aging of, 93–98
  arrival in Miami Beach, 38, 39
  and Bernice, 37–38, 52–54, 87–88
  death of, 98
  and Eden Roc, 72–75
  financial problems of, 93–97
  and Fontainebleau, 24, 35–37, 55–62, 64–71, 80, 81, 86–88
  money-making schemes of, 39
  and Mufson, 50, 53, 55, 58, 72, 74, 75, 76
  and Sans Souci, 38, 47–51, 56
  and World War II, 39–41
Novack, Ben Jr., 34–37, 55, 70–71, 88, 97–98
Novack, Bernice Drazen, 34, 35–36, 37–38, 52–54, 55, 69–70, 87–88
Novack, Hyman, 39

O'Donnell, Rosie, 178, 181
Omarion, 2

O'Neal, Shaquille, 17, 178–80
Operation Greenback, 151
Oppenheim, Chad, 7
Otto, Siegfried, 184–85

Paciello, Chris, 222–25, 230–37
  arrest of, 249–53, 254
  and Capponi, 225, 233–37, 243–44, 246, 247–49, 250–51, 253
  and Casares, 238–40, 242–45
  and Liquid, 240–46, 247–49, 250, 252
  and Risk, 223–25, 237, 245
  in Witness Protection Program, 252
Pacino, Al, 67, 113, 238
Page, Patti, 62
Pahlavi, Mohammad Reza, shah of Iran, 51
Parks, Arva Moore, 9–10
Patterson, Floyd, 77
Paul, David, 104, 157–60, 163–64
Pei, I. M., 158
Percal, Esther, 19
Persico, Alphonse, 250, 251
Phillips, Lisa, 114
Piazza, Mike, 2
Picasso, Paloma, 114
Pliner, Donald J., 178
Pommier, Michele, 170, 189, 191–92, 194, 208–13, 216, 221
Pons, Luis, 7
Pooch, Tommy, 169, 202
Portale, Alfred, 101
Prest-O-Lite, 29
Prince, 114, 225
Puente, Tito, 42

Quinn, Michael, 243

Rayder, Francesca, 226–27, 228, 230, 234, 236, 258–59
Raye, Martha, 42

Raymond, Max "Little Maxie Eder,"
    85–86
Redford, Polly, 11, 12
Reilly, Thomas Francis Jr. (Brother
    Louv), 181
Revson, Charles, 66
Reynolds, Thomas, 232–33, 251
Ricardo (model), 194–97, 210
Rickard, Ted, 42
Rickter, Alicia, 2
Ridinger, Amber, 1–7
Ridinger, James "JR," 4–7
Ridinger, Loren, 4–7
Rieff, David, 15
Rizzo, Johnny, 224
Robins, Craig, 7
Rodriguez, Alex "A-Rod," 179–80
Rodriguez, Juana M., 97
Rodriguez, Tito, 42
Roland Group, 100
Roosevelt, Eleanor, 41
Rosenbaum, Ed, 45
Rosenberg, Abe, 56
Rothschild, John, 119
Roudner, Leonard "Dr. Boobner,"
    186–87
Rourke, Mickey, 202, 223
Roy, Rachel, 3
Rubell, Don and Mera, 19n
Rubens, Peter Paul, *Portrait of Man as
    Mars,* 158, 163
Rudin, Milton, 86
Runyon, Damon, 12, 41
Ruszczynski, Michael, 9

S&G Syndicate, 45, 76
St. John, Jill, 81
Salvey, Harold, 45
Sans Souci, 38, 47–51, 53, 55, 56, 77
Savage, James, 85
Saxon, George, 46
Saxony Hotel, 46–47, 51
Scarface (film), 113, 238
Schaller, Dennis, 253

Schlesinger, John, 241
Schnellenberger, Howard, 211
Schnellenberger, Tim, 211
Schrager, Ian, 79–80, 241
Schultze, Leonard, 9, 10
Schwartz, Richaqrd, 201
Schwarz, David, 7
Scull, Haydee and Sahara, 119
Seikaly, Rony, 179
Senator Hotel, 117–22, 136
Shemtov, Judith, 232–33, 245, 251,
    252
Sherry Frontenac hotel, 46
Shore, Pauly, 200
Short, P. R., 44
Siegal, Edith, 130
Siegel, Bugsy, 49
Sinatra, Frank, 36, 77, 81–85, 86–87,
    111, 118, 202
Singer, Isaac Bashevis, 91, 92–93
Siskind, Steven, 107, 108, 109
Snowden, James, 54
Solomon, Tara, 2, 5
South Beach:
    Art Deco district, 113, 116–17,
        128–30, 131–34, 136–38, 173,
        175, 255
    color scheme of, 132–34, 175
    condominiums in, 256–57
    as modeling destination, 211–12,
        221
    revivification of, 113–15, 134, 138,
        184
South Beach Diet, The (Agatston), 256
Spector, Charles, 48
Spinks, Michael, 156
Stallone, Sylvester, 67, 178, 230
Starck, Philippe, 175
Star Island, 177–83
Stevens, Harry M., 12
Stone, Sharon, 67
Streisand, Barbra, 76
Sukhanova, Julia, 243
Sultan, Donald, 114

Tahlawi, Sheikh Wadji, 79
Taylor, Nikki, 243
Teriaca, Craig, 201
Tilson Thomas, Michael, 18
Toby, Lenore, 70, 88, 93, 94–95, 96
Toffel, Harry, 47
Tony Rome (film), 81, 84, 111
Travolta, John, 201
Truman, Harry S., 41
Trump, Donald, 156
Tucker, Sophie, 42
Turlington, Christy, 211
Tyson, Mike, 156

Vaccarezza, Carlo, 223
Vanderbilt, William Kissam, 41
Vergara, Sofia, 243, 252
Versace, Gianni, 254–56
Von Drasek, Woody, 119

Wagner, Robert, 62
Wahab, Walid, 7
Warhol, Andy, 113
Warner, Albert, 72

Warren and Wetmore, 49
Washington, Rudy, 245
Weaver, S. Fullerton, 9, 10
Weber, Bruce, 113, 192–93, 211
Weinhardt, Carl Jr., 129
Weiss, Merle, 240
Wilhelm, Dennis, 138
Wilhelmina modeling agency, 169
Wilzig, Naomi, 19
Winchell, Walter, 12, 41
Windsor, Duke and Duchess of, 41
Winfield, Sandy II, 67
Wolfson, Mitchell Jr. "Micky," 7–12,
    114, 117, 129, 130, 131
Wolfsonian–Florida International
    University Museum, Miami
    Beach, 7, 8–9, 10, 19
Wood, Ron, 113
World War II, 39–41
Wright, Frank Lloyd, 68

Yagoda, David, 244

Zimmer, Marie, 119